Rhys Alun Wilcox first picked up a pen sometime between his first and second birthdays and has never looked back. Literature took a more serious turn at Portsmouth University whilst reading Media & Design. There, he found he had a lot of spare time on his hands so wrote some plays for the drama society, tried his hand at stand-up comedy and conceived the idea for the *Blood Lust* series.

Most people think he thinks he's funny but this is wrong; he knows he's funny. It's not his fault that other people lack the pragmatic understanding to fully appreciate his jokes.

He currently exists in Bedfordshire with his wife and two children. There, he attempts to complete at least another dozen novels between parenting, procrastinating and dying. Not necessarily in that order.

He seems to spend most of his time not updating his website *www.thebloodlust.co.uk*.

Also by Rhys A. Wilcox
Blood Lust
Blood Lust 2: The Carrion
Blood Lust 3: Revelations
Blood Lust 2.5: L'Hunch Est Dos

Blood Lust: Sound Bites
(free dl from www.lulu.com/spotlight/zorga)

**Also by Rhys A. Wilcox
(but not in the *Blood Lust* series)**
Aftermath

Rhys A. Wilcox

Blood Lust IV
Being Supreme

RAW!

© Copyright 2014
Rhys Alun Wilcox

The right of Rhys Wilcox to be identified as the author of this work has been asserted by him in accordance with the Copyright, Designs and Patents Act 1988

All Rights Reserved

No reproduction, copy or transmission of this publication may be made without written permission. No paragraph of this publication may be reproduced, copied or transmitted save with the written permission or in accordance with the provisions of the Copyright Act 1956 (as ammended).

Any person who does any unauthorised act in relation to this publication may be liable to criminal prosecution and civil claims for damage.
I dare you!

ISBN 978-0-9561559-2-4

<u>For:</u>
My wonder woman.
My dynamic duo.

<u>Major Props to:</u>
Stan Lee
Neil Gaiman
Jim Lee
Steve Dillon
Alan Moore and Kev O'Neill.

"To be a real hero, you must have a real weakness: something that can be exploited, something that can make you lose, something that can still connect you to normality. If there is no flaw, no dent, no humanity, then what's to stop you just going off and doing whatever the hell you want? Who do you answer to? What's left to ensure you do the right thing? That very thing that defines heroism. What's to stop you from becoming just like them?

On the other hand, if your weakness is that you're just a fuck-up, then it's probably best to avoid conflicts with beings who could incinerate your spleen with the merest inflection of their pinky finger."

How To Be Supreme, Daniel J. Knight

It was Daniel Knight's eighteenth birthday and, in true British tradition, he had decided to celebrate by going to the same pub he had been frequenting for the previous two years.

Of course that made it rather awkward with the landlord, what with the celebratory nature of the event. Danny was a mature looking boy: very tall for his age, an athletic build (which had burnt away any vestiges of puppy fat a long time ago) and was able to pass himself off as eighteen very convincingly so now had to remember, and try to pretend, to be 21. This, of course, became increasingly more difficult the more he imbibed throughout the night.

It was on this evening when he, and a close friend, came close to realising that they possessed powers beyond the understanding and abilities of normal men.

Theirs was the ability to talk shit.

Not just talk drivel like the majority of people can. Nor was it simply expounding without sense and purpose, which many develop the skill of as they progress up the corporate duodenum of success. Neither was it the talent of waxing lyrical with hyperbolic effect to romanticise and poeticise the mundanities and irrelevances of life, which few are capable of but do with such artistry and prose that could make the most hardened of souls weep at the plight of a dust mote caught in an cyclonic updraft.

No, their oratory skills were of such that they could defy the very laws of science and nature within the depths of postulation that they would dig. They could reconfigure the intrinsic innateness of being through their communicative dexterity. Their verboseness could turn gravity on its head; have Satan worshipping Krishna; put the most hardened insomniac to sleep.

Tonight, they were going to have to embark on the rite of passage of all beings of heightened abilities: that of pitting their skills against each other. Only time would tell whether this would be a battle that would reinforce their kinship or be a wedge that would one day become an unspannable rift between them.

At first, Cameron Mortice had not wanted to go to Danny's party. But that was not because he did not like him or did not like parties or did not drink: he did – all three. It was more to do with the fact that all Danny's friends seemed so much younger than him: immature, childish and underaged (if you catch his meaning). On top of that, he was absolutely skint. University life had been taking its toll on his bank account and the colour of his overdraft had gone well beyond the red to drift off the visible end of the spectrum into infra red. He was sort of hoping that if he continued spending it might find its way into ultraviolet and eventually back to black.

Cameron was in his early twenties, plainly faced with darkened fair hair. His impoverished living conditions reflected in his physique: unkempt moppish hair, slenderness to the degree of emaciation, paleness that suggested malnourishment. However, there was a deep-set manner about him that made him stand out amongst the more 'beautiful' and youthful around him. He held himself with some sort of sense of pride and confidence whereas perhaps he should curl up and hide away from eyes that might judge his ragtag appearance. There was a defiance in his sparkling, dirty blue eyes that dared anyone to connect with him with the slightest indication of derision. The way he sat, positively screamed, 'Fuck off,' and, 'Fuck you,' to all around him. It was sort of noble, considering the time and place.

Everyone kept a wary distance apart from Danny, who was completely oblivious to the body language because he was very drunk. But it was his insobriety that was his utility belt, his speed force, his ring of power.

On the opposite side of the small round table, Cameron's state of impecuniosity and irritancy was his spider's bite, his Mjolnir, his gamma radiation.

The boys sat, staring, contemplating the weaknesses of each other. And in that moment, the room went silent as every conversation in the building found a natural pause. The effect was overwhelming; voices felt too self-conscious to break the silence so it prolonged beyond startling, outlasted awkwardness and evolved into something almost sacred.

The jukebox had no sense of propriety and cued its next song. The first beats of some synth driven pop tune tore through the building like a powerful derailed locomotive.

"Prince," Danny declared. "*Partyman*, from the soundtrack album to *Batman*."

"You're very clever," Cameron sneered. "It was a stupid soundtrack that highlighted the ridiculousness of a stupid film that laid the cornerstone for a stupid franchise that nearly destroyed an icon. Seriously, Bob Kane should have sued."

"Take that back," Danny ordered with a threatening staccato.

"Leave off!"

"I fucking mean it, man," he growled and drew his body forward over the table.

Cameron sighed. "Look, Batman in itself isn't too far-fetched a concept but the whole premise of-"

"Pardon me? 'Far-fetched'? You had better be talking about your Pokèmon collection, mutant boy."

"No, no, no," Cameron groaned. "Please don't go there."

"Well, if we're going to question the feasibility of one concept then it only seems fair to consider the genre as a whole."

"Fair enough," Cameron conceded. "Batman is stupid. End of."

"And yet you consider the ability to fire laser beams out of someone's arsehole based on a genetic quirk to be quite acceptable," Danny elucidated with a surprising level of sudden sobriety.

Cameron rolled his eyes. "Genetic mutation is NOT fiction so, on the basis of that alone, X-Men holds more credibility than Batman does." He folded his arms in triumph.

"Your argument is bunk, dude! Just because a degree of credence exists, does not validate an entire concept," Danny squealed. "If that's the root of your argument, then let's look at the facts: rich men exist, fast cars exist, body armour exists, martial arts expertise exists, caves exist, insane criminals exist. Should I go on? BLUE FURRY HUMANS, WHO CAN CLIMB UP WALLS, DON'T!"

Cameron gave him a dramatic moment's pause. Then, "How do you know?"

"Fuck you!"

"How do you know what extents of evolution humans have reached?"

"Fuck you and the X-Jet you came in on!"

"How do you know what wondrous things people can do somewhere out there? Every year, mere mortal men and women are getting faster, stronger and more intelligent. Isn't that all the evidence you need of human genetic evolution? Who knows where our DNA will take us next."

"Not with metal-laced bones and the ability to facsimilate ourselves. Batman is just a story about a well-trained man with limitless resources doing a bit of good in the world. A slight embellishment with the sci-fi elements for the sake of entertainment but with practically everything firmly embedded in social, psychological and science-fact."

"Batman fails entirely because of one simple primary concept! Maths. The sort of money he spends on his high-tech gadgets couldn't possibly be hidden from the taxman! X-Men is more believable because its premise is rooted in the core of human behaviour: discrimination, segregation and intolerance. It's contextually relevant to the atrocities and harmony of our very existence."

"Batman deals with the inimitable nature of human resistance; the ability, desire and - often - reasoning to do good or bad. It deals with darker and more real social issues than X-Men pretends to."

"Like paedophilia?"

Danny convulsed as if having been attacked by a live, cold eel down the back of his neck. "By the hairy whores of Hogwarts!"

Cameron had won. Time to deliver the finishing blow. "If Batman is so real, how come he isn't?"

"..."

Cameron leaned back in his seat and smiled smugly. "Kracka-fucking-thoom," he said.

"This is not the last you have heard of me, Cameron Mortice. You're feeble victory here merely spurs me on to achieve that very goal."

"You what?"

"I am going to become that paragon of virtue and show you that it is possible."

"You're going to become Batman?"

"Of a sorts."

"You can't be a superhero."

"I can be whatever my spirit wills me to be."

"But your name's not even alliterative!"

Danny faltered again for a brief moment but, this time, he was not searching for a response but trying to fathom the statement. Was it truly as flawed as he thought it was? Or was it a devious trap?

No, Cameron had displayed his weakness: his overconfidence, his eagerness to utterly destroy and humiliate his opponent.

"Nor does Bruce Wayne," Danny said, stood and walked away.

Cameron considered shooting him in the back with some existential rebuttal based on the fictional qualities of his QED but remembered his own, equal, tenuous position. "Buy me a pint, you tosser!" he shouted and Danny gave him an over-the-shoulder thumbs-up.

Cameron took this moment of solitude to peruse the peers of his friend. His eyes finally settled - and widened with interest - when they settled on an exceptionally tall, and strikingly attractive, auburn-haired girl. He had hit the jackpot.

CHAPTER 1
THERE IS NO 'I' IN 'TEAM'
OR THE DAFT KNIGHT RETURNS

3 YEARS LATER...

Danny Knight was an undeniably handsome young man. He was six-foot-six, broad shouldered and neatly muscular. He had tidy dark hair with a perfect side parting. Dark smouldering eyes hid seductively behind perfectly shaped eyebrows and were delicately bordered by long lashes. White, straight teeth and a permanently tanned complexion made him an ideal candidate as a model for any arty, brand name cologne commercial. Everything except for the fact that he was heterosexual.

He was distinctly unaware of his good looks, which frustrated girls and some boys alike. Extreme naivety and confident optimism often made it appear that he was flirting with those he met. To use a popular stereotyping out of context, he was a bit of a blonde at times.

Which was probably why he was partnered with Cassandra Twee. She was a very attractive girl. After all, even if Daniel was not fully aware that his physique gave him the pick of the crop, he still was not going to go out with an ugly bird. She was only just over five-foot, which looked ridiculous when they went out together but love cares not a jot for the opinions of others. There were other reasons that compounded their oddness: the first was that simple fact that she was five-foot-five. In heels. The second was down to her overall colouring. It seemed that a secondary school science class may have conducted a bizarre chromatography experiment on her head and that had spread into her choice of attire. Either that or some retro-hippy had tried to tie-dye her. On top of that, she had shiny bits of metal that were slowly spreading up around the outside of her ears. When she had been at university there had been a saying: 'If you're caught in a thunderstorm, don't stand under a Twee.' Daniel thought this was hilarious whereas she thought it was just plain immature and that summed up their personalities perfectly.

They had been seeing each other for a few years now and were very comfortable with each other's company. Most people think that the perfect relationship is one where both people can be in the same room and not feel obliged to talk. They can generate a 'comfortable silence'. This is not the case; the perfect relationship is one where either partner can be in a crowded room of strangers and comfortably call the other a 'fucking cunt' and still end up going home together to have sex.

Recent developments in their lives had brought them closer together than ever. These events involved a multitude of near death experiences (in the sense that their lives were put in jeopardy on many occasions and also that they were physically near (and responsible for) the death of others quite a few times).

They, along with four others, had been in Leeds when vampires had decided to try to take over the world and were instrumental to the safety of mankind. I guess you could call them heroes. Not that anyone outside of Leeds knew what had gone on because those six surviving 'heroes' had just slipped out the back door when all the fuss had ended. Annoyingly, they had metaphorically left the lights on and had not flushed the toilet properly so those who came after were a bit ticked off with clearing up to do.

Having been a part of the destruction of an entire city's population, they were, understandably, a bit shell-shocked so decided to have a short break with Danny's parents. They lived just outside Brighton's town centre: a thriving hybrid metropolis of commercialisation and socialist liberalism – a place where you could be exactly who you wanted other people to think you were as long as you were rich enough to afford it or in so much debt that you no longer cared. Danny would describe his parents as being 'hippies': they did not work, they had longish hair and they had a couple of *Pink Floyd* albums. The truth, however, was something far more conceited and seditious. They wanted to appear to be free living, peace loving, open-minded spirits of the Summer of Love generation. They had dabbled with pot (but it left a smell in the upholstery), they had attempted swinging (but all the invites came from housing estates that they would not even have considered as a first-time property purchase) and even went as far as getting a divorce and second marriage because it seemed the thing to do. The deeper reality was that they religiously voted Conservative, believed everything *The Daily Mail* wrote and were born in 1969 – not even as a result of the Summer of Love but more of an afterthought – and were, in turn, descended from a long line of social chameleons. "The paper says everyone has been having free love, dear." "Really? How very bohemian. Put the kettle on then and let's get started."

They loved Danny very much and displayed their affection by giving him lots of money. Luckily, he was far too naïve to allow this materialism to affect him negatively. Instead, it had desensitised him very early on to the idea of possessions, ambition and egotistical self-worth: he was all about the id, karmic forces and *que sera sera*. Inadvertently, and somewhat ironically, his parents had managed to raise him to be the sort of person they wanted everyone to perceive them as being.

He and Cassandra packed their things and made the six-hour journey down to the East Sussex coast and were barely quizzed for their premature arrival or their escape from one of the UK's largest cities' sudden evaporation from existence. Nothing more than his mother's statement of the obvious, "Daniel! You're home!" and father's, "Did you see the new motor outside, boy? Take her for a spin later?"

His mother, Angela, was of Afro-Caribbean descent and she had probably not cut her hair since the day Danny was born. Gentle black curls fell unencumbered from her head down to the middle of her back, fanning broadly around her waist; her dark skin shone radiantly from consistent application of a variety of expensive skin products specifically engineered for use at different times of the days, humidities and, more specifically, delusional women with too much money and not enough sense to realise they were being taken for a ride. 'Hydro-regenerative-peptonucleides' indeed. Although not ashamed of her heritage, as such, she had deliberately crafted her dialect away from her homegrown patois to fulfil the requirements of the true-blooded upper middle classes.

Danny's father went by the name of 'Charles', 'Charlie', 'Chaz' and even 'C-Dawg' depending on the age of pretension he was attempting to indoctrinate himself to (and, as was the level of his hypocrisy, when in the presence of his select mates, he even answered knowingly, with a smile on his face (which made it okay) to 'Chalky'). He had the misfortune of being born and raised in an environment of extreme deprivation: deprived of the feeling of need; deprived of moral conscience; deprived of a sense of responsibility. This had ensured that Charles had grown up without an awareness of the plights of the world which leant itself to a degree of disbelief that they even existed. "It's not that bad," he would say, "people exaggerate these things to get votes or money. The real issue is -" and then go on to espouse the latest theories presented by *The Daily Mail*.

Angela embraced Cassandra to drown her within the frizz and multiple layers of chiffon, then air-kissed each cheek. "Cassy, I'm so glad to see you still making an honest boy of him."

Charles gave Danny a playful elbow in the side. "Man, eh, son? Not boy," and winked at him in a manner that would have made Sid James blush.

"Charles, I need to get to Waitrose," Angela declared abruptly.

"For goodness sake, Angel, you went yesterday," Charles responded with mock derision.

"I didn't pick up any green tea yesterday," she huffed and wafted around the room in a seemingly industrious manner but, ultimately, not achieving anything: moving papers, adjusting ornaments and straightening the perfectly straight throws that were minding their own businesses. "And now that Daniel's home, we need some *Sugar Puffs* and *Billy Bear Ham*."

Cassandra stifled a snigger.

"Don't forget *Ribena*," Danny interjected without any kind of reaction and ensconced himself into the family dynamic by dumping his bags on the floor - which Angela swept up and carried through to an adjoining room - then dropping himself onto the sofa and activating the TV remote.

"Well, we'll take the X3 then," Charles stated deliberately, which stopped Angela in her flusterous steps.

"Oh Charlie, really?" she whined. "It's a lovely day out and I wanted to go out with the top down."

Cassandra had immediately picked up on the possible innuendo and was automatically prepared to chastise Danny for being entirely inappropriate but, apparently, the double entendre had passed him by unnoticed. Perhaps he did have a sense of standards; perhaps he did have some sort of primordial code of ethics that governed his life; perhaps there was a line that should not be crossed and it had something to do with anything that might refer to his mum's 'bits'.

"Angela, we took the Corvette out yesterday when it was a 'quick trip for the papers' and I had to drive home with a box of Proscecco on my lap because we ran out of boot space!"

"You shouldn't have bought such an impractical car then," Angela retorted weakly.

"You wanted the convertible! I wanted the XF."

"But people wouldn't see us in that."

"When did you become so vain?" Charles demanded but received nothing but a faux admonished, exaggerated lip-pouting stare in return. It would have been 'mock admonished' had she not have taken a French evening class five years ago. "Give me five minutes to get changed," he instructed and left the room in his perfectly pressed, light grey Chinos and dark green Ralph Lauren V-neck jumper to return, fifteen minutes later, in a pair of perfectly pressed navy Chinos and charcoal grey Ralph Lauren V-neck jumper.

Danny's parents departed with an emphatic, "Are you *sure* there's nothing you need?" and the youngsters were then left to their own devices.

"I am knackered," Cassandra announced and slumped heavily into the seat next to Danny. "It is going to be so nice having your parents look after us for a while."

"Tell me about it," Danny concurred whilst skipping through channels at a seizure-inducing rate.

"I know I take the piss out of them a bit," she continued, "and how much money they have, but after uni', poverty and all that running around, I don't mind taking advantage of their generosity for a bit."

"You go for it," he commended and stopped on a cartoon channel where a collection of familiar-looking super heroes was being presented in their teenage years. "I hate it when they mess around with the continuity of stories just as an excuse to repackage and sell them again."

She did not acknowledge. "I'll give the exam board a call and sort a re-sit, have plenty of lie-ins and maybe go shopping with your mum."

"What's next? *Justice League Animals* and a range of cuddly costumed pals to collect?"

"I am *so* going to kick back and do nothing."

| TWO DAYS LATER... |

"I am *so* bored!" Cassandra declared.

Danny flinched in his seat and turned to see her pacing by the front door. "What's up?"

"I need... to do something," she told him.

"There's a *Carry On* marathon starting in a minute; come watch -"

"Aaargh!" she screamed. "No more telly! You sit there watching cartoons and old films all day and they watch quiz shows and soaps all evening! It's boring!"

"You want a drink?"

"No more alcohol!" she wailed. "I never realised what a bunch of lushes your folks are. I swear, as soon as that clock hits pm, the bottle opener comes out."

"You said you wanted to go out with mum? How about -?"

"You are *not* leaving me alone with that woman," she warned him. "It's like trying to hold a conversation with a QVC presenter: she talks lots but has nothing of any substance to say. And your dad seems to think he's a stand-up comedian, always adding a punchline or a nod-and-a-wink to everything. Which is just plain wrong."

"Well, what -?"

"Your parents are so weird," Cassandra concluded.

"Aren't all parents?"

"Mine aren't."

"Yours were divorced when you were young; your mum has had five kids with three different blokes and your dad married a woman only four years older than you!"

"That's normal, twat-face," she spat. "Your parents being together for twenty-five years -"

"Twenty and three."

"- is a clear indication that they are either living in denial or sociopathic. They can't do anything independently: they go to the gym together, they cook the dinner together, the load the dishwasher together, they drive down to the corner shop for their morning paper... TOGETHER!"

Danny, well-known for his super powers of sarcasm, ignorance and 'saying exactly the wrong thing at the wrong time'[1] and not known for his tact or common sense, was sometimes able to engage his lesser known, secondary talent of insightful or profound observation that could cause her to reel as if being physically assaulted. He replied, "They met at uni when they were our age." His remark was counterpointed with a non-committal physical reaction: not straying his eyes from the TV screen.

WHAMMY!

She studied him carefully as his words rattled around in her conscience. She hated these moments when he made her think about him; it was always so much easier when he was predictable. Had he made an idle comment or was he questioning her expected level of commitment? How much he thought she loved him? Perhaps worse, had she just revealed an aspect of an inherent, unconscious attitude towards commitment?

The moment of instability was only a brief one and, instinctively, she was able to regain control of the situation, conversation and, ultimately, him. "Cunt!" she stated and stormed upstairs, ensuring that the amount of noise each foot made on the floor rose proportionately to the distance she was away from him. The ceiling light's crystal teardrops quivered in fear as she entered a room above him.

---

[1] An actual super-power utilised by many supremes but first exhibited by the D-list, French meta-criminal, Faux Pas.

Danny desperately tried to watch the telly but the resounding silence that now screamed at him from every corner of the house prevented his peace of mind. "By Odin's eyepatch," he muttered and hauled himself from the sofa.

She sat on the edge of the bed with her back tactically facing the door. The room was not even to the guests' room. It was, however, the one right over his head. She waited.

"Cass?" he called up to her. "Would you like to go shopping with me tomorrow?" And she knew she had won.

The train journey into the city was quick and uninspiring (considering the proximity of a coastline, it was all very urban scenery that the track passed through) but did give Danny enough time to figuratively lay himself prostrate before Cassandra until she finally forgave him. He sat in a window seat and she squished herself up so close to him that there was still space next to her for another passenger. Her embrace was far too affectionate for someone who might have truly been pissed off - it is all very well to say that an apology has been accepted; another thing entirely to actually mean it. She wrapped her arms around his and rested her head against his shoulder, curling her feet up under her bottom, thereby reclaiming the rest of the seat.

"No pubs," she said softly.

"The *Fortune of War* on the seafront has just been refurbed," he responded. "I thought it might be quite nice to finish off there for a swift one out in the garden and watch the sea."

Dammit! He had done it again. "That sounds nice," she conceded but felt a need to reinforce her dominance; his guilt needed testing. "No comic shops, though." She could feel his muscles stiffen in his arm. "You know how long you can spend in those places and you promised me this would be my time."

"What if I knew exactly what I was after, go in, get it and come out?" he negotiated.

She released her embrace and sat upright. "It never works out like that," she told him. "You probably 'know' you want to get fifty-odd titles or, more likely, will get distracted by some new titles that you didn't know about."

She knew him too well, he knew that. There had been too many trips to *OK Comics* in Leeds that had taken multiple hours of their time with him rifling through back issues, searching for one of those elusive editions to make up the continuity of his collection, or discovering a collection of brand new titles or publishers, or - as it was during that five hour session - uncovering a mass crossover story that required trawling through every title and their multiple spin-off sister, daughter and second-cousin titles. That was a bad one. Even he looked back on that day with regret and a sense of disappointment: he had spent - he calculated - an absolute fucking fortune, not only through having to purchase titles that he normally would not touch with the Oak Staff of the Druids, but to the extent that the two leading publishing competitors had gone as far as teaming up with each other for this story and he had to buy all the oppositions puerile, juvenile titles too. *New Titans* was bad enough but having to buy *X-Factor* was an all-time low. The aftermath of which was having to hunt out some back issues of these second-rate rags to fill in narrative blanks. He felt utterly betrayed by the industry he had loyally served for a dozen years of his life and, by way of protesting, ended up cutting back on three of his regular titles. That would teach them.

He had, since then, picked up six new series.

"Baby," - he was playing a trump card now - "I'll write a list of the ones I want and if you think it's too many then I'll cut it back. You can hold the list and count them off. If I go off-piste then I renege the lot. How's that?"

Where was the control? He was negotiating terms but he was giving her charge of them. He was letting her be in charge. Did that mean he was in charge and that he was giving her temporary control? She could not work it out but realised if she simply said 'No' then she would be in danger of releasing another of his alter-egos - Obstreperous Man - and the entire day could be shot. "Okay," she acquiesced, "but we get your stuff out the way first." *Still in control*, she prided herself.

Dave's was a modest establishment situated a short stroll from Brighton station. Ensconced within the eclectic boutiques of the small streets, its primary discursive feature seemed to be the store's resilience to overcome the stormy economic seas of fickle comic fandom. Originally, it was a seedy-looking, second-hand book shop a few short strides away from the more trendy *Forbidden Planet* at the northern end of the road; at the opposite end was a far more interesting purveyor of back issue pornographic literature. Ten minutes' walk westward would have the comic consumer at the doors of one of the largest *Virgin Megastores* in the country and their own, sanitary and well-stocked comic department.

Cassandra tried not to listen as they weaved their way through the mismatch of social subcultural representatives – Danny had always boasted about the number of famous people he had brushed shoulders with while wandering the avant-garde streets but she was always left unsatisfied.

"That was Norman Cook," he declared between breaths of documentarian exposition.

"Who?"

"Fat Boy Slim!"

She spun around, eager to catch a glimpse of the rich and famous but everyone in Brighton was dressed like they were rich and famous: designer sunglasses; weird hats; bizarre, multi-layered homemade clothes that made them look like a walking jumble sale.

"The guy in the green t-shirt," he said.

He was possibly the most 'normal' looking middle-aged man she had ever seen and, by that account, was incredibly unimpressed. "I don't like his music anyway," she grumbled.

"What?" Danny demanded and began bobbing his body in a most disturbing manner as he walked. "Fwuff the wipping widdit, fwuff the wipping widdit, fwuff the wipping wid de Fat Boy Slimminginnit!" he chanted loudly and drew no attention from anyone other than a punch in the arm from his girlfriend. "His beach gigs used to be mad," he continued unabated. "Up until they got popular and stupid big."

"Here," Cassandra stated, very eager to end any conversation her over-eager man had to offer. He did not seem to know much about a lot of things, but those things he did know a lot about tended to be delivered with such passion and enthusiasm that she wished he never broached the subject.

"Not this one," he said, "we want the next. *Dave's* survived thirty years of fluctuating interest in the genre -" she rolled her eyes "- and where the mighty comic emporium of *Forbidden Planet* failed, and the mass media monopoly of *Virgin* quit, *Dave's* persisted and has become a firmament which comic readers can guarantee will fulfil their needs without fail and without judgment and, more importantly, will continue to do so despite the economics of trends."

"Why have they got two stores separated by a different one," Cassandra demanded.

"Dunno," he replied and disappeared into the shop.

"Hurry up!" she bellowed after him.

She tried to stand and wait impatiently but it was very difficult when considering the colourful ebb and flow of humanity around her. She got distracted by the visually stimulating, contentious and, sometimes, ostentatious displays of individualism. She also found herself having to constantly shift position from her vigil as those people, deeply concerned with their own being, walked straight towards her with no intention of diverting their route. Here was probably the only place where her dress and self-expression failed in its attempts to be noticed. She was unobtrusive in stature and in dressage now. "I hate this place," she grumbled and, as a result, was in a steamingly foul mood when Danny returned in a very timely manner.

"What's up?" he asked with genuine concern (albeit, concern for his ears and arms).

"I want to go home," she muttered sullenly.

"He wrapped an arm around her shoulders and pulled her body into his. "Did somebody say something?"

"No, I just don't like being a nobody."

This, he was not expecting and took a step back. "You're not!" he exclaimed. "You are my everything."

She thrust herself back into his embrace and allowed him to rock her gently.

"You are a force to be reckoned with," he stated. "You are an undead-killing, karate machine. You are a real-life superhero and I am in awe of you."

BLAMMO! He had done it again. She looked up into his deep brown eyes of absolute sincerity and she melted. How could she possibly think she could control this beast of emotion? "Drink?" she questioned.

"Cool," he replied and returned his attention to the comic shop. "I just wanted to show you-"

Danny stood motionless, staring at the shop front and its plethora of science fiction, fantasy and comic memorabilia.

"What?" she prompted.

"It's weird," he stammered. "I get this strange tingling sensation like I'm seeing it for the last time."

"What? The shop? Don't be silly, you can come back any time you want," she comforted. "In fact, why don't we go back in now?"

"No!" he screamed irrationally, turned, grabbed her by the waist and launched the pair of them towards the far curb. He rolled his body to land on his back, her falling on top of him. However, as he landed, he rolled again to shield her.

Nothing happened. Although, finally, these actions had been deemed odd enough to draw the attention of passers-by.

"What the fuck are you doing?" Cassandra screamed when the air had returned to her lungs.

"I -"

A cacophony of sounds assaulted the scene: a distant whistling of the wind that got louder, indicating its nearing proximity: an almost Christmassy tinkling of glass and metal; a pained yawning of a large structure under stress; and beneath all that, the unmistakable screams of fear and pain of tortured souls.

It was the strangest of sights. Cassandra had a clear view of the blue summer sky over Danny's shoulder. It started as an ovoid shadow, sailing gently across the sky but she did not have time to attempt identification because its true momentum became horrifically apparent as it hurtled directly towards them. Disk shaped, about four storeys diameter, a lattice of metal beams, orbited by small orbs, trailing tendrils of varying thickness in its wake.

It landed horizontally and perpendicular to the row of buildings, crumpling *Dave's* like a stamped-on can. Bricks and glass erupted across the street, indiscriminately slicing and bludgeoning the hoi polloi to the ground. The flailing vines were a variety of decorative bulbs and thick support cables that whipped through the street, dismembering those who were in their paths. Then the remaining detritus rained down: lumps of sheered metal embedded themselves firmly into concrete, steel and flesh; finer splinters of glass hailed down, tearing and blinding; bodies fell with the force of speeding cars, hammering cars and victims flat into or exploding as they met the concrete. Those fortunate enough to avoid the assault were felled either by the shockwave or an instinctive survival dive for cover.

As dust settled and the volume of cries rose, Cassandra could finally start to identify the missile. The orbs were large buckets big enough for two and, indeed, many still had people within them, although they dangled lifelessly over the edges or had lost extremities during their flight and impact. "It's a big wheel," she said.

Danny dared to turn his head for a glance; he blinked the dust from his vision. "It's *the* big wheel," he stated. "From the pier."

Something caught his attention from the corner of his eye and he whirled back to Cassandra. "Can you move?" he demanded urgently.

"Yes?"

"Then we have to move, now!" He hauled himself off her and grabbed her arm but, rather than waiting for her to get fully to her feet, he began dragging her through the debris.

She was about to start complaining; about to suggest that they try to help the wounded, but her voice was cut short when the wheel emitted a ferocious metallic growl, indicating that it had not quite come to a complete stop. Cassandra found her footing and a burst of energy and was overtaking Danny, dragging him to keep up as the wheel rolled forward into the street then toppled over, ending the suffering of many but adding more to a few.

The couple paused when they considered the danger might be over and looked back at the carnage.

"What the hell could have caused that?" Cassandra demanded.

"An explosion?" Danny suggested.

"We would have heard that, no?"

The dust was slowly settling, thinning, allowing sights and sounds to become more distinct. Ghostly shadows shambled around in the murk, groaning with piteous wails - a mixture of pain, loss and helplessness. They crawled through the forest of debris: thick trunks of girders that thrust resolutely from the ground were entwined by the vines of cables, wires and fabric; twisted limbs with too many joints or whittled ends twitched with their waning vestiges of life; gnarled fingers clawed at the air.

Then, from out of the depths of the fog came a deep, rhythmic bass pounding that resonated through their bodies: a heavy beat that got steadily louder with each thump and made the ground tremble. The dust and smoke seemed to coalesce around one space in the middle of the street and an undefined shadow began to emerge. It gradually increased in size forming a silhouette of striking proportions. It stepped purposefully through the aftermath as if on a brisk ramble but, more than that, it just kept getting bigger. Not growing but, as it drew nearer, the youngsters could approximate that it was about nine foot tall and half as much in width.

"What is it?" Cassandra demanded.

"Incredible," Danny whispered in as much awe as fear. "He radiates with an overwhelming aura."

"Vampire? Like Cameron?"

"No, not giving off light like him but effusing a magnificence."

"What the fuck is that supposed to mean?"

Danny watched with uninhibited awe as the thing stepped out of the murkiness and surveyed its surroundings. Through his eyes, not only was it a creature of unprecedented physical proportions but it also radiated with an aura that filled the street; the patterns and colours of nobility, decency and pride: stars and stripes: red, white and blue.

A few years after Danny's crossover battle of verbal dexterity with Cameron, their paths crossed again but, this time, as comrades rather than combatants. He was a fairly average student at Leeds University, finishing his final year and preparing for the next stages of his life when everything changed and his path of destiny was altered forever. He was thrust into a world of death, destruction and damnation; from this point, nothing would ever be the same again.

Vampires.

For too long had they kept confined to the recesses of society; contented themselves with being the things of myth and nightmare; satisfied themselves with simply sustaining their existence rather than making their presence known to the world around them. Now they were ready to feed without fear of reprisal and without mercy. It was not so much an invasion but more of an uprising as they poured from the shadows, drowning the city from within its populace.

Many had no time to comprehend the manner in which their lives were ended let alone have the chance, inclination or capabilities to react.

A few did and Daniel Knight was one of them.

He was wandering through the university campus, about to meet with Cassandra at the library when a furore broke out and people were panicking, running, screaming. And it was radiating away from his intended destination. Despite the waves of distress that buffeted against him, his steadfastness and size allowed him to wade against the current until he caught sight of his multi-coloured girlfriend staggering hesitantly amongst the throng. He placed his hands on her shoulders and turned her around.

The immediate expression on her face was one of abject fear – something he had never seen before in his life and filled him with a mix of dread, confusion and anger – but passed into elation as she acknowledged it was him.

"What the fuck's going on, Cass?" he demanded. His first thoughts had been of terrorists, psychotic student gunmen or even the formation of a tectonic fissure pre-empting a pyroclastic eruption.

"You want to die too, huh?" a gravelled voice declared from amidst the bustling bodies. People parted to reveal a boy in his late teens, dressed in jeans and olive green hoodie striding calmly yet purposefully towards them. The distinguishing features about him were the shining bloodiness of his eyes and that his teeth seemed to have been replaced with shards of glass. It reached forward, took a firm grip of the scruff of Danny's chest and lifted him off the floor.

"Cass?" Danny called out with desperation and increasing confusion.

And that was what Cassandra needed to bolt her back to her senses, to engage her courage, to transform her from distressed damsel into vengeful valkyrie: the pitiful cry of help from the man she loved. She leapt onto the vampire's back and dug her sharp nails into his neck, unhindered by the sensation of splitting skin.

The vampire squealed from the pain, dropped Danny, unhooked Cassandra then nonchalantly threw her down on top of him.

"What the fuck?" Danny bellowed with frustration. "Is that a fucking vampire?"

As if to answer his question, the monster grabbed a passer-by, popped his head open like a Pez dispenser and captured a spray of blood that spurted from his rent neck.

With a gleaming razor-blade grin, the vampire returned its attention to Cassandra, lifting her and drawing her towards his moist, reddened face. She twisted, kicked and punched, trying to get free but the creature displayed such strength and resilience, all that she achieved was force him to waver on the spot, reasserting his balance.

Danny knew about vampires - the ugly, limb rending ones like *From Dusk Til Dawn*, the emo ones that pine for their mortality like Rice's, even the wussy, glittery ones that are like misunderstood teens and just want to be loved - there were loads of variations but there was always one solution. He picked up a picket fence post that had been destroyed during the chaos: one end had the cliché arrow point; the other had a more interesting split along the grain. There was no hesitation, no compunction, no dilemma; vampire or not, this thing was out to kill them and had to be stopped. He brutally thrust the post upwards into the centre of the vampire's back and felt it sheer off its spinal column at an angle. He readjusted his force, levering the stake around the spine and feeling the popping of the dislocating vertebrae resonate through the wood into his hands. There was a slight resistance, like slowly puncturing a balloon, and then a wet crack from its chest along with an eruption of wood and bone.

"Stand away from him," an old man instructed.

"Why?" Danny asked. "Hasn't that done it then?" And he watched the convulsing creature warily.

To the casual viewer, the vampire exploded into a ball of light. For those beings capable of watching the paths of a breeze, however, it could be discerned that the creature's entire molecular structure underwent an instant atomisation. Each particle breakdown released and carried a sum of necromantic energy which radiated like light. Due to Danny's proximity, a significant portion of that energy accessed his nervous system via his optic nerves. It killed parts of his visual cortex turning him blind but, as is the nature of necromancy, reanimated those neural cells into inhuman receptors capable of seeing otherwise imperceptible energies. The first sign of this enhanced ability displayed itself in the form of seeing vampires slightly differently to how he perceived normal humans. "Humans," he would explain with great authority, "look normal. Whereas vampires," he would continue with a flair for the dramatic, "look well fucked up."

Obviously there is a limit to the level of imagery that can be conjured by such a figurative narrative and, driven to further elucidation, the bard would continue to justify his metaphorical exposition by stating, "Literally, dude, their faces look like the angry prolapsed urethra of an old-aged whore's over-used, engorged, corpusculent fanny."

Normally, the audience's desire for a continued poetic conceit would end there unless he decided to describe the exception to the rule. This came in the form of co-vampquishers, Cameron and Gillian, who inadvertently found themselves demised but lacking the conventional characteristics and motivations of their brethren. They carried with them an almost heavenly glow that prevented him from looking at them without sunglasses.

In practical terms, his ability did not serve much purpose other than preventing him from mistakenly driving a shaft of wood through the sternum of an innocent mortal. But, eventually, even that aspect became redundant when every mortal (apart from himself and immediate allies) had been turned into similar state of face-blendered monstrosities. And that ran out of kudos when every vampire was then extinguished.

Now, he was Daniel Knight: ex-hero. He had come so close to fulfilling his childhood dreams only to have them so cruelly taken away. When he pondered upon it, there were times, when he felt he could cry. There were times when he wanted to ball his fists and punch the walls. There were times when he wanted to punish the world; seek blessed revenge on the fates that had stripped him of his glory.

Then he would remember that that was the path of doom and that, perhaps, destiny had other plans for him. So he bided his time patiently.

CHAPTER 2
THERE IS 'META' IN 'TEAM'

For all intents and purposes it should be described as a man; only, a man who had been inflated beyond the limitations of skin, tendons and bones and had found a way to take advantage of his personal space. His humanity was defined by a geometrically immaculate, right-side-parted blonde hair that peaked atop his granite-chiselled head; a solid square jaw that underlied his thin, stern lips that were clenched in abject consternation; and steel-blue eyes that were tightly focussed ahead of him, staring above and beyond his present calamity.

"I need clean up," he growled into the air in a baritone American drawl. "About a mile north from the conflict. Multiple injuries and casualties, heavy structural damage. Looks stable, though."

His metahumanity had him towering two foot above Danny, forcing the boy to crane his neck in his attempt to catch eye contact. Shoulders billowed out in all directions like someone had stuffed double thickness, king size mattresses up his costume with memory foam pillows for muscles. His costume required a double take: some sort of material but was so tight that they could (if you will pardon the extended analogy) clearly see the stitching around the manufacturer's label.

"Dude," Danny gushed.

"Stand aside citizen," the malestrom simply said without looking at him. His voice effused so much confidence that, despite being a few feet away from him, Danny and Cassandra could not help but take a step backwards. He leapt forward with a powerful thrust of his right leg and landed heavily at the end of the road: a good five hundred yards away. His landing leg coiled, absorbing the impact, and then released, propelling him over the row of buildings that impeded his immediate path.

As he disappeared beyond the rooftops, the shockwaves reverberated along the street and up the youths' legs.

"Able to leap tall buildings in a single bound," Danny cited hypnotically.

"Technically, it was two," Cassandra stated, "he had a run up. And those shops aren't that tall."

Danny's trance snapped and he directed his attention to his cynical partner. "How can you not be amazed by that?" he demanded.

"What? The big man jumping over the house?" she sniffed. "Cameron can fly. Anything else seems a bit blasé."

Bookmarked as a rare moment in Danny's life, he was momentarily lost for words and could only emit gagging noises from the back of his throat. Eventually: "That there was a real life superhero!"

"Different to Cameron in what way?"

"His persona, his costume, his poise."

"'Poise'?"

"We need to get down to the sea front," he decided and started pulling her along by her sleeve.

"We need to get the hell out of here, Daniel," she told him, literally digging her heels into the cobbles. "Something is throwing Ferris wheels around like Frisbees. We do not - cannot - get involved with that."

He turned to her, crouched down to be at her eye level and placed his hands firmly on her shoulders. "I need to go," he reiterated. There was no begging or tones of coercion in his voice. There were no words of flattery, bribery, pretence or excuses. He released her, turned again and ran away.

Cassandra stared. **KAPOW!** "What the fuck?" she demanded. That was something entirely different: not his normal predictable behaviour or his customary unpredictability; this was unprecedented unusual unpredictability, almost as if he was being completely and utterly serious and, with Danny, whatever he did, there was always an iota of silliness, joviality or irony. When they battled their first vampire, he uttered some pithy aside about bats; at his relative's funeral, he corpsed at the 'purple headed mountains' line in *All Things Bright and Beautiful*; and, in his final dissertation, he managed to write a comprehensive conclusion on *Gramsci's Cultural Hegemony in The Matrix Trilogy* which had the acrostic 'lick my balls' in the final paragraph. This was not a man who did serious and, yet, there it was: totally and utterly.

"Danny!" she called and raced after him.

With his stature, intent and intricate knowledge of the winding lanes versus her high heels, ballast and topographical ignorance, she did not catch up until he had stopped running at the end of East Street. There, where the kebaberies and boutiques ended and The Channel began, she beheld the sight of a national landmark torn apart and cast into Neptune's necropolis. The shadowed mass of the pier thrust out of the murky thrashing sea like an untended gravestone. Barbed branches of metal and wood entwined the defiant mass, clutching at its body and trying to drag it down.

"That's West Pier," Danny told her. "It's always been like that. You should be looking this way, at East Pier."

She turned her attention to the opposite horizon to what Danny was staring at.

He bore witness to the realisation of a lifetime of dreams and aspirations. The pristine blue ocean sloshed against the Autumnal pastels of the pebble beach, the summer sun was hanging heavily in the cloudless sky and heading towards the western horizon. The moon was hovering over a negative space on the east horizon: a space that should have been filled with the gaudy, bustling pier. It used to thrust boldly out into the ocean with its stolid wooden girth and engorged, brightly lit tip but now it drooped embarrassingly in the detritus of its own prolapsed entrails. It had been crushed into the sea from the end to the beach and now, progressing westwards along the shore, was a small group of humans attempting to stave the continued movement of a beast that stood at twenty storeys high.

The creature must have dredged itself up from the depths of the ocean floor; seaweed clung and writhed from the ridge of every car-sized scale that armoured its immense frame and, with every step, hidden reservoirs of water held between the scales cascaded to the ground that cracked and tremored beneath its behemothic weight. Tree-trunk legs thrust into the concrete and sought extra purchase with radial, retractable claws that penetrated the floor like grasping fingers. As it raised each leg again, it hauled its fistful of hardcore and released it at the apex of its stride, adding another calamitous ingredient to its stroll along the promenade.

It was efficient in its path of destruction: if not dowsing, crushing, rending or burying during its forward movement, a girder-like tail being dead-weight-hauled behind it carved a metre-deep trench with its tip flicking irritably from side to side, displacing any structures that may have escaped the preceding mindless destruction.

And what made it literally 'mindless' was the expression of absolute disinterest it displayed across its facial features. Its eye line, physically above the roof of the highest building, did not waver from the middle distance beyond its present place. Nary a glance at the vehicles crunched underfoot like autumnal leaves, no inflection of remorse as an errant leg slighted the front of a building and scraped away its facia to expose its interior decor, not even the shadow of a sadistic grin as it stamped on a collection of recumbent bodies and they popped like bubble wrap. All the time, its unblinking, bulbous, yellow eyes were staring emotionlessly into the distance, its downward V-shaped mouth not emoting, its two fin-like horizontal extrusions from the back of its head gave the impression of a predatory cat - an overall expression of sedate calmness - its arms, however, flailed about like a melissophobe in an apiary.

The 'bees' came in the form of projectiles of various sizes being hurled at the creature's skin. There were, in relation to it, insectal spheres that showered its torso from multiple directions; there were apple sized lumps of rock that seemed to explode intermittently around its thighs; and there were more discernible objects that managed to reach head height: bins, bicycles and bits of cars. Then, whipping around at its ankles was a horizontal human - it was not apparent what it was doing other than weaving in and out of each stride. Around its body, Danny was able to perceive a border of electrical interference: something akin to TV static.

Other humans' interaction became more distinct: the oversized, tri-coloured man was in front of the creature, bounding backwards to stay ahead of each tennis-court step. He was responsible for the concrete nouns, grabbing anything that was not nailed down (although some things that were deep set into the pavement did not concern him) and hurling them at the monster's head. There was a short, stocky female emanating a purple hue, who was picking up bricks and rubble then throwing them into the air on a trajectory with her head. Then, before it made contact, it would rocket off at the beast and detonate against its armoured hide. Another male, of an average size, build and greenish glow, was just keeping up with the pace, he was whirling his hands in the air which seemed to stimulate clouds of inch sized spheres into swarming at the beast. Then, on occasion, another figured caught the corner of Danny's eye. She would slink out from the shadows of side streets and shop fronts, aim and fire a plethora of advanced technological gadgetry, then merge with the darkness again. She carried a cloud of darkness around her that obscured her from his sight.

Would it have been that the leviathan was overwhelmed by the variety of attacks and the unerring fervour of them but, alas, the incessant onslaught achieved nothing more than the creature wafting them aside like they were unpleasant gastric gases. Each stroke of its mighty arms deflected elements of the barrage and the resulting wake of tumultuous air staggered the assailants and offered a moment's respite.

The two youths were rapt with awe (well, one was 'rapt', the other was 'wrapped').

"Excelsior," Danny sighed.

"What the fuck?" Cassandra reiterated.

"Look: a real-life team of superheroes with super powers and super gadgets and everything."

"Ooh yeah," she mocked, "and look: a real-life fucking huge monster destroying everything in its path and heading straight for us. Can we go, please?"

Danny woke up. "No, Cass. This is it, this is everything my life has been leading up to: real-life superheroes."

"Do stop saying that."

"This is that rare moment in someone's life when, suddenly, everything makes sense, everything has meaning, everything has had purpose."

"Don't do it," she warned. "This is too big."

"I gotta."

"No you don't," she urged and held on to his arm desperately. "For once, we can leave it to someone else."

He held his focus on her eyes for a long 'serious' moment. "What if..." he said solemnly, "... there was no one else."

She stared back at him, trying to comprehend the logic going through his mind that would make him willingly throw his life in front of such extreme peril. "That was some sort of comic reference, wasn't it?"

"My whole existence is a comic reference, baby," he stated, turned and jogged calmly towards the battle.

"Twat," she muttered. "Don't get killed!" she ordered and he gave her a backwards wave. "Why does shit like this keep happening to us?"

Danny trotted closer to the action, keeping a careful eye open for bits of shrapnel that ricocheted towards him. The creature was further away than its perspective had suggested; its size was so gargantuous that it seemed a few metres away but, as he approached, its higher features began to get blocked by its shoulders and torso and he finally started to have doubts about his presence. He kept a safe distance, edging along the path, and approached the Greenish Master of the Flailing Arms Technique.

"Dude," Danny said but received no response.

The man was dressed, in what looked like, an old fashioned, American boy scouts' uniform - khaki short-sleeved shirt, baggy three-quarter length shorts and wide brimmed hat - but with a khaki cape and dirty brown under suit that was on display after his shirt sleeves stopped and in the gap between his shorts' cuffs and shin-high socks. He continued to whip his arms around frenetically, controlling the clouds of spheroid objects.

"Dude," Danny called again - slightly more forcefully this time - and tapped the man gently on the shoulder.

He screamed and wheeled around with a look of utter fear on his plump, red-acne-ridden face.

The clouds dropped around the ankles of the beast.

Danny was taken aback to discover this particular hero was at least five years younger than him and the outfit had been completed with a yellow cravat, woggle and black eye mask.

"Oh, er, citizen," the boy declared with uncertain boldness and an American accent. "Try to take to some cover until -"

"I'm here to help, dude," Danny interrupted.

"I - ah - oh, no thank you, citizen, everything is being taken care of and if you -"

"Look out!" Danny pulled the boy forward a moment before a gilded mermaid careened through the window he had been standing in front of.

"Thanks, I -"

"What can you do?"

"What?"

"What can you do? I can see shit different, what can you do?"

"You're supreme?" the boy asked.

"Supremely mother fucking awesome, dude," Danny replied and puffed his chest out. He did not notice the hero wince and look around nervously.

"You really need to speak to Bob," he advised. "Or even Floater. I don't know what to suggest."

"Well, the rules of crossover suggest we either have a misunderstanding and battle each other until our common goal is revealed," Danny told him, "or team up!"

"'Crossover'? What are you talking about? Who are you?"

"You're on my turf, dude," Danny stated. "Technically this is my threat to thwart and you're the visiting team."

"'Thwart'? Who talks like that?"

"So, I need to know what you can do to know how we can best combine our powers." Danny turned his attention towards the beast and scrunched his eyes in concentration. There was something odd about it, something like seeing a *Magic Eye* picture in reverse: there was a three dimensional image but if he changed the focus of his eyes slightly...

"I have an empathic link and telekinetic mastery over Brussels sprouts," the boy recited awkwardly, stumbling over the 'telekinetic mastery' bit.

Danny was concentrating and, therefore, unable to listen properly at the same time. "You can control Brussels? The city?"

"No, the vegetable," the boy explained.

Danny looked at him and then at his feet. Sure enough, there was a blanked of small green leafy orbs spread across the road and path. He looked back at the hero again but did not read his expression of expectant embarrassment. "That is fucking awesome!" he squealed. "You can create a shit-storm of green death to rain down on your foes or use one to infiltrate the most secure of bases."

"Er, I suppose."

"I was going to say that control of a city was probably a bit limiting in its potential unless you could animate parts of it like the Manneken Pis or something but then what would you do with it? Have it piss on people?" At this, he laughed loudly and pulled the boy up the street, getting ahead of the monster's progression.

"I have no idea what you're saying to me right now," the boy responded and, unprotestingly allowed himself to be dragged along.

"Boy?" a seductive female voice called from the darkness beside them.

Danny peered into the shadow, willing his eyes to become accustomed to the darkness but all he could make out were faint reflection lines that hinted at shiny curvatures.

"It's okay, Cat," Boy replied. "He's a local supreme."

The darkness shifted in tone as her presence slipped away; it seemed to get slightly lighter.

"Who was that?" Danny demanded. "And what can she do?"

"That's Cat, she can see things that have happened."

"Can't most people?"

"Not if you weren't there."

"Cool."

"On top of that, she is proficient in multiple forms of hand-to-hand combat and an arsenal of amazing gadgetry."

"A cross between Batman and Cat Woman, then," Danny suggested.

Boy's hand slapped so quickly over Danny's mouth that he instinctively said, "Sorry, Cass."

"Don't say that," Boy growled. "Don't ever say anything like that ever again. The swearing? Okay, you might get away with a bit but don't ever do that."

With eyes wide, Danny nodded and the hand was slowly pulled away. Boy darted his head from side to side, checking for anyone who may have been within earshot.

"Identity issues?" Danny whispered.

"Don't even think about it," Boy hissed. "Literally. Don't think it. There's always someone listening."

The monster grabbed their attention by changing its path to head inland, up Western Road. It used the cinema on the west corner for support as it turned; it seemed to have some problems with the vector change and maintaining its balance. It pivoted on its left leg, its right rose into the air searching for a point of counterbalance as its body teetered over. Its left arm stretched out and obliterated the promotional billboard for '*X-Men Babies: Mojo's Irony*', its body toppled part way into the building and it took a few moments to try to correct itself.

This hiatus allowed Danny the time to concentrate on the beast, desperately searching for something he did not know the identity of or even if it was actually there. Like a prank page of 'Where's Wally'. The monster's physicality shifted in and out of focus, blurring at the edges to the point of intransience and, all the while, a form started to become more definite within its mass until it coalesced into the shape of a man: naked, suspended in mid-air, echoing the creature's movements. As he pulled his vision back into perspective, he assayed the tactics of secret compatriots: big guy hits head, flying girl attacks ankles, the rest target the thighs and chest. And where was the actual target?

"Right in the happy sacks," he said.

"Nobody told me speaking to the English was going to be so hard," Boy moaned.

"You need to get a wave of sprouts and whack it in the nuts," Danny told him.

"In its...? What? That's a bit below the belt, isn't it?"

"Have I ever given you reason to doubt me before?" Danny demanded. "After everything we've been through, I need you to trust me this one more time."

Words and sentiment filtered through. Luckily, sense and meaning did not.

It started as a delicate pitter-patter and quickly built into a stormy cacophony of thumps. Multiple, non-synchronous drum beats hammered off concrete, metal and glass. Boy stood with his eyes closed, head lowered and fists clenched as a trickle of green became a tidal wave, crashing around the stabilising creature's midriff then amassing to form a bobbly simulacrum in front of it. It swung a leg backwards, held it for one breath-drawing moment, then swung it forward to connect with the monster's crotch. The resulting impact created a shock wave that knocked the on-looking heroes off their feet and shattered windows in a half-mile radius.

The exertion of the action was too much for Boy and he collapsed to the ground. Danny managed to catch his head and cushion his fall.

The sprout monster, disconnected from its puppet master, disintegrated, its elements rolled down the hill towards the beach.

The creature itself contemplated the situation, folded at its waist then fell forward, taking out three more buildings on its way down. The heroes gathered themselves around the recumbent mass, warily watching for signs of recovery. Danny hauled Boy to his feet to join them; Cassandra emerged from a side street to share the load. The creature's moist, armoured shell began to glisten more lustrously. Sharp edges softened and scales fused together. What green orbs were still lying around found themselves being lifted on a rising tide of swamp water. The creature was melting, losing all distinctive features, gradually pooling into an amorphous mass of mulch. Then, as the core of its substance diminished, a solidity remained: the unconscious body of a naked man.

Boy wearily lifted his head and managed a self-satisfied smile. "I did it?"

"You did... something, Boy," the hügerman replied with concern scrawled across his bulbous forehead. His body had begun to deflate but not uniformly; random areas had bigger leaks than others: the lower half of his head had been sucked in giving him a light bulb effect and his whole body was leaning to one side because his left leg was shrivelling faster than his right.

A golden haired, slim female had taken it upon herself to act as a prop for him until things balanced themselves.

Danny found his inspection of her taking a little bit longer than any of the others (later, upon being interrogated by Cassandra for an explanation of the events, he would explain that it was her static aura that was causing him to have to stare so intently at her body).

She had a harness strapped around her body that was collaged by a plethora of technological doodads - wires, LEDs and circuit boards. There were wrist and ankle cuffs of a similar design and a pair of flight goggles pulled up to her forehead, holding her sunshine hair out of her face. Bright blue eyes stared suspiciously at Boy's assistants and the stern expression was made even more intimidating when framed by high, round cheekbones, button nose and full, pouty lips. Where she had been adorned with an abundance of gadgetry and aesthetically pleasing features, karmic balance had reneged on ample material for her uniform. Although it was the same muddy shade as her compatriots, it had probably been designed by a costumier who had a long and illustrious career making horse bridles. The two widest strips covered her shoulders. They traced the curvature of her collarbone down to her breasts, which were largely covered by the electronics but still displayed profiles of her firm, fleshy orbs. A single, tapered stripe continued down to her belly button where it bifurcated horizontally to loop around her pelvis to join at the base of her spine. Strands stretched down from her hips to merge into just enough coverage just in time. The wispy entrails briefly continued slithering and cross-hatching down her legs until they buried themselves under her thigh-high boots. From behind, it could be seen that a meshwork of straps offered some additional top support, thereafter attaching themselves to the equatorial belt. A single, central narrow ribbon tapered from there down between her legs, precariously straddling the inner boundary of each buttock.

Danny found the need to swallow.

Cassandra wrinkled her face with disgust.

"Who are you two?" the woman demanded with a Southern States' accent.

"I'm..." Danny peeled off because his brain wanted to announce a cool codename to the world - something about seeing stuff. How had he described it earlier? The Shite Seer? The Watcher? "... Danny," he said weakly.

"They're supreme," the woman of black stated coldly. She was decked in black leather; a trench coat that looked denser than its airy movement suggested, revealed glimpses of her undergarments: tight-fitting leggings wrapped around toned calves and thighs; a halter-top veed precipitously into her cleavage; shiny silver adornments laced the lining of her coat and winked maliciously whenever the panels wafted open. Her eyes were covered by green oval lenses that curled up at the outer edges, giving her an Egyptian appearance. Her shoulder-length, brown hair had been pulled back into a tense tail that seemed to flick at the end with irritation. "Apparently," she added.

There was a long silence that went beyond the realms of awkwardness and fell into the pits of confusion. It felt like someone was supposed to say something but s/he missed their cue. It was now up to the other players to adapt and improvise to get the script back on task but they were wary as to who was going to lead.

"Mother fucking supreme," Danny blurted instinctively.

The heroes took a synchronised step backwards so quickly that Danny and Cassandra retaliated in measure.

"Watch your mouth, boy," the lesser-than-big-but-still-larger-than-average man instructed.

"I didn't say it," Boy protested. "I warned him."

"Not you, Boy," the man explained, "the boy next to you."

"Who are you calling 'boy'?" Cassandra demanded.

"Him," Danny replied and pointed to Boy.

"And you," Boy stated and lifted himself to support his own weight.

"That's not my name, though," Danny said.

"He's not using it as a handle, Danny," Cassandra barked, "he's being insulting."

"Zounds," Danny gasped. "Consorts!"

The shorter, purple tinted woman stepped forward, pulling a hair band from the back of her head and shaking her straight, brown to fall into a neat bob. She was shorter than the others and more overtly toned. Her skin-suit displayed the curvature of every muscle from her shoulders down to her ankles. Her body rippled with waves of raw power, plunging into each other, reinforcing each other at peaks and flattening briefly when there should be troughs. "What can they do?" she demanded and folded her arms defensively.

"I-" Danny started.

"'They'," she repeated.

Boy looked between them in anticipation of something kicking off. When it was obvious they were just going to glare at each other, he replied slowly, carefully choosing each word, "He has some sort of optical enhancement that allowed him to identify the bad guy's weak spot."

"Good report, Boy," the man praised (and even though his body had shrunk to relatively meagre proportions, his suit had remained steadfastly adhered to his contours), "but 'bad guy'?"

"Oh, er, antagonist? Antagonist," Boy corrected himself.

"I see," the emaciated man pondered. Then, when he had finished evaluating, he thrust his arm forward, extending his hand. "I'm Bold Bob Jaw and this, our team, is the Genetically Altered Squad."

Danny shook his hand and felt rather queasy by his limp, flaccid grip.

"This is Floater -" Bob indicated to the static woman at his side who, despite his state of normalcy, still held his arm. "- she is our technology expert and has devised the equipment that can create and manipulate gravitational fields.

"This is the Cat." He pointed at leather girl. "She has retroactive acuitive perception."

"And bad-ass Ninja skills!" Danny added.

Bob needed to consider the word 'ass' and its implications, resolving to scowl as he continued. "Block, over there," - defensive stance woman - "has a self-generating, reflective kinetic shield."

"You've already met Boy Sprout -"

"Ha!" Danny laughed. "Boy Sprout. I get it now. I wondered about the Cubs outfit."

"The what?"

"- and his empathic link and telekinetic mastery over Brussels sprouts." It rolled more easily off his tongue. "And then there's..." He trailed off and looked around his team, settling his vision on a very obvious gap between Block and Cat that could have been construed as a body language thing. His gaze flowed around and settled on Cassandra. "... you."

"Me?" she squarked. "I haven't got anything to do with this. I'm normal."

Again, the heroes took a step back. Block positively oozed with seething indignation. "And we're not?" she demanded.

"No," Cassandra replied in utter surprise. "You're not normal. People who do the things you do aren't normal."

"Paranormal," Danny interjected quickly. "She means 'more than normal'."

"Ab-fucking-normal," she muttered under her breath which caused Boy to bristle and scamper across the divide to show his primary allegiance (just in case the verbal turned to physical).

"Cassandra," Danny said, "her name's Cassandra and she's with me."

The heroes all nodded and 'Ahed' with profound understanding. Cassandra eyed them suspiciously, daring any of them to make their understanding clear to her.

"I was wondering if I can join?" Danny asked with a huge grin on his face.

The heroes looked at one another with varying shades of uncertainty.

"I haven't really established a persona or what-not yet cos I only just had my origin last week."

"Shhhhhh!" Bob commanded (the others looked around themselves as if having been told there was a shape-shifting alien infiltrating humanity with the intention of undermining its defences to eventually overthrow the entire race... and it could even be one of them!). "We call it, 'a genesis'."

"Don't even think it," Boy hissed.

With the threat finally dealt with, the heroes convened in private to discuss this new complication: should they (could they) consider enrolling a new member into their ranks given that he was obviously altered and certainly displayed the right gumption required of heroism. He seemed keen and confident (perhaps overly?) but was his ability something that could be utilised within the team? And what was it with his sidekick?

While they were discussing Danny's attributes, and being completely disinterested by the calamitous aftermath around them, a squadron of black transit vans and army styled trucks arrived. Each vehicle housed similarly attired occupants: stern and stereotypical men and women dressed in black tailored suits, white shirts, black ties and sunglasses emerged and stood in strategic places. Some had been given bits of equipment to take readings and samples from the scene: still and video cameras; boxes with aerials, dishes or microphones presumably capable of detecting an array of energies or emanations; someone had a trowel and box of nappy sacks.

The green trucks with tarpaulin backs spewed too many combat clad passengers than apparent space should have allowed onto the streets. They dutifully set up perimeters and point and pincer positions; medics finally started to tend to the wounded and others started shifting rubble from one place to another so a compatriot team could move it to somewhere else.

It looked very well organised even if, ultimately, not much was being achieved. Somebody was doing something.

Two of the suited clichés approached Bob. They were both middle-aged but that seemed to be the only common likeness between them. As is the way with most buddy-buddy partnerships, the best team is devised when there are as many contrasting features between them needing to be bridged during their adventures. She was tall and angular: he was short and round; her hair was dark, straight and glossy: his was bright, curly and mismanaged; her eyes were half closed and piercing: he wore glasses that enlarged his eyes like he had been in some sort of iguana gene splicing experiment. The three of them had a brief discussion, which involved Bob pointing in various directions and at various people (Danny being one of them). Eventually they nodded to each other, shook hands and went their separate ways. Bob turned in Danny's direction and waved him to join them all.

"Looks like they've made their mind up," Danny whispered and Cassandra rolled her eyes. "I haven't been this nervous since losing my virginity."

"And your mum's not even here," she mumbled.

"Step mum," he corrected her and picked up his pace to put a bit of additional distance between them.

Bob was holding his right hand out for Danny to shake. He reciprocated the offering and gripped the hand firmly. Bob winced slightly from the boy's over exertion but smiled through the pain. "Congratulations, Danny," he boomed. "By a unanimous decision, I hereby indoctrinate you into the Genetically Altered Squad as a novice supreme."

"A padowan?"

"Novice supreme," Bob repeated.

"But everyone said yes?" Danny enthused and completely missed the shifty expressions and sideways glances of his new colleagues as he scanned around the group.

"Well," Bob replied cautiously, "at first, we thought the team was at its optimal size. After a recount, we realised we actually had an empty seat on the van so there was no *rational* reason -" He shot a look at Block. "- why we couldn't take you on."

"Sweet!" Danny called and raised his arm for high-fives. Everyone - Cassandra included - managed to avoid reciprocation by various degrees of nonchalancy; only Boy felt awkward and intimidated by the exuberancy to limply raise an arm and received an almighty **WHAP** across his palm as recompense. "You and me, dude! We can be like Blue Beetle and Booster Gold!"

"What are you saying?"

"You need to be led through an induction and training period first," Bob stated. "Uniform, policies and team ability acclimatisation."

Cat was the first one to notice; a small, green LED winked urgently at her from the cuff of her right glove. "Something's not right," she declared.

"A second wave?" Bob asked, his body already beginning to expand.

Cat checked some sort of read-out on her wrist and shook her head. "It's something... different."

A piece of rubble shifted itself from the collapsed wall next to them and they took a preparatory step backwards. It wobbled on the peak of the pile then gently plinked its way down to the base. The constituents on the next level became unsettled and rattled down the slopes as debris emerged from within; a rubbly mouthful of saliva before the gutful of vomit.

The metaphor extended itself more relevantly as shardy, earthy browns made way for a fluid, bright primaries: the shades of tomato soup and sweet corn. But, no, the conceit did not last because it quickly became apparent that the moistness was only the surface lustre of a limb. The puke was actually a person, pulling themselves free of the hardcore.

"A survivor!" Bob declared and deflated. He leapt forward (close observers would note that his team members had pre-emptively stepped back) and grabbed the sprouting appendage, offering support and anchorage. He pulled and a torso blossomed: horrifically bloody, shredded and twisted - more so than one would imagine a motile body should be able to sustain - and Bob's desperation to aid this poor soul grew so he pulled harder.

The torso displayed deep impact craters and overt bony extrusions and Bob realised the hand he pulled on was backwards for its expected angle. A head sprouted and lolled around loosely on its shoulders. An eye stared unblinkingly into the distance, taking in everything that its dislocated neck directed its head to. Its other eye was swollen shut, freshly purpled and seeped pustulent, rhubarb coloured tears. Straggles of blonde hair had been streaked pink by the weeping holes in its scalp. Deep trenches had raked down the side of its face revealing its jawbone and molars through flaps in its cheeks.

Bob jerked back in revulsion and instinctively bulked up again. In doing so, his strength multiplied exponentially and he inadvertently ripped the gashed being's arm out of its socket.

The heroes had continued their retreat - through fear or effective reconnaissance was unclear - but now Floater screamed as the lump of meat disconnected from the body with a wet suction-cup of a **POP** and a pent up reservoir of crimson gobbed out over the road. They skittered and scuttled backwards as the splash grabbed for their toes.

"Zombie!" Danny squealed with excitement.

"Don't hit me," the creature ordered with a greater level of eloquence and clarity than its mandibles should have allowed. "It's me, Gillian," it continued through its loose hanging maw.

"Gill?" Cassandra enquired with a tremor of fear in her voice. "What happened to you? Why are you even here?"

"You know her?" Block demanded.

"It's a girl?" Boy squealed.

Bob raised the spongy limb over his head, ready to strike.

A peculiar, yet familiar, sound pervaded the group's awareness: a quiet but close voice, not quite a whisper and not projecting from a great distance. The secondary voice was coming from the fresh corpse; from its mouth. It was someone else speaking in the background: speaking but trying not to be heard.

"I'm trying to," the primary voice said without moving its lips (which, incidentally, were hanging below its chin), "but he's threatening to hit me with an arm!"

"There's a lot of interference," the backseat voice stated.

"Okay! Listen, Cass, I'm talking to you through this reanimated vessel. I'm in Portsmouth and need you to get here as quickly as you can because Cameron has an emergency. 66b, Manners Road. Got that?"

"O-kay," Cassandra replied uncertainly.

"See you soon," the voice said brightly and the body folded to the ground, displaying a collection of too many joints that had been hidden during its vertical state.

"Awesome! A mission!" Danny enthused.

"A personal calling," Bob said. "I can't endorse team involvement if we haven't been called via the appropriate channels."

Now, Danny was crestfallen and it was something akin to the look of a lame puppy... being fed into a wood chipper. "Like what? GASphone?"

"Direct interaction, governmental instruction or interstellar-stroke-pan dimensional foreboding of doom."

"'Kay."

"It would be morally wrong of us to intervene in, what could be deemed to be, a path of personal development," Bob explained.

"Can you give us a lift, though?" Danny asked. "It's only a couple of hours down the road."

Bob searched the inside of his mind for a response and only came up with, "I suppose so."

The Gaswagon (as Danny hailed it) was unimpressive in every way other than its design, upkeep and colouring: a 1974 VW camper van with clashing splashes of purple and green around it. Tinted windows gave it a vaguely cool look but the flaking patches of paint and oversized Thule on the roof swiftly plummeted it back into the realms of middle-aged scrap heap.

"You travelled in that thing?" Danny asked Boy. "You're braver than I thought." He looked around the group in anticipation of some kind of acknowledgement but they all just glared at him.

"Ah'll have you know," Floater sniffed and took a hip-swinging step towards him, "this Microbus has been optimised for efficiency, safety, comfort, defensive and offensive capabilities."

"I didn't mean -"

She thrust her hands on her hips and locked one leg so her pelvis jaunted. She pulled her shoulders back slightly, projecting her breasts, and widened her tantalising blue eyes. "Ah personally oversaw the retuning of the engine for performance and ecological factors."

"I was only -"

She pushed her head forward, strands of her gossamer hair drifted over her alabaster cheeks, and her lips pursed together. "Then, Cat and Ah devised a hydrogen propulsion engine which runs the thing off water!" A delicate redness rose in her cheeks as she jabbed her slender index finger at him.

"IT WAS A STAR WARS REFERENCE!" he uncharacteristically barked.

They all stared at the over-reaction, which made Danny feel even more uncomfortable.

"It was just a Star Wars reference," he whimpered and desperately tried to not lock eye contact with Floater.

She, in turn, inhaled heavily, calming her emotions. She bit into her full, red, bottom lip thoughtfully, contemplating whether her own actions had been uncalled for. Her eyes moistened and she blinked slowly.

"What is the matter with you?" Cassandra hissed into Danny's ear.

He flustered on the spot: head down, fidgeting, trying to escape. "She was messing with my head, Cass."

Cassandra stared daggers at the blonde and growled out of the corner of her mouth: "If your brain wasn't in your dick, you wouldn't have such difficulty dealing with the tart."

"Block," Bob barked, "take the boy through concept costuming and ethical guidance orientation."

It looked like Block was trying to scowl but, because her face was still bunched from whatever earlier comment was still causing her offense or consternation, any further concentration of her features was sure to cause a density anomaly so she had to relax. "Okay," she said and led the newbs around the side of the van to the cab. There, she activated a hidden panel just above the wheel arch, which released a section of the radiator grill. A slim tube extended vertically to head height, angled at ninety degrees then continued to snake horizontally for a couple of meters. When it stopped, a thin but totally opaque sheet dribbled down from its length to the floor.

The effect was completely lost on the couple.

"You're being paranoid," Danny told Cassandra.

"'Paranoid' my arse," she retorted. "You was slathering over her like a rabid dog."

"Seriously? You need to back off, Cass," he warned.

"You practically inseminated her with your eyeballs."

"For f-" He stopped himself. "For goodness' sake."

"It's bad enough that she's parading around in something that shows off the contours of her urethra," she continued.

"Oh my god! And that's my fault?"

"No, but you trying to crawl inside and stake some territory, is."

"Leave it out!"

"Oh, don't you worry about that, mister," she declared. "It is being well and truly left out until you sort your head out."

"You can't cut me off over this!"

"You've been cock-blocked for less."

Block closed her eyes while the couple continued their debate as if trying to focus on a happy place, or maybe testing her powers to see if they could deflect sound waves and the conjuration of mental images. Her eyes sprung open after a physical shudder ran up her spine in response to Cassandra's reference to, 'ham-fisted sink plunging'. "You must be a paragon of virtue, an epitome of righteousness, the embodiment of morality which means you have to follow a strict set of codes. One of which is, 'romantic interests shall never be treated in such a way as to stimulate the lower and baser emotions.'"

"What?" Cassandra sneered.

"It means, it's okay for you to two to be romantically involved with each other, as long as your relationship does not cross the boundaries of common decency."

"No public displays of affection?" Danny asked.

"No, no, no," Block exclaimed. "We are not the Taliban. Holding hands is acceptable, as is closed mouth kisses and two-second embraces."

"Thank god you're not the Taliban, eh?" Cassandra mocked.

"Ridicule or attack on any religious or racial group is never permissible," Block told her.

Cassandra rolled her eyes. "Jes-"

"Cass!"

In 1971, the British Government's space programme consisted of a consortium of the top astrophysicists from around the commonwealth and a chimpanzee called Cosmo. No rockets, no resources, no money, just a whole bunch of theory, hypotheticals and men with an average IQ of 437 changing a simian's nappy before it could get its hands on its faeces and add a few shit coefficients to their already dodgy calculations on the blackboards.

Bizarrely, had they allowed Cosmo free reign with his excremental expression, they would have discovered that he was that infinite monkey that could, with enough time, not only write the complete works of Shakespeare but also, inadvertently, construct the equations and environments for successful, safe cold fusion. Written in shit, mind.

However, that was the British Government's space programme and their parallel dimension *Coulda World* stories. The Welsh Independent Party's space programme consisted of Evans the Professor and his silver mobile home.

Evans was actually the Professor of Astrophysiometry at Aberystwyth Polytechnic: a very lightly undertaken course which - by nature of its unique specialism, links to the Independent Party and background of the student body - was able to accumulate huge amounts of funding and corporate sponsorship to eventually build their own rocket, administer their own launch and perform a semi-successful expedition to the moon. He was in his mid-fifties and wore an expression of deep-seeded concern: his eyes were not much more than blackened slits, intensely scrutinising everything his gaze fell upon; they were bordered by heavy wrinkles which webbed his whole face, causing the corners of his mouth to be set in a tight-lipped grimace; his bald head accentuated these harshities. Upon getting to know him, he was actually a very personable and light-hearted man most of the time. He saw the positive outcomes of most situations and could draw a humorous perspective from most crises.

Most.

There were times when his mood would swing and it was best to avoid him completely. He could become intolerant, agitated and aggressive.

However, there were only four people who took his class and they quickly worked out the monthly pattern to his biorhythms.

Erich Wodenson was a big man in height, width and charisma. Wherever he stood, it felt like he was standing too close and always looking down. Supposedly, he was a descendent of Nordic royalty – his lustrous blond hair and blue eyes validated his genetic lineage but geography could not. He claimed to be the ruler of a small principality that sat between Sweden and Norway that no one had ever heard of, nor could they find it on any map. Although his previous known address was questionable, his knowledge of the cosmos was not. He was able to map the heavens (day or night) simply by looking up and without having to reference star charts, a clock or by having to find the shiniest star on the Big Dipper first. Aside from his innate knowledge of celestial bodies, Erich also brought with him an almost bottomless purse with which he had no problem funding the slightest enterprise. He was a very important student.

Next was Kevin Keane: dark brown, bowl cut hair and thick-rimmed glasses; skinny, awkward and angular; unwashed, unkempt and smelly; possibly the most intelligent man on the planet. His ability to calculate and formulate and postulate was as innate as breathing. His ability to communicate, however, worked by some rule of inverse exponentials to his mathematical abilities. At that time in history, diagnosis of autism on a spectrum of extremity was performed using the empathic psychometric parameters of, "Are you mental, or what?" So Kevin had lived a confusing and upsetting childhood being victimised by his peers and the medical professionals who were ignorant in the field. It was not until he reached his late teens that he started to mingle with people who - although not necessarily understanding - were certainly more accepting of his 'eccentricities'. Especially when he was capable of writing a few numbers on a piece of paper that could be worth thousands of pounds. He was a very important student.

Larry and Elizabeth Lockwood came as a joint deal. They were the two children of American global industrialist, Harry Lockwood, who had the resources to allow them to explore whatever niche in life they so desired. This year, it was spaceships.

Larry, the oldest, was as many would describe him, a hot head. He had grown up in an environment where everyone would do whatever he wanted and there were very few negative ramifications to any of his actions. With no sense of consequences, he had grown to be impetuous: quick to fly off the handle, quick to jump to conclusions, quick to wade into a fray. Now he was 'somewhere in In-gr-land,' he had decided to play on social stereotyping and so nurtured the cowboy persona he thought everyone thought he had. Even though he seemed like an airheaded, arrogant bruiser, he was actually an exceptional chemist and anthropologist. So, he was not *just* an airheaded, arrogant bruiser. He had an intimate understanding of the human body and how to manipulate it through exposure to a variety of stimuli: physical, chemical, emotional. Specialised knowledge and more financial backing ensured that Larry was an important student too.

Elizabeth was Larry's proviso: where he went, she went. On the one hand, it meant that she got to see a bit more of the big world, on another it kept her from interfering in her father's more morally ambiguous business ventures, and on the third it meant she could chaperone Larry and diffuse potential embarrassments before they could ignite on the front page of the media. She did not come with the same level of intellect or specialised knowledge but did come with the cash so was important by proxy. What she did absolutely offer to the project was her unerring eye-hand coordination and spatial awareness. She could pilot any vehicle. From a child, she would have been given cycles with varying Roman numerical prefixes and master their controls within minutes. Skates for all sorts of surfaces proved to be as if they were natural extensions of her being. It came to pass that anything that had the potential to move - even the most stubborn, squiffy-wheeled trolley - would eventually acquiesce to her manipulations. Panzer tanks, Boeing 747s, office chairs: as soon as she had worked out pitch, yaw, start and stop, they were slaves to her ministrations.

Despite their genetic bonds, there seemed to be few physical similarities between them: his divine Michelangeloesque curled blond hair condescended her near-black-brown, flyaway bob; his authoritative six foot diminished her five foot frame; his slim proportions cast a disproportionate comparison to her stolidity. But for all these differences, the one thing they shared was their unshakeable convictions and, when they clashed, their disputes could be akin to two unmoveable objects travelling at each other unstoppably.

Evans the Professor (or 'Evs' as Larry disrespectfully called him) headed up the faculty. Undisputedly a genius in the fields of astrotheory, astrotheology and astrophilosophy (and a couple of other self-imparted astro-epithets) but actually knew very little about the practical applications. He was the driving force who would conjecture the most abstract notions and push his students to turn theory into practical. And, more often than not, they succeeded: bouncing ideas off one another; where their field became limited by the boundaries of their science, a teammate would be able to offer an element from their specialism until some of the wildest sci-fi imaginings became realised.

Artificial gravitational manipulators, recursive kinetic field generators, atomic bond reduction: these discoveries, amongst others, should allow a craft to accelerate to potentially unlimited speeds without resultant g-forces being exerted; produce an aura of exerting energy which could repel any solid matter; and reduce the physical size of the fuel which thereby reduced the necessary size of the fuel tanks which would cut down the amount of fuel required to achieve escape velocity.

Each member of the team played an integral role to the development of the exploratory space craft they constructed in a clearing in Cwmcynfelin Woods. Its placement there was quite innocuous and went relatively unnoticed by local ramblers, dog walkers and perverts. It was constructed more like an extra large caravan than it was a rocket. Due to the fact that the students had managed to negate the negative effects of acceleration, wind resistance and friction, there was no real need to worry about things like aerodynamics. The craft was therefore constructed to fulfil its primary purpose of housing five people comfortably while they travelled a long distance. There was the laboratory, which had been customised to suit each scientist's specialism; each had their own cubicle for 'r and r' and 'getting the hell away from the nerds'; there was also a shared social area with TV and eight-track player; and, of course, everybody had a window seat in the cockpit.

This was achieved by making the flight deck spherical; a transparent orb that protruded through the top of the block body of the craft looking like it was blowing a snot bubble through its roof.

People thought it was just a forester's cabin or BBC bird hide but, otherwise, paid it no more attention than that. Unless a hiker was caught short mid-ramble and looked for a door to get in.

The only thing about it that had ever caused any contention was what its name should have been. It had to have a ring to it, be collectively relevant and appropriate to its purpose. Roman gods were often a good one, also science fiction novelists or mythological creatures. But it had to be nothing that could be used ironically against them.

"The Phoenix," Larry suggested with an elaborate wave of his arms as if the name was emblazoning the very space above his head. His blue eyes stared in awe at the imaginary scene before him; his chest puffed outward with masculine pride; his legs stood astride with noble confidence.

"Point of order," Beth interrupted, "surely for a phoenix to rise from ashes means it must, at some time, end in ashes?" she questioned.

Larry desperately wanted to argue but, for a change, could see the irrefutable logic in her argument and swiftly backed down.

He took back to his seat like a deflating balloon and Erich stood with unerring purpose; his blond hair billowed around his granite chiselled cheekbones. "Ares," he declared with boldness that even the most hardened contrarian would have trouble disputing. "God of war. He is a most hardened and most worthy god; a name that wouldst bring much resolute fortune to our craft." And with an additional dramatic flourish, he scribed the word, 'Ares' in regal italics across an acetate sheet that was on the overhead projector in the centre of the table.

"Arse?" Larry read phonetically from the projector screen and that was that decision made.

Kevin's pale and emaciated face lowered itself to direct the crown of his greasy brown hair at them. This was his signal that he was preparing to speak to them; the only time they got to see his thick, black-rimmed bespectacled face was when he was lost in thought and unaware of company around him. "How about 'Hubbard'? After L Ron Hubbard who is an excellent writer of science fiction who wrote *The Ultimate Adventure* and has some very interesting ideas about humanity's origins that have been rivalling Christian beliefs," he said with his usual dispassionate but confident monotone.

"You want us to name our highly explosive spaceship – a craft that will be skimming past the doors of God himself – after a man who defies the word of the Big Man?" Professor Evs demanded. "Now, I'm not a religious person, as such, but I don't think upsetting *any* potential deities is a good idea."

In the end, to solve any further debate, Professor Evs made the final decision: '*The Dandare*'. None of the students understood the reference so at least there was some continuity there.

The launch date was a very underrated affair: at first, it was planned for Saturday evening, straight after Professor Evs had checked the results from Match of the Day against his pools. Unfortunately, this had to be postponed because he managed to accumulate twenty-four points, which meant a big win, and he insisted treating everyone to fish and chips and a few pints down the *Moonraker's Arms*. This, in turn, meant that it could not be held the next day, the Sunday, because of hangovers.

It was not rescheduled, or even mentioned again, until class on Wednesday. The four students were waiting patiently in the lecture theatre when Professor Evs burst in, out of breath and a bit anxious. "Right then, you lot," he puffed. "Pack a spare pair of knickers; we're going to the moon today."

And that was it. No pomp. No ceremony. No student news reporter. Just five people with lightweight holdalls taking an afternoon stroll through the woods. They entered The Dandare, wiped their feet on the mat and unpacked their belongings in their cubicles; Professor Evs put the kettle on.

"Right then, last minute checks," he ordered and tossed computer printouts across a broad underlit table. Respective students grabbed the documents that made most sense to them, spread them out in front of them and poured over the data. Evs liberally spread some biscuits over a poppy decorated plate and poured out the tea.

"This is interesting," Larry announced. "There's been a recent, unexplainable shift in the sun's solar radiation spikes. We should reconsider our trajectory."

"Whatever you think, boyo," Evs muttered through a spray of biscuit crumbs. "Just make sure we get to the moon safely, now."

"Sir," Kevin stuttered.

"Permission to speak, boy," Evs commanded with a knowing wink at Beth.

"With Larry's altered trajectory, I calculate a potential erroneous incurrence."

"In English, boy!"

"A problem, sir," Kevin corrected himself with a scrunched up face of concentration (whether this was due to trying to think his vocabulary down to a more primary level or holding back his frustration at being so obviously patronised to was not clear). "There are readings here that indicate a mass of matter – a meteor cloud – that we should compensate for."

"Serious?"

"It might get a bit bumpy."

"How will it affect our journey?"

"To circumnavigate would consume an additional forty per cent of fuel and take twenty extra hours."

"We can handle a bit of bumpy, right boys?"

The students looked at each other dubiously.

"Thine shields willst hold most verily," Erich declared.

"English!" Evs demanded.

"The shields can cope with debris up to half a meter diameter, weighing up to 500 kilograms travelling at thirty kilometres a second," Larry reiterated. "This course is the best suited."

They all looked at Kevin while he scanned through his printouts. "We should be fine," he deduced with consternation.

"My liege," Erich hailed. "Mine calculations dost contend with our intent. Forsooth, our final destination wouldst befit a recourse."

"Make it so, boyo," Evs commanded. "Just get us on that moon."

The sun was drifting below the treetops, casting long, cold, finger-like shadows across the roof of The Dandare; its compound eye cockpit peeked through a pair of knuckles at the waxing moon. They stared at each other with silent intent. Oh yeah, it was on!

Five dark orbs found position in the eye: four at equally placed points around a centre one. They bobbed back and forth; an excess of energy making the little atoms vibrate excitedly within the fixtures of their bonds.

Something activated around the perimeter base of the craft and it began to blossom outward: thick sheets of dense metal delicately slid over each other, sighing at their gentle caresses until, finally, locking into position with a jolt that indicated a lot more power had been exerted than first seemed. The Dandare's base had increased its surface area by fifty per cent and was now resembling a caravan had it been owned by some Egyptian Pharaoh who had not fully accepted his godhood and wanted his children to grow up with a sense of the real world.

A thrum reverberated through the craft, commencing in its perimeter and waned into its centre. Its pitch intensified though and, as it reached a pinnacle, erupted into a roar of violent indignation. Brilliant blue flames spewed from its underbelly and flooded around the woodland floor, incinerating flora and fauna unfortunate enough to fall in its waves. Green shrivelled to brown, flesh hardened to charcoal, dirt fused into glass.

The Dandare shifted on its moorings - only slightly at first, as if caught in a rough gale - gently rising, fighting against gravity's lure. One would have imagined a greater struggle as this unwieldy block attempted to defy the laws of an entire planet's will, trying to break through barriers of attraction, resistance and forestry. But no, The Dandare continued to rise gracefully to the treetops, gradually gaining momentum as it gained height. Branches across the canopy reached out in one last desperate attempt to hold it back but they were forced to recoil before the craft had even touched them as if having changed their minds at the last minute.

The Dandare was finally free of earthly constraints and now, away from the contrasting reminders of gravity, with its juxtaposition to the clouds high above, it looked less like a brick trying to perform ballet but more like a star, regally surveying its surroundings. Without any immediate counterpoints, the momentum of its continued ascension was difficult to judge. It could have still been rising with its slow but steady purpose or it could have been perfectly stationary. It gently rotated on its vertical axis; a freshly hung Christmas bauble unwinding itself from eleven months of hibernation.

A streak of white whipped past like a tissue in a hurricane. Then there was another. And another. Another. The Dandare was consumed by a dense fog in an instant and now its relative speed was discernible; trailing whirls of mist churned in its wake; spiralling strands evaporated as quickly as they formed; it erupted through the roof to be faced with a midnight blue vista of infinity, speckled with diamanté flecks of unattainable wonder.

The scientists, despite their collective intelligence and practical understanding of the universe, could not help but stare in quiet amazement at the sight. Without the refractive interference of the atmosphere; without the distortion effect of air-borne evaporated water molecules; without the manipulation of gravity disguising their true position: these remnant markers of light radiation from burning balls of hydrogen were really quite mesmerising.

"Nearly there, kiddies," Evs declared in a soft lilt that could have been perceived as just speaking his thoughts aloud had it not been for the obvious company. But they were so enraptured in their own thoughts, the students bade it no notice. "Nearly there."

Their passage continued. The students checked readings and made calculations and pottered around the craft with no real intent. Everything was now up to Beth to stay on course but even that only required a slight adjustment of her instruments every hour or so. Right up until the flight system alerted her to a more extreme manoeuvre that unsettled her inner navigator. She checked the flight plan against the coordinates she had been given, activated the autopilot, released herself from the cockpit and calmly sought Evs, who was making another cup of tea.

"Professor," she announced quietly.

"Use the head whenever you need, love," he replied, "no need to ask for permission."

"It's not that," she said. "Erich's calculations won't get us to the moon. His course will make us overshoot and head into space."

He poured the boiled water into his mug; the clarity of the water transmogrifying into murky brown. "A slight miscalculation, perhaps?"

"We will miss by over a hundred miles."

He added a heaped teaspoon of sugar, allowing the microcosmic mountain to gently avalanche into the liquid then plunging the metal in after the last crystals had submerged. He stirred, slowly and deliberately, causing the outer edges to rise to the brim of the cup as they tried to escape the suffusing eddy in the middle. "Can you make the corrections, pet?"

"Not with the navigational computer, sir," she confessed, "but manually? Yes."

"Make it so. I'll deal with Erich."

They parted ways calmly; Beth returned to the cockpit, switched the autopilot off and manipulated buttons on the console that made the stars wheel around. She became aware of a presence behind her and did not need to turn.

"You dare?" Erich demanded.

"You would have killed us all," she replied.

"I wouldst bring you such glory, the likes of which bards would herald during the feasts of Ragnarok for all eternity. You must revert to my suggested course," he growled at her.

"I'm taking us to the moon," she stated.

"I say thee nayergh!" His pitch started the statement as a commanding roar but ended as a strained croak.

She turned around now, wondering what malevolence awaited her. She was completely unprepared for the spectacle before her: Erich was towering above her; his blonde mane billowing around his face; his jaw fixed in a garish grimace of violent intent; every muscle in his huge frame, clenched. The most disturbing aspect, though, was his body was radiating pure electrical energy. It arced between his fingertips, sparked and crackled across his skin and created an incandescent halo around him. His steel-blue eyes had been fixed upon her but now wiped to white as they rolled up into their sockets. His hand reached out to her, fingers stretched as if about to release the pent up charge within him. Then he collapsed to the floor and twitched.

Evs had been standing behind him. In his hand was a two-foot pole with a two-pronged fork at the end. Behind him were Larry and Kevin looking torn between being defensive and offensive.

"Cattle prod," Evs said pre-emptively.

"Erich's coordinates had us drifting off course," Beth placated the boys.

Before any further questions or explanations could be engaged in, a sharp thump resonated through the hull of The Dandare.

An expression of extreme consternation engulfed Kevin's face. "If you have readjusted his course," he contemplated, "then it could have serious implications on our trajectory through the meteor cloud."

"You said we could handle it, boy," Evs reminded him. "A bit bumpy, I believe."

"On Erich's course we would have skimmed its periphery," Kevin clarified. "Now we will be heading through its heart."

The tension in Larry's body escaped with a flap of incredulous indignation. "Oh come on! How can you possibly know that without crunching some numbers? Not even you could have memorised that much data or know what course correction Beth made."

"No," Kevin snarled; staring intently at the floor in front of his feet. "But I do recognise a huge piece of rock when I see one." He pointed out through the cockpit at a gently twirling, pebble-shaped obstruction.

"That doesn't look too bad," Evs commented.

They climbed up into the cabin so the full panoramic vista of the heavens was put into its proper perspective. The pebble appeared to be about the size of a football pitch but had to be re-evaluated when it became apparent that it was a very long way away. Its smooth, metallic surface glistened moistly in the sunlight and its mellow movement mesmerised the crew until one of its more hyperactive offspring leapt at them from nowhere and **SPOINGED** as the repellent shield bounced it away.

"Will you look at the size of that thing," Larry gasped. "It must be at least a mile in diameter."

"Two miles," Kevin corrected him. "Two miles at its widest."

"Can we avoid it?" Evs enquired.

"I can try," Beth replied and strapped herself securely into her seat. She pulled at the lever in front of her and The Dandare pitched suddenly to the left.

Larry took the seat beside her.

"How do you know this thing's size, boyo?" Evs demanded with a direct insinuating glare at Kevin.

"Radio-cartographic readings," he replied without a trace of trepidation. "Early spectroanalysis indicated the existence of core elements otherwise undiscovered on our periodic table; a metal that remains in liquid form at absolute zero and becomes a non-Newtonian fluid at body temperatures and only solidifies at temperatures over two hundred degrees Celsius."

"And you thought a head on collision would help identify it?" Evs bellowed, causing Kevin to physically recoil, turning away from the man.

"No. No. Not collide. Coordinates would circumnavigate, allowing me to take samples from the edges of the cloud."

"Why didn't you tell us, boy? This is a tremendous discovery we could have worked on together."

"NASA told me not to say anything."

Even the pebble seemed to stop in mid spin for that one dramatic moment.

"NASA," Evs repeated in an almost sub-sonic baritone. "Fucking NASA!" He brandished the cattle prod and jabbed it at Kevin. "Get off my fucking ship."

A short spark of electricity jolted through Kevin's body and he threw himself away from his tormentor. "Can't get off in vacuum of space; death is almost instantaneous through suffocation, freezing and depressurisation."

Evs jabbed him again, steering him towards the entry. "I'm not a monster, boy, you can take a suit."

"Death is still inevitable - starvation, dehydration -"

Jab. "I'll give NASA a call, let them know where you are. GET OFF MY FUCKING SHIP!"

Kevin thrust his palms over his ears and howled loudly, attempting to block out the external and internal noises. Evs kept prodding him though, and he involuntarily shuffled into the airlock.

Meanwhile, Larry had been keeping a careful watch on their new trajectory, occasionally triangulating a projected path and swearing under his breath. "Sis," he muttered, "I don't suppose there's any chance you could change course?"

"Are you fucking kidding me?" she growled. "At this speed, we're going to be lucky we don't end up like a pancake on this rock. There is no other route other than hoping its density is as compact as polystyrene and going straight through."

"It's just that..." Larry's voice trailed off as the landscape of the pebble became more distinct.

It was anything but a smooth surface. Skyscraper sized splinters of gleaming animosity reached out to eviscerate anything that got in their way. The circulating meteors were reduced to shrapnel shaped sharps of swarming savagery.

Years of unspoken sibling understanding set an alarm ringing in her head. "'Just' what?" she demanded. "What have you done?"

Larry stared through the dome at their impending doom. Despite the perfectly regulated climate conditions, a heavy splatter of perspiration had appeared across his forehead. His eyes shifted quickly between objects although they did not focus on anything beyond his inner thoughts. "There are some unusual radiation spikes that I wanted to explore," he explained. "Initial hypotheses suggested that, when harnessed, could be an easily farmed renewable energy: Dad would monopolise the global energy market."

"Dad?!" Beth exclaimed. "Oh, Larry. You sold your soul to the devil."

He turned to her. "Not just mine, sis. On these current settings, we'll fly through the core of the radiation. I don't know what the result will be; if we're lucky, we'll die."

"And if we're unlucky?"

"We'll be horribly mutated and die in extreme agony."

"Isn't there anybody on this mission who hasn't conspired to kill us all?" Beth questioned, pulled back on the flight lever and pushed forward on the thrusters.

"What are you doing?"

"If I can navigate the slivers of instant death and penetrate the surrounding clouds of razored obliteration, I'm hoping to face a penetrable frozen crust and liquid centre."

"What the hell would make you think it might be liquid?" Larry demanded.

"The outcrops remind me of the old crystal growing experiments we did in fifth grade."

"But they were solids grown in liquid!"

"Exactly."

"What!? Your theory has no foundation to it."

"Kevin said it was solid at temperatures over two hundred degrees which would explain its crystalline structure on this side in direct sunlight, any part of it in shadow could be in liquid form: below the surface, hopefully, and on the opposite side."

"How thick's the surface, though?"

"Which death would you prefer? This one or yours?"

It took a fraction of a second to consider. "Gun it," he said.

The Dandare was equiped with RaDAR, SoNAR and vector encoded determining entity emplacement (which needed a better acronym than VeEDEE) which could predict and plot the position of multiple objects based on a range of factors including mass, momentum and external resistances then project them as three dimensional outlines a lot like an advanced version of *Asteroids*. But Beth did not need them; she relied on what she could see with her own eyes, what was right in front of her. And with that, she rotated the Dandare on multiple axes, skimming the surface of fractal knife-edge brachia and slaloming through the chicanes of sharp meteor fragments.

"We still won't avoid the danger zone of these galactic beams," Larry informed.

"Perhaps we will find some protection if we break through the surface," Beth hoped.

"Right then," Evs called from behind them, "that's that sorted. What have I missed?"

Larry and Beth turned to eye him with as much condescension as they could muster, given the circumstances, while his eyes widened in an attempt to take in the expanse of metallic lustre that now blocked out the infinity of space that he was expecting to see.

A small red light blinked rapidly on the console in front of them.

"That's just the airlock," Evs minded as he watched the surface of the pebble come into further HD clarity to reveal a pristine mirror reflecting their rapid kamikaze approach.

"Fire torpedoes?" Larry suggested.

"The heat will only solidify it," Beth replied.

"Do we have anything that will cool it? Liquid hydrogen missiles?"

"Only the contents of the mini-bar," Evs said.

"And our shadow," Beth stated and adjusted their course to target a rapidly enlarging darkness. As she did, a body-sized projectile was seen darting away at a tangent. "If we block the sunlight, it might be enough to reduce its temperature to melting."

Another red light flickered more urgently.

"Radiation levels are spiking," Evs commented with an air of concern.

"We're not going to get clear," Larry muttered.

"Brace yourselves!"

Long before its actual impact, The Dandare slowed dramatically. The repelling field attempted to push the pebble out of its way but was as effective as an ant shoving at a juggernaut. The energy generator within the ship strained with the exertion being reversed upon itself and more red lights winked on the flight consol. The buffer between field border and hull lessened and the resultant pressure increased. Another alert flicked on, warning of an imminent breach of The Dandare's outer shell. Then the surface of the pebble bowed and cracked.

Despite inertia dampeners integrated across all planes within the ship, even they could not compensate for the precollision deceleration or the intracollision stoppage. Anything that was not battened down was sent hurtling through the craft: papers, cutlery, furniture and bodies careened around the interior, bouncing off surfaces like a tornado was late for an appointment.

The seat straps dug into Beth's shoulders and stomach as her mass tried to join in with the momentous calamity. Then the surface tension of the pebble broke, the thrusters resumed their propulsive powers and The Dandare jerked forward again. The moorings of Beth's chair could not handle the sudden direction change of inertial forces, wrenched themselves clear and sent her flying to the back of the craft, pinballing between the banks of generators.

As The Dandare sank below the surface, the sun's rays reheated the metal and it crystalised again as if nothing had happened and the literary perspective moved around the pebble, past the shadow line, into pitch-blackness. Under normal circumstances, the lack of light radiation would prevent any detail of this side of the pebble being contrasted from the blackness of the void around it. However, literary no-light vision can compensate by blinking a few times until its omniscient perspective irises are fully dilated. On this side, the pebble's name was better suited than before. Its surface was perfectly smooth and gently curved outwards, creating a convex surface that refracted the extremely potent and mysterious spacial rays into its core where The Dandare was passing.

White lights flickered intermittently; sparks crackled and rattled through open panels; for some reason, the rest of the craft was illuminated by red underlighting that cast ominous, prowling shadows up the walls. There was movement from one pile of clutter and Evs pulled himself to his unsteady feet.

"Anyone alive?" he called and included himself to sound off to make sure.

Only the damaged areas of the craft replied with strained groans and metallic 'plinks' while he staggered back to the cockpit, holding on to the walls for support. Amongst the dials, metres and digital readouts that flickered and flashed incomprehensibly at him, one light glared with singular menacing intent.

"Radiation levels are in the red," he muttered. "We're all about to be cooked from the inside out." He looked through the port to be confronted with absolute darkness: no reflected sunlight, no pinpricks of starlight. He pulled a drawer open and took out an ornate silver tube about the size of a katana handle with two buttons at one end. He held it firmly in both hands, raising it parallel to his face as he took a lingering inspection around the derelict ship. His thumb hovered over one button. He depressed gently, received a soft click from the device and a brilliant beam of blue light rose into the darkness. Evs pressed the second button and the beam changed to a gleaming red. Another press and it changed to white and, satisfied, he aimed the torch up at the window to reveal mercury-like, swirling metal streaming across its surface. With that, he also discovered fine hairline fractures in the reinforced glass.

"At least it can't get any worse," he said.

Something – or someone – tapped him on the shoulder and he wheeled to face the emptiness of the craft. Again, there was a pat on the other shoulder to which he just directed his head and, there, found a moist, viscous drop of fluid. While he analysed the substance, it was joined by another heavy droplet. He warily angled his head upwards to seek its source: the ceiling.

There was a puddle gently oscillating above his head. As the ripples crossed and reinforced each other, a peak would become too heavy, globulate and break away from the mass's surface tension, begrudgingly complying with gravity and dropping. Another one GLOLLOPPED onto Evs' shoulder and the combined volume began to run forward, over his chest but stopped, solidifying at the end of its course like ice-cream crispy topping. He dabbed it tentatively with his index finger but it still rippled at his touch. He returned his inspection to the ceiling to discover multiple pools of metallic ooze penetrating the cracks of his craft. Evs slouched with nihilistic resolve into the nearest chair and shrugged his eyebrows with disinterest when he saw the radiation levels had defied the limits of the meter and simply displayed 'E'.

The metal seeped through the gaps between the molecules in The Dandare's hull while the waves of galactic radiation soaked through the craft, staining every atom it washed over: splitting, reforging, moulding, distorting. Different substances suffered different effects to the exposure and there was little consistency even between similar states. One stack of papers burst into flames, whereas another pile liquefied into a pool of mulch.

A mass of clutter shifted and Larry pulled himself free, bearing his weight against a blue, plastic chair that reduced to atomic dust. Its disintegration spread from the chair's centre out. Larry watched the atomisation with rapt curiosity until it reached his hand and he whipped it away as if being burned. He checked his fingertips, seemingly oblivious to the dematerialisation of all solid matter around him. "This is what I came for," he mumbled. The skin on his index finger whitened and began to blister; he lifted the digit closer to his face for critical inspection, his eyes crossing to focus intently. The bubble continued to inflate and spread down the finger's length; his other fingertips displayed similar symptoms.

From the other end of the craft, Beth wrestled herself free of her seat, pulling herself upright using the generators on either side of her for leverage. They huffed out intermittent breaths of smoke, still indignant by the excess labour they had been forced through. Then the space beams streamed through and rid them of their burdens by evaporating their intricate network of wires and releasing the energies constrained within. These, along with the intergalactic powers, coursed through Beth's compactly interwoven DNA and unseamed it, strand by strand. As each helix strand began to flap freely in its protonucleic fluid, the discombobulating forces recombobolated her genetic blueprint but filled gaps and forged new bonds using the data from the excess energies drifting through her. The disintegration and reintegration was instantaneous and simultaneous, creating a blast of pain that passed so quickly it barely registered in her mind. She wavered on her feet uncertainly, postulating an idea that something somewhere had just violated her with extreme prejudice. Her sight caught the eyes of something that looked like a human sized potato at the opposite end of the craft. The pulsing amorphous blob stared at her with a pitiful expression that she recognised from years of bailing him out of trouble. "Larry?"

A hole at its apex opened as if to say something but the hull wall behind it ripped open and the pebble poured in to engulf him.

"Larry?"

The interior of The Dandare had been swept clean of all extraneous matter, only the walls of the craft – with their unusual uplighting – remained. The silver soft innards of the meteor covered the entirety of the ceiling with multiple stalactite formations dripping to the floor. The mass incursion that had just claimed Larry was now creeping around the walls.

"Never mind, eh, girl?" Evs said from the floor of the cockpit. The metallic fluid had continued to drip to the floor but Evs had refused to move. Each droplet that landed on him had dribbled a little further down his body and congealed up until this moment where his head and left arm were the only visible parts of his body, protruding from the glistening stalactite.

She approached him hesitantly: worried that a sudden move might cause the embodying mass to react in some negative manner; worried that too heavy a step would plant a hole in the floor of the fragile craft; worried that the professor, just for the sake of maintaining the status quo, was about to reveal some diabolical plan to destroy them. In all fairness, it looked like they were going to die anyway so she reconsidered her movement and decided on a slightly more bold approach. "Do you need some help?" she asked.

"That I do, girl, that I do," he replied. "However, unless you have access to a matter transporter, time machine or another spacecraft, I doubt that there's any way you could assist."

"I could help pull you out of that... that... stuff."

"Shhhh," he warned. "It's sensitive. Try not to upset it."

"What?"

"Sentient, it is girl," he told her, "not quite on our scale but alive none-the-less. It shares properties with non-Newtonian fluids but has some sort of shape memory. It's fluid." He gently smeared his finger across the surface of the pile and it yielded under his touch. "Yet it sustains sudden pressure." He slammed his hand down violently on an area over his chest and it seemed to have no effect. "I didn't feel a thing," he commented. "And it remembers its shape." He dipped the tip of his finger in and gouged a deep groove through it, which slowly sealed up again in the finger's wake. "Bloody amazing stuff, it is."

"Can we use it to help us?"

"Oh, I doubt that, love. Not unless you plan to wrap yourself up in it and find some way to hurl yourself back in the general direction of Earth."

"Really?"

"Theoretically, like, its density and insular properties increase proportionally to the forces applied to it so should dissipate the temperatures encountered as you re-enter Earth's atmosphere and could even protect you from the kinetic forces upon impact but to be able to navigate your way back from here and do it before your air supply runs out would take the piloting prowess of God himself."

"Or Herself," Beth corrected with a tenacity that belied her circumstances.

Evs just eyed her, contemplating this child who was always the odd one out in the class: completely out of her depth academically, severely limited within the scope of her imagination and a girl to boot. However, at no stage did she ever let the posturing of her peers put her down or put her off. Even now, as Death skulked towards them with invites to a party no excuse could get them out of, she stood there ready to tell him she was washing her hair that night.

He slowly pulled himself upright, the excess malleable material dribbled away from him and left a silvery gilt that lined the atoms of his clothes and exposed areas of skin. "Right, pet, what do you want me to do?"

"Damage report and systems' status," she ordered and, while he scanned over the controls of The Dandare, she bathed in the pools of metallic mulch that had been steadily thickening around her feet and creeping up her heels.

"Amazingly, we still have primary thrusters and any hull ruptures are being supported by the asteroid goop which threatens to drown us. However, we should be leaving it in about thirty seconds, travelling at approximately one-hundred-and-seventy miles per hour," Evs reported. "All generators are kaput, though. No shields, no life support, no power that isn't coming from the main and reserve capacitors. All piloting will have to be done manually."

She nodded her understanding. "Do we have enough fuel to turn back?"

He tapped at a dial and turned back with deep concern etched through his features. "This density shift has depleted the tanks considerably; a stop and turn around will leave very little to allow you to make any trajectory alterations. There is an alternative, –"

\/^^^\/

"Slingshot around the moon?" Danny interrupted from the other side of the opaque sheet.

Block eyed it with suspicion. "That's right. Are you a science man?"

"Science fiction," Cassandra snorted from behind Block.

"Was it a million-to-one-shot?" he asked.

"After he had crunched the numbers," Block continued, "he said it was a one-to-one sure shot as long as I thrust away from the moon at the right point. We made it back without any further complications."

"Oh," Danny muttered with unbridled disappointment, "it doesn't usually happen like that."

"Well, I say that but there was the cosmic force that offered me limitless power in return for hosting its ethereal spirit so it could experience the frailties of being human," Block said matter-of-factly.

There was a contemplative silence from behind the curtain followed by, "And?"

"I told it I wasn't interested."

"Oh."

"But what about your powers?" Cassandra reminded.

"The generators and cosmic rays!" Danny chastised. "Weren't you listening?"

"Space beams," Block corrected. "Aren't you ready yet?"

"Just putting the mask on," he replied.

"I know how she got them, Daniel! When did you find out you had them?" Cassandra reiterated.

"Oh, I see. When we crash landed. The ooze sustained a lot of the impact and heat just as the professor said but we hit in New Mexico travelling in excess of five miles per second. The Dandare crumpled like a soda can and, eventually, people came and cut us out. I was fine, suspended in the middle of a foot-wide clearance of the ship around me. The professor, though, was like an individually canned sardine. He had broken his back and was paralysed from the waist down."

"And now you can create a force field on demand to repel anything that comes near with equal but opposite force," Cassandra cooed.

Block scrunched her face with embarrassment. "Not exactly. The field is actually always there and intensifies the more agitated or irate I get. I have to be completely relaxed and concentrate to drop it."

Danny leapt from the cubicle and posed before the women: standing side on, feet shoulder width apart, fists thrust upon hips, head held high looking into the middle distance. He was adorned in a charcoal grey stretch fabric, which covered his entire body apart from a circular gap for his face and another for the crown of his head. Black gloves and boots rose midway along their respective limbs and flared flamboyantly at the cuffs. His mask was black, thick rimmed and square cut around his eyes and a pair of black boxers attempted to flatten his manliness. "Tremble, evildoers, for your crimes will not escape the gaze of *THE PERSPECTRE!*" he declared.

Cassandra snorted at the back of her throat as she failed to suppress a burst of laughter.

"Good name," Block praised, "and nice costume choice: it fits the ghostly nature of the name, simple in its colouring but still has stylistic flair. You just need a logo."

"How about a huge knob," Cassandra suggested. "Which could also be your superhero name. After all, that seems to be your most obvious power."

Danny looked down to his crotch. "It is a bit snug, isn't it?"

"Rule number one, children: profanity, obscenity, smut, vulgarity, or words or symbols which have acquired undesirable meanings are forbidden," Block recited.

"Gotcha," Danny acknowledged obediently.

"That's rule number one?" Cassandra asked with incredulity.

"Rule one of the Code of Metahuman Dialogue," Block explained. "It is a basic premise of respect. Careful considerate choice of the language you use shows your level of respect for those around you and is an indication of the sort of person you are."

"What do you mean by that?" Cassandra demanded defensively.

"If it sounds like a duck..." Block replied and stared dispassionately at her.

Cassandra's eyes narrowed and her lower jaw jutted forward as her teeth ground together. She inhaled a long and controlled breath until she came to some internal decision, exhaled and allowed her facial muscles to relax again.

"This is The Complete Code," Block told Danny and handed him an A5 booklet. It was thin, containing only a few pages. It looked like it had been printed and compiled at someone's home: the cover image of a heavily pixelated GAS emblem had lost some colour about half way down the page and was slightly off kilter; the folded pages were not quite flush, creating a fan effect when they were closed; the staples were binding the pages a couple of millimetres to the left of the fold.

He flicked through the pages, more to see how many there were rather than to sample any of its content.

"You have to learn those and abide by them," Block ordered.

Danny shrugged. "Shouldn't be a problem."

Block turned to the open compartment and retrieved an encyclopaedia sized book and proffered it to him. "And this."

Danny and Cassandra stared at the volume and, despite the time it took them to relieve Block of the strain, her arms did not tremble from the exertion.

Cassandra adjusted the tome in her arms until its title could be discerned clearly. "International Laws and Decrees," she read aloud. "Why?"

"Code of Metahero Dialogue, four-point-eye and four-point-eye-eye."

Danny flipped through the booklet and eventually rested on a page, reading, "Metaheroes will always give villains the opportunity to surrender before engaging in combat: 'As a duly appointed member of G.A.S., I am authorised to command you to cease and desist in all nefarious activities forthwith. Failure to comply with said instruction will be considered to be a violation of (cite criminal code relative to state/nation/principality) and will be met with proportional physical retaliation until all nefarious activities have ceased or you have been incapacitated. Do you understand these stipulations as I have declared them?'" He raised his head with wide eyes and a curled lip. "I have to learn every country's penal code?"

"Every country, nation, principality," Block cited, "and - when you are thinking of advancing your role in the group - religions, sects and subcultures."

Cassandra realised he was taking this all very seriously; not only had he used the word 'penal' without a hint of derision in his voice, he had not even flinched when Block had said 'sects'. "I'll help you, Danny, don't worry. We'll treat it like that time you were trying to learn Klingon."

"You need to learn it too," Block told her.

"What?"

"Although you may not be genetically altered, you have been deemed to possess qualities and or skills that warrant you to be a valuable side-kick and therefore-"

"What?"

"- it is imperative," Block continued unperturbed, "that you are entirely familiar with the ins and outs of the code for your benefit but also to fulfil your supporting role."

Cassandra's glare was intensifying and her jaw muscles were protruding fiercely as her teeth ground together again. Her attention moved from her antagonist to her partner with the expectation that he would, if not actually be laughing, at least have a humoured glint in his eyes.

There was a look but it was not of amusement; it was utter consternation. "She's not my side-kick," he stammered. "She's my partner."

THWACK!

Block re-evaluated her opinion by dragging her gaze from Cassandra's face down to her feet and then back up again. Her opinion showed no visible sign of change.

Cassandra, however, had not noticed the appraisal or the conclusion but her posture had changed again. She was staring at Danny with her head tilted, her shoulders drooped forward and her arms hanging limply at her sides. Her eyes were wide and watery, her bottom lip pouted and delicately trembled.

"If that's the case," Block continued, "if she's neither in your care, an assistant or a ward - and without the prerequisite genetic enhancements - she cannot become an affiliate member."

Without shifting her position or poise, Cassandra allowed the inference of her words and tone to relay her current feelings: "I wouldn't want to join a club that would allow someone like you to be a member."

Danny slipped behind the screen again. "What's with the dirty brown outfit?" he called out - this could have been a tactical ploy to derail the current imminent head-on train wreck or a characteristic oblivious topic shift. "Do they come with a promotion?"

"It's standard affiliate gear," Block replied. "You'll get one when we next pass HQ. You can wear it, like Boy does, as protection under your costume if you want. It's the metallic alloy we discovered in the asteroid field. It adheres closely to the body and can withstand extreme blunt force trauma. With that, it has a malleable sentience which allows it to adapt to physiognomic powers and self repairs if damaged. We call it 'dress': design retaining sentient suit."

"Nice," Danny commended as he revealed his mild-mannered persona. "What's with the colour though?"

"We tried to dye it in our standard costume colors and patterns but due to the material's fluid nature, the colors mixed and always turn brown."

"Like plasticene," Danny commented.

"If you want," Block replied, having now learned the right way to react to many of the incomprehensible things the boy came up with.

"It's time to meet the team captain," Bob interjected from the rear of the van.

"It's not you?" Danny asked.

"No!" Bob roared with unbridled amusement. "Whatever gave you that idea?"

Block, Boy and Cat exchanged glances.

"Our team leader is Ultimate," Bob said. "Possibly the first supreme. Definitely the most powerful. This is him." He pulled a photograph from somewhere and thrust it out proudly for Danny and Cassandra to inspect it.

It was worn at the edges, had dog-eared corners and had faded with age but the man stood in the centre was still very prominent. The photographer had taken the shot from a low angle, peering up at what could have been mistaken for a golden statue of a Roman god. For he stood with noble purpose and confidence:

firm-set legs astride, clenched fists pressed against his hips, expression of determination angled high and looking to the future through a glittering eye mask.

Glistening white, curly hair flowed backwards, caught in a gentle updraft and whiting out the photograph at reflection spots. And he smiles with proud, self-satisfaction at a job well done, displaying both rows of teeth and a chip between his upper incisors with uninhibited joy.

"If it hadn't been for Ultimate," Bob sighed reverently, "there would be no Squad."

"Cool," Danny gushed. "So where is he?"

"In the box," Bob replied and thumbed over his shoulder at the luggage carrier on the van. He pressed a discreet button above the wheel arch initiating a gentle whirr from within the van and a movement on its roof. The Thule was slipping backwards and, as it began to overhang, it slowly transposed to horizontal then touched down onto the ground.

Danny waited with unrestrainable excitement but nothing else happened. He looked for elucidation. "He's dead?"

"No, he's not dead. This container was specifically designed to prevent Ultimate inadvertently destroying the planet with his cosmic powers," Bob explained. "He comes out during times of extreme peril, when we have no other choice but to risk using them."

"How many times has he been in action?"

"One," Block stated coldly.

"When he wiped out the last of the vampires," Bob said.

Danny and Cassandra allowed the information to bounce around their brains before jumping to any conclusions.

"Vampires?" Cassandra asked innocently.

"I know," Bob said, "it's hard to believe, isn't it?"

"He destroyed the last of them?" Danny repeated, jabbing a thumb at the box.

"Block can fill you in on the details later," Bob said. "None of us would be here today had it not been for the united efforts of Block and Ultimate."

Block reddened and humbly looked away. She also raised her arm and placed it affectionately on the side of the Thule. She jumped suddenly as the box ascended again and slid back onto its final place of rest.

On the roof rack.

Danny felt like there was a distinct lack of respect for the founder and leader of the team. Even less considering he had cosmic powers! But the whole vampires thing...

"Holy Chris O'Donnel," he blurted. "Just wait 'til you meet Cameron. You're going to love him!"

"Vile, disgusting creatures," Bob growled.

"The scourge of the Earth," Floater added.

"Evil incarnate!" Cat spat.

"Er," Boy stalled, "nasty... things," he said weakly.

Block said nothing. She clenched her fists and screwed her eyes shut. The van shifted sideways slightly.

"Perhaps not, eh?" Cassandra mumbled. "Most people end up hating him, anyway."

"Or getting slaughtered," Danny added under his breath.

There was a collective calming sigh through the group and Bob pulled a key fob from nowhere, pressed a button at the van and made its doors swish open. The front doors swung outwards, two side doors drew back on themselves and a rear door swung upwards: slowly, silently and controlled.

"He's supreme as well, is he?" Bob asked idly.

"Yeah," Danny replied. "But don't say that to his face; he'll let it go to his head."

"To your places," Bob hailed and the team began piling into predetermined places. "Grab an empty seat," he told the youths and climbed into the driver's seat on the left side.

Danny mooched forward. "That's the rousing cry into action? We had better at least get a, 'Turbines to speed,' before we set off."

Cassandra took his hand in hers and squeezed it supportively. "I think you need to re-evaluate your expectations," she advised. "You're judging everything against your idealistic comics and, to be perfectly blunt, these guys are shit. Plain and simple. Stupid powers, socially retarded and sluttish."

They clambered in through the back and took the two empty seats there. While everyone strapped themselves in, the doors sensuously returned to their respective housings with a relaxing sigh and satisfying click.

Danny noticed another, lone empty seat and, straining against his seatbelt, tapped boy on his shoulder. "Who sat there?"

"What? Where?" Boy replied and scanned the interior, seemingly missing the obviously vacant place that was across the aisle from him. "Oh, there," he remarked as if seeing it for the first time or, perhaps, being unable to keep up a pretence any longer. "Er, no one, actually. No one has ever sat there."

"Bachman Turner Overdrive!" Bob declared and Danny sat up excitedly.

For some reason, the rest of the team members lowered themselves further into their seats.

Bob held aloft an inch-thick cartridge for all to see, about the size of a paperback book.

"What's that?" Cassandra asked.

"Atomic power core?" Danny suggested. "Maybe just condensed nitrous oxide."

The van's engine roared into life with the growl of a territorial dragon. Bob slammed the cartridge into a slot in the middle of the dashboard; the team stiffened; Danny jiggled his legs excitedly.

"You ain't seen nothing yet!" the stereo sang. "B-b-b-baby, no you ain't seen nothing yet!"

"What were you saying?" Danny minded and, this time, Cassandra could not find any words to console him with.

William Russels was a well-liked, polite and hard working boy. His parents had been together for a long time before they were married and they had established safe careers from which they were making a comfortable income. When they had finally reached this point of stability, they were able to evaluate their lives, expectations and relationships, arriving at the conclusion that they were ready to start a family. From that point on, their love-life became even more passionate - now unencumbered by plastic and chemicals - and their love for each other blossomed. It was like they were teenagers again: excited about being in each other's company; tactile to the point of inappropriate; constantly exchanging knowing, lustful glances. It did not take long before she became pregnant, carried the pregnancy to full term without any major concerns (sickness, heartburn and haemorrhoids aside), and they shared ten arduous hours together until little William made his final, full and safe arrival.

Life continued normally. His parents had another child when he was three - a sister - and they were friends for most of the time and enemies some of the time.

On his thirteenth birthday, things began to happen; more than hairs, hormones and horns but unexplainable emotions, irrational behaviour and unpredictable mood-swings. Although his parents put this down to another symptom of adolescence, William (being unusually rational for his age and gender) believed there were external forces responsible. He became aware of his tempestuous temperament and began to record where and when it happened.

At first, it seemed as though it was whenever his mum asked him to do something. A great wave of belligerence would flow over him if she asked him to set the dinner table, his intolerance would escalate when required to bring the groceries in, and he could be reduced to tears if she so much as suggested that he accompany her to the supermarket.

However, tidying his room was not an issue, mowing the lawn was undertaken without even a huff, and removal of the garbage was performed with a dutiful acknowledgement. So, perhaps it was not the instructor but the instructions themselves.

He had rallied himself and joined his mum at iMart for the weekly food shop. They traversed the various aisles in a logical fashion - tinned, frozen, packets then fresh produce - and, all the time, he kept a careful check on his physical and emotional feelings. Apart from feeling unnaturally frozen to the core around the freezer section, his constant apprehension was only superseded by immense oppression when they arrived at the fruit and veg.

Specially designed lighting made the primary colours more verdant and lush. A delicate chrome framework had been constructed over the shelves and displays to emit a fine, chilled mist over the produce to accentuate its freshness, adding a gleaming lustrousness to, otherwise, past-their-due vegetation. Each products' positioning had been carefully mastered: colours contrasted against each other, shapes and sizes evolved along the displays and, all the while, were sectioned and subsectioned by socially accepted genus groupings: fruits, salads and cooking vegetables. Everything was packed in as tightly as possible, racked on top of each other as high as would allow; so much so that each aisle slightly distorted the gravitational field around it and was able to attract trolleys towards them.

William had to stop. He could not breathe. He was trapped, weighted down by his own mass, each step was a labour. He was a tiny speck surrounded by the enormity of his own being. He was insignificant fodder awaiting slaughter, one of thousands of individuals who were ineffective, weak and replaceable. His pleas went unheard, his pain was ignored, nobody listened or understood him and his problems. At that moment, he wanted to curl up into a ball and die and it was only fear of death that made him want to scream and escape.

His mother had noticed her son's beyond-the-standard-irrational behaviour and had her arms wrapped around his hunched shoulders when he jerked himself upright, his arms thrusting outwards and his head arched back. He inhaled to erupt a heaven shattering scream but then a section of the vegetables silently exploded. Hard green bullets ricocheted off shelves, trolleys and customers. People threw themselves to the floor, protected loved ones or ran for their lives thinking it was the start of a variety of end of world scenarios.

All except William.

William stood there, arms akimbo and silent screaming while the barrage continued around him. But never on him. Despite the apparent chaotic nature of the eruption, William remained unscathed. Careful observation would have revealed an avoidance of contact: shards of green shrapnel changed their course around him like tuna avoiding a shark. They veered to the sides, found impossible energies to soar ceilingwards and even double back on themselves.

And then it was over.

Customers and staff picked themselves up, dusted themselves off and ventured nervously in search of reasoning. But there was nothing to be found: no device, no chemicals and no call to claim responsibility. The investigating fire department concluded that it must have been as a result of pent up gases from moulding vegetation (of which, none could be found). The more popular explanation came from the fisherman versions, which usually ended with something along the lines of, 'The Brussels sprouts obviously didn't want to be cooped up any more.'

During the subsequent months, William's behaviour became even stranger. He became more introvert, spending long hours confined to his bedroom, moving quickly through the house to avoid interaction with anyone else. He skipped mealtimes, developed a sickly pallor, and was often caught sneaking in or out of the house during the early hours of the morning.

When his parents finally built the courage to raid his bedroom, they prayed to God that they would find pornography, perhaps even alcohol, but anything other than the drugs they 'knew' it was going to be. What they found was far more disturbing and, ultimately, more damaging to them as a family dynamic than jazz mags, vodka or weed could ever be. The first thing that struck them was the odour. A pungency so acrid that it felt like a physical force attacking their senses. Even when they held their breaths, it seemed to bypass their noses and pervade their pores. It was the ripe smell of farmland in summer; a mulchy, swampy mouldiness that caused their throats to constrict in self-defence and their eyes watered acidic tears that stung more than they soothed.

Windows were thrown open and air-fresheners were emptied; eventually they could stomach staying in there for an indefinite time but now worried that the worst they might find was rotting corpses. Yet again, their expectations were surpassed.

Now, given the time and the light to inspect the room in detail, they discovered a carpet of vegetation; a chromatograph of stages of decaying greenery radiating from a bucket of seething mush by his bed; through semi-solid pulp by his wardrobe; out to crispier foliage by the door.

As they stood, pondering the possibilities, William approached from behind.

He could have exploded into an embarrassed rage of betrayal - privacy invaded, lines crossed, liberties taken - but, being the boy he was, he cleared his throat softly so as not to startle his mesmerised parents. When he had their attention - his head lowered in shame - he said, "Mum, Dad: I have something to tell you. I think I'm a *genetically evolved metahuman*[2]."

It would be nice to report that, after the shock of the confession and the practical demonstration, this hitherto supportive and well-balanced family

---

[2] This is not the actual nomenclature he used. Due to the constraints of publishing copyright legalities, editorial restraints are in operation that prevents the use of generic idioms. - *Lawyer*

worked through the trauma until understanding and rapport were established. But no, they freaked out beyond measure. At first it was shouting abuse because of ridiculous lies and callous damage that he had done to the room. Then, when he showed them how he could get a Brussels sprout to dance around in the palm of his hand, they progressed to insults accusing him of insensitive trickery. Finally, when he resorted to creating a green, bobbly replica of the Statue of Liberty on his bed, his mum passed out and his father threatened to kill him if he did not get out of his house immediately.

William wandered the streets feeling sick and stupid. Why had he explored this strange thing that was happening to him? Why had he practised his powers in his room? Why had he not cleared up after himself? What on earth had been going through his head to think that leaving his room in such a squalid state of putridescence was acceptable behaviour and would go unnoticed?

He had not walked far when a green and purple VW van pulled up alongside him. He was too disenchanted to be overly concerned by the suspicious overtones and so, just peered vacantly at his reflection in the tinted window.

It scrolled down to reveal a skinny, blond-haired man behind the steering wheel. "Are you sure?" he called over his shoulder. A response could not be discerned but the man nodded. He turned to William. "I have reason to believe that you are supreme," he said. "We can give you a learning environment that will allow you to explore your skills and hone them so you can use them to be a benefit, saviour and paragon of righteousness."

"Okay," William replied.

A side door opened and he climbed into the vehicle.

\/^^^\/

"That's it?" Danny demanded.

"What else should there be?" Boy returned. "I was born with latent - I mean, 'hidden' - powers, which eventually showed themselves and, from which, I became a victim of persecution and discrimination. Then the Squad found and saved me."

"Pfft," Cassandra huffed. "Your parents telling you to tidy your room can hardly be considered a hate crime."

"I dunno," Danny confessed resignedly. "A huge emotional conflict should ignite your powers, not a strop in the middle of Tesco."

"But that's the way it happened," Boy protested. "And since then, I've been training and getting better at controlling my abilities."

"That's nice," Danny commended, gave him a half-hearted smile and sank back into his seat, staring out of the window at the world blurring past.

CHAPTER 3
THE 'M...E' IN 'TEAM'

The rest of the drive to Portsmouth was surprisingly swift - even though they were subjected to forty-five minutes of 70s soft rock - the Gaswagon's heightened specs gave it incredible speed and manoeuvrability. Block commentated something about inertia dampeners negating the effects of acceleration within the vehicle and the gyroscopic chassis stabilisers made cornering control safer and more accurate. The overall effect was that the scenery flashed by with no more impact than a scene on a TV screen and the indicators of passing time were absent.

There was a brief stop at the city's edge as they had to pass through a military blockade - not a rest stop, though, much to Danny's discomfort - and they continued their journey without further hindrance. Absolutely none at all. No taxis cutting in and out of bus lanes, no proliferations of orange cones, no school mums blocking the road with their seven-seater four-by-four for one child to be picked up. No one-way systems, no traffic lights, no giving way. No motorists. No cyclists. No pedestrians.

"Where is everybody, Bob?" Floater asked.

"'Everything,' Mary," Bob corrected and pointed to the skies.

They were clear. Blue stretched from horizon to motorway allowing the sun unfettered access to scorch the earth below. Even at the height of summer, this was unusually clear of cloud cover but, even more disconcerting, being a seaside city, was the obtrusive lack of aviary activity.

"Oh mah," Floater gasped. "Look at the fields. Ah thought they were just muddy but..."

The passengers stared out of the windows as Bob decelerated to allow a clearer view. The sweeping open plains were a deep earthy colour but, as detail became clearer, they could see the individual blades of brown grass; either an unusual strain of Gramineae or the colour had been swiftly drained from every leaf.

"Everything's dead," Cat announced after checking the back of her wrist.

They continued to survey the environment and, slowly, they began to spot lumps of humanity or, perhaps more appropriately phrased, humanly shaped lumps. It was upright, by the side of the road and, in the mid-distance, resembled a six-foot bowling pin. As they got closer, it became more obvious that it was a body without upper limbs and they all had time to see the open wound of its sheared shoulder because of the crawling pace Bob had slowed the van to. Fractured shards of bone jutted through torn meat; clothes were shredded to limp, dangling strips; the skin beneath was bruised, bloodied or peeled back to reveal ripe flesh.

"I'm going to be sick," Boy warned and fumbled with the latches on the window beside him.

"It's still alive," Floater observed as its body twitched from an involuntary spasm.

"No, it's not," Cat corrected. "Everything is dead: people, animals, plants. I'm not picking up any kind of life signs in our immediate vicinity."

Bob attempted to pick up speed again but was quickly impeded by more upright undead loitering with untent in the middle of the road. He pressed down on the horn which elicited no reaction at all: none moved out of the way, none flinched with shock, none of them even turned around and belligerently raised a middle finger at them.

"Just drive through them," Danny called. "They're zombies. Undead. They won't feel anything."

"I... can't," Bob replied. "What if...?"

"What?"

"What if they're not actually dead?" Bob stated. "What if this is a trick and I end up killing someone?"

"What if this is just a sickness and they can be cured?" Floater added. "How would you feel knowing that someone wouldn't come back because of your rash actions?"

"What if they can feel?" Block pondered. "But can't express themselves. Perhaps they're trapped inside their own bodies."

"What if one of them is the future King of Botswana?" Cassandra mocked and opened the back door.

"I'm not entirely sure of the relevance," Bob mused, "but we appreciate your contribution."

"Cass! Wait!"

She cautiously crept around the van, checking her corners for the approach of anything she may have been unaware of. The creatures were the distance of the van from her: some had their backs to her, some were face forward so she concluded that visual stimuli did not set them off.

"Halloo," she cooed softly, which achieved nothing. "Hey!" she snapped but still nothing happened.

Danny jumped down from the back to join her and picked up a rock from curb. He threw it at the closest body and missed. The stone overshot and dinked off the scabby scalp of another further in. It did not even turn around to blame the one behind it.

"I dunno," Danny murmured. "Is this one of those moments when you reach out to touch one and when you're about a centimetre away it SUDDENLY WHEELS AROUND - GRAAARGH!"

"Danny, you fucking arsehole!" Cassandra screamed and punched him repeatedly on the arm. "What the fuck do you think you're fucking doing? I nearly pissed myself."

"Sorry."

"Fucking idiot!" she shouted and marched forward.

The passenger window slid open and Floater peered out. "Everything okay?"

"Fuck off, bimbo," Cassandra growled. She walked up to a corpse directly in front of the van, grabbed its arm and pulled it to the side. Its legs instinctively compensated for the movement and shuffled to stop itself toppling over. She turned to face all onlookers and opened her arms as a voiceless, 'ta-daa'. "If you don't want to hurt them," she called, "you're going to have to get out and push them out of the way."

And with that, she gave the one next to her a shove at the shoulder. Its torso moved sideways but sheered at the waist - she had failed to see that its midriff had been removed and it was only standing upright because of the precarious balancing of its vertebrae. Its body slipped off and **SHLUPPED** to the floor, upright, next to its feet. The impact sent a shockwave into its neck, which caused its head to jar then pivot to stare up at Cassandra. Its jaw hung open as if having exhaled a huff of inconvenience and its eyes rolled accusingly upwards.

"Oh crap," she spat. "Sorry."

Then its head wobbled and dropped onto the floor.

"Some of them are a bit more fragile than others," she warned.

The gathering was duly dispersed with minimal acts of aggression; any injuries that occurred to members of the disenfranchised were entirely accidental, were followed by profuse apologies but were generally incredibly severe in nature. The way ahead was cleared, sanitary hand gel overused and progression resumed.

Urbanry started to become denser and, after clearing the occasional pocket of loiterers, the Gaswagon swept along a narrow passage of terraced houses to stop outside one that was entirely similar to all the others around it: a frosted glass front door stood politely beside a large bay window, both overlooked a foot-wide 'garden' and brick wall that marked the boundary between pedestrian and private property.

Danny and Cassandra exited the vehicle again, stepped up to the door and pressed the doorbell. It emitted a low tone bing-bong.

From the street side of the door, Cassandra could see a flurry of movement from a lightened space at the end of a long hallway. The reinforced, rippled, frosted glass initially made the movement look like a blob in a lava lamp. But like it was being observed from inside. The blob got bigger. Very quickly. And as it got bigger, it also became more distinct: it was tall, it was female, it had lots of reddish-brown hair.

Even though Cassandra witnessed the approach, she was still taken aback by the forceful opening of the door. With the added support of the doorstep, Gillian loomed over Cassandra's diminutive form nearly twice over. Her dominance was enhanced by her sturdy physique: toned yet shapely. Her firm-set face was counterpointed by her dazzling green eyes and bountiful curls of chestnut hair that billowed to her shoulders. She was as young as Cassandra but looked weary. Her clothes were ragged and dirty; an entire sleeve was missing from her jumper. She smiled with unadulterated happiness when her eyes met Cassandra's[3].

Danny was waving to the tinted windows, delightfully oblivious to the fact that the heroes were all staring eyes forward. He turned to the house to see the girls in full embrace. "It's not even been a week," he tutted but neither resisted nor complained when Gillian transferred her attention to him.

"You'll never believe what's been happening to us," the two girls screamed, paused, laughed and then hugged each other again.

"Gillian," a formal female voice called from deeper within the house, "don't keep them waiting on the doorstep. Let them in so we can all get acquainted."

Gillian ushered them through the prim, flower wallpapered hallway towards a living room and Cassandra reminded Danny to put on his sunglasses before he saw Cameron again. He slipped his shades over his eyes as they walked into the conservatively furnished room: matching comfortable armchairs and sofa; glass coffee table placed equidistant from every seating position; a small, practical TV tucked in the corner of the room as another piece of furniture rather than a focal point. This was the room of someone who like to socialise.

Danny was aware of a few people in the room but one stood out more prominently than any other. His old school friend and perpetual ligger, Cameron. It was hard for Danny to pinpoint specific physical features of his colleague due to the luminescence that radiated from his body, but it was obvious that he was in bad shape.

He looked skinnier, his fair hair - although never coiffured per se - looked like the proverbial hedge that one might get dragged through to end up looking messy. His arms hung wearily from his shoulders and his whole body was curled over on itself like an unhindered marionette.

"Despite the angelic glow," Danny said to him, "you look like shit, man."

Everyone fell into a nervous silence.

Cameron looked up at him to display a pair of fiery-red irises.

"There's no need for that," Danny blurted and took a defensive step backwards, "I was only saying."

"I can't turn them off," Cameron explained and, for one of those rare moments, Danny seemed unable to come up with a response.

Introductions of all the main players were exchanged and narrative catch-up summarised. They then went out and saved the world[4].

\/^^^\/

The skies had decided to take a break for a few days. The last twenty-four hours had been dealt with and, in retrospect, had been completely outside of their job description: collapsing theological dimensions and haemorrhaging precipitation

---

[3] See forthcoming solo adventures of the auburn angel in *Necromancing Queen*.
[4] See the actually existing accounts in *Blood Lust III: Revelations*.

was someone else's department and, in return, maybe they could sort out any resulting issues that might arise while sky was not at its desk.

There was blue above and that was it. The ocean lapped at the pebbles beneath their feet: the browns to white froth to marine, which converged with sky at the horizon, without any visible border, and stretched over their heads and behind them until it hit the grey of the city.

No one really noticed. No one really cared. They all had other things on their mind.

There was a petite, blonde woman who had her back to the rolling seas to face the crowd and a cloud. She was dressed sensibly (albeit perhaps not for a beach party): pastel green cardigan, cream, A-line dress, white blouse buttoned to her neck. Her hair was shaped into a nice, neat bob: long enough to be obviously feminine, short enough to not require lots of maintenance or get in the way.

Among the crowd were GAS, looking a bit dishevelled but dutifully solemn[5]; Danny, who had his arms wrapped around Cassandra; she, in turn, had her face buried in his chest and her shoulders jerked with the rhythms of uncontrollable sobbing; Cameron, who seemed to have come through the experience positively: he had added some pounds to his bones, some colour to his skin and a spark to his eyes that no longer resembled illuminated blended flesh but a vitalised grey-blue. There were two other adults (a male and female) and a free-floating blob of mist that, when looked at closely, had facial features and limbs.

Between the crowd and the sensibly dressed woman was a wrapped package, approximately five foot in length and resembling the shape of an embalmed Egyptian pharaoh but presented in a manner if the priests had run out of white linen and had to use their aunt's Laura Ashley curtains.

"I've never had to do something like this before," the woman stated, "and am not sure what to say. It's hard to hope for a peaceful afterlife for a loved one when you have had personal experience of the afterlife you know they are definitely going to be moving on to. All I can say is that I am thankful for Belinda Wollstonecraft being a part of my life. For, if she had not been, then I would not be here now. I would not have had the chance to evaluate my life and realise that, although I was content, I have not been happy for a very long time." She turned her attention to the package. "Linda, you became a friend and mentor too late in my life and too briefly but no doubt have had the biggest impact than anyone else I have known." She lifted her eye-line to gaze above the onlooking crowd before her. "With her passing, this world has become a slightly greyer place and I envy the world she has moved on to." She bowed in private musing then looked up. "Would anyone else like to say anything?"

Cassandra disconnected herself from Danny's body, wiped her eyes and gulped back a couple of breaths to calm herself. "I hate it," she stated. "I hate this life and I want my old one back. I don't want to know that there really are monsters and demons out there, and that they really maim and kill, and they really maim and kill the people I know. She saved my life. Not in some indirect

---

[5] See hypothetical four-part, Brittastic GAS mini-series: *To be or not, Zombie*.

action but deliberately and individually and it's not fair that someone that nice and selfless should be the one to die. There are thousands of shitty people out there in the world; why is it the good ones that have to sacrifice themselves? It's not fair."

She turned again and buried herself in her partner; the woman standing next to her placed an affectionate hand on her shoulder.

Cameron cleared his throat and the people who looked to him looked on with trepidation.

"You're both right," he said. "There are no words of comfort for us anymore. No blind faith to pull us through the dark times. No naïve hope for a silver lining. We've all seen behind the curtains and the illusion has been broken. The sooner we can accept that, the sooner we can, at least, find peace of mind and then we can hope for some joy. She knew it, she had encompassed it and that's why, I think, she was such an irritatingly positive and optimistic person and, ultimately, why she was able to face the end with such gravitas and dignity. I can only hope I can muster half the courage of her when I can see it's my turn."

The group was silent.

"I'd like to lead us in the Lord's Prayer," Bob declared. "Our father -"

"Are you fucking mental or something?" Cameron demanded and Danny slapped his hand to his face.

The body had been pushed out into the Solent, the small blonde said some more words (that were unfathomable to all but her) and the body dissipated into a spray of colourful pyrotechnics. The mourners then made their way back up the beach; many had more than the death of their compatriot to grieve.

"She just walked away," Cameron said. "Just like that. Ditched me. After defying Satan, after escaping the bowels of Hell, all it took was a couple of words from some random bint claiming she was God and she was off. Talk about just looking for an excuse."

"Dude, getting personal mission from a god is a pretty big deal," Danny counselled.

"Not 'a' god," Cameron corrected. "'the' God."

"Even more so."

"She could've waited a bit," Cameron suggested. "Talked about it. Checked in with you guys to see how everyone was. It's just so fucking selfish and irresponsible."

Danny and Cassandra exchanged a look.

"And what's happened to Penny?" he continued ranting. "Hadn't we better go looking for her?"

"I'm sure she's fine," Danny attempted.

"He's actually right, Danny," Cassandra added, "we don't even know if she's alive or not."

"Okay, okay! So we'll try to find her even though she's a fifty year old vampire arse-kicker."

"And I want to catch up with that bastard, Nutter," Cameron growled. "I've got a few things I need to sort."

"Like?"

"I need closure."

"You mean you want to kill him."

"I'm going to rip that cunt's head off and shove it up his fucking arse."

This outburst caught the attention of the GAS members.

"Dude," Danny whispered, "you've got to keep the swearing down."

"Why?"

"Cos I'm trying to get you a gig with those guys." He jerked his head in the direction of GAS, who had noticeably distanced themselves from everyone. "They're a touch moralistic."

Cassandra snorted derisively.

Cameron did not even try to conceal a sneer of contempt. "Seriously? They look like a bunch of tossers. 'Lord's Prayer'! She was spawn of Satan for fuck's sake."

"He didn't know that," Danny explained, "and it's probably best that they go on not knowing that sort of stuff." He gave a knowing look. "They think all vampires are dead."

"They are."

"ALL vampires," Danny reiterated. "And they think they did it."

"Whatever."

"But they are genuine superheroes, man," he enthused. "This is our chance, you know? Proper superheroing and everything!"

Cameron stopped walking and just stared at his friend. He turned to Cassandra. "How long has he been like this?"

"Since he first saw them," she replied.

"Like what?" Danny demanded.

"Like *iCarly*," Cameron said. "'Superheroing and everything!'" he mimicked in a high-pitched, nasally American accent and clapped his hands together excitedly.

"Listen, you might have become all jaded and serious about your responsibilities and this new world you're in," Danny said, "but I still see this as a gift, as something that can be offered to aid others around me, as a part of my destiny." With that last statement came the look into the middle distance.

Cameron attempted to follow his eye-line to see what caught his attention but saw nothing except empty sky. "Good luck with that then."

He snapped back to reality. "What else have you got to do?"

"Ouch."

"Seriously, what? Are you going to try to make happy families with your demonic dad and ghost mum? Hunt Gillian down? Or sit around feeling like a victim?"

Cameron seemed to give it some serious thought. "Can't I do all three?"

Danny slapped a solid hand, squarely on Cameron's shoulder and pulled him in. "Dude, I want you in on this," he confessed. "I think I need you in on this to make it work. I know my powers aren't all that special and I need my wingman. They're dissing me and I need some back-up."

"What about her?" Cameron nodded at Cassandra.

"'Her'?" she snarled.

"Cass has got less clout than me," Danny said.

"Even with the mad Power Rangers skills?"

"I think she's keeping them under wraps."

"I'm right here, boys," she sighed. "I'm not interested in peacocking for these arses."

"Nice," Cameron commended. "Keep that back for a shocking reveal later, eh?"

"Oh don't you start," she moaned and wandered away.

Danny stepped in even closer. "Seriously, check them out."

"Who?"

"The girls! They are just like the covers have them: all curves and little imagination needed."

Cameron gave GAS another cursory inspection and lingered over the uniforms on Floater, then Cat, then Block. "What are you suggesting?"

"This might seem cold," Danny whispered, "but you're a free man now."

Again, Cameron considered the targets. "Which one?"

"Well, the blonde is with the skinny guy and the S and M chick is probably out of your league -"

"The fat one!" Cameron cried with indignation. "I think my league might be a little higher than that."

"She's not fat," Danny defended, "she's a powerhouse. The Cat would probably destroy you what with you... You know."

"What?"

"Having only ever done it a couple of times."

"You cunt." Cameron stormed up the beach.

"Dude! I only say it because I'm your friend and want to look out for you."

"Kuh uh nuh tuh!"

"Go on then," Danny called while following behind. "How many times?"

"Fuck you!"

"Two? Three? You haven't had the chance to get it on since you gave Gillian your cherry and killed her!"

There did not seem to be any movement: at one point, Cameron had been stomping up the pebbly dune with Danny matching pace a few steps behind; in the next instant, they were half way back towards the ocean, Danny had had the air thrust out of his lungs and his back had dug a deep trench through the stones with Cameron straddling his body, fists clenching his collars. Cameron's eyes were burning red and his incisors had extended through his gums.

DON'T YOU EVER FUCKING TALK ABOUT THAT AGAIN! YOU FUCKING HEAR ME?

Danny sucked air in to compose himself. "Sorry," he gasped. "I wasn't thinking."

Cameron stood up, his features returning to a state of normalcy. "That wasn't me." He held a hand out for Danny to take and hauled him to his feet.

"That's what I'm talking about," Danny puffed. "You're not you. You can be whoever you want to be."

"Thank you, Bugsy Fucking Malone."

The boys returned to their trek up the beach only to be confronted by GAS and Cassandra watching from a few steps further back.

"*This* is him," Bob stated.

"Yeah, Cameron," Danny introduced.

Cameron tried to be bolshie and defiant but found it hard while being confronted by breasts and bonnets.

"What was that?" Bob asked. "Accentuated acceleration?"

"Er, possibly."

"You're a speedster?" Boy enthused.

"Amongst other things." He could not help but notice how their looks of disdain changed to intrigue, folded arms uncrossed and Cat raised her eye visor. He was in control. Sha-fucking-zam.

"I was thinking of going with 'Self Elating Man'," Cameron suggested and it even took Danny a second to catch on. "What with my stretch powers, I have the ability to make myself very happy."

The heroes' expressions blanked. "How do you use that power?"

"He's joking with you," Danny interjected. "He can fly."

"Ah can fly," Floater said with enthusiasm that she might have found a kindred spirit. "What tech do you use? Gravitational manipulators? Magnotronic influxors?"

"I flap my arms really hard," Cameron said and, with a burst of wind that ruffled all present, lifted himself off the floor. He ascended until the temperature got a bit chilly for him and dropped gently to the ground again.

The heroes' jaws had dropped.

"What?" Cameron asked.

"Do you have any idea of the energy that's required to achieve that kind of propulsion and altitude?" Floater demanded.

"No," Cameron replied without trying to mask his disinterest.

Floater faltered. "Lots," was all she managed.

"I can also do this," Cameron said. He placed his hands on his hips, turned his head to one side and angled it upwards. Without any other atmospheric change around them, the tails of his trench coat billowed behind him.

"What's the point of that?" Bob commented.

"Cool," Boy praised.

"Nice effect," Cat commended.

"Bob, even you have to admit that's quite a nice touch," Floater said.

"He's also fairly invulnerable," Danny blurted and that seemed to be the icing on the cake. All but Block and Bob stepped forward.

"That is fantastic news," Boy gushed.

"How much pressure can your body withstand?" Floater asked.

"Is your skin really hard?" Cat asked and almost floored Cameron with the steely stare she gave him.

"What's the big deal?" Danny asked. "You've already got Bob as a bruiser."

"It just takes the pressure off," Boy explained. "Those that can take a bashing go in the front lines. It's just a good job he doesn't have accelerated recuperative abilities."

The team all shared a knowing chuckle over that one but quickly shut up when Cameron said, "I do."

"Oh dear," Floater muttered and looked to Bob for support.

"I'm not sure we can take you on," Bob said.

"Why?"

"It may sound odd but we have found that the degree of your defensive capabilities dictates the severity of your aggressors," Bob said. "The more you can take, the harder they'll give. It just puts some of the more vulnerable team members at more danger."

"Shut up!" Cameron scoffed. "Are you trying to tell me that you don't face any enemies with the ability or intentions of slicing you up but if I was to join, you would?"

"Exactly," Bob said and the others nodded.

"That might explain all your escalations," Danny suggested to his friend.

"Evil katana wielding Samurai are out there regardless of if I'm in your team or not," Cameron argued.

"True," Bob conceded, "but they'll be looking for you."

"We just get the bo staff Triads," Floater said. "No guns, no shuriken, no sais. Your presence will inject that more lethal dynamic."

"I say we give him a chance," Cat said from nowhere. "I think we need an injection and he certainly is supreme."

"He seems volatile," Bob observed.

"Then even more reason to help guide him," Floater added. "These boys need our help, Bob. Regardless of their talents, it would be against our basic tenets to turn them away."

"Remember Dog Boy," Block said and they did, bowing their heads in either reverence of an attempt of memory suppression.

Bob lifted his head and locked eyes with Cameron. "Very well. You do what I tell you to do, when I tell you to do it. Is that clear?"

"Absolutely," Danny replied.

"Sure. Why not?" Cameron concurred.

"Good," Bob conceded, "get your gear together because we've received a call. There's trouble in London."

Farewells were bid, vague promises made and uncharacteristic thanks were made. The newly initiated took their places at the back of the bus and one started intently reading through the rule books.

"I can't read while driving," Cameron had said, "it makes me feel sick."

The van zipped past mobile infantry units that were shovelling corpses into dumper trucks and sweeping debris from the streets. The urban backdrop morphed into open fields and stretching motorway. A backlog of traffic was trying to get into Portsmouth but being diligently, and sometimes ruthlessly, turned away with words of bureaucratic spinnage and the occasional barrel of a gun. Their progression was impeded slightly by confused and disconcerted commuters not knowing where to go but, eventually, the road opened to a clear journey into London.

They passed landmarks in correct geographical order: the high-reaching chimneys of Battersea Power Station twirled by; they swept by the immensity of Waterloo station and roared eastwards, parallel to the Thames. The austerity of the House of Commons, exclamated by Big Ben, was eclipsed by the girth of The Eye. They turned north at Waterloo and plunged into the milling city, winding their way through traffic immune to the thwarting powers of red lights; pedestrians impervious to speeding motorised vehicles; courier bikes that could phase through the smallest of gaps between cars.

The Gaswagon took a sudden turn up a back alley; walls, seemingly a couple of inches away from the van's windows, blurred past at frightening speeds. Another turn, then another and finally a stop at a residential courtyard: four-storey town houses had been packed in so tightly they were not much wider than their front doors. They crowded around a small patch of green which was being protected (or entrapped) by a wrought iron fence. The houses' windows stared down on the park, daring it to try to escape and devalue them. In the middle of the green was a gathering of figures with a path of prostrate bodies trailing towards the gate. Around each body was a gently expanding aura of viscous redness.

"I suppose I'll get the blame for this," Cameron commented.

The collective was made up of half-a-dozen suited individuals of varying ages and both genders. They were kneeling on the ground, radiating from a man dressed in fluorescent blue overalls; orange shin-length boots, gloves and eye mask; his face was bleached almost pure white albeit with over exaggerated bright red lips and pink irises. His hair was a multi-coloured afro, twice the size of his head. On his back was a large red backpack and on his chest was a crudely drawn, thick red 'O'; presumably a representation of his mouth.

"Bob, those people," Floater observed.

Bob swivelled round in his seat to face the whole team. "Boys, this is Clown Face -"

Cameron barked a loud guffaw whilst Danny and Cassandra buried their faces to hide their mirth.

Bob paused and checked with his compatriots for any indication of what the joke might have been. He received no response. "Clown Face -"

Another eruption of giggles but Bob remained undeterred this time.

"- is a particularly unpleasant psychopath. He is supposed to be undergoing life-long therapy in Barker Asylum[6] - the world's most secure penitentiary for the supremely insane. It seems he escaped. Again. Get out there and incapacitate him."

This stopped the laughter. "Us?" Danny demanded.

"You want our first official trial to be against a murderous sociopath with hostages?" Cameron enquired.

"Psychopath," Bob corrected.

"Whatever."

"What better way to train than on the job?" Bob explained. "What better motivation to do it right than when lives are at stake? Cat, give them an earpiece each."

The boys held their hands out and Cat dropped an oval bud into Danny's palm and placed another in Cameron's, allowing her fingertips to linger a fraction longer than was necessary.

"These are two way devices," she said.

"Just follow my leads," Bob added.

"Let's go, Boy Bum-der," Cameron announced and opened the back flap.

"Don't order me around," Danny complained, "people might think I'm your sidekick."

"You are."

"Shut up!"

"Are you sure about this, Bob?" Block asked. "This is quite a serious encounter for a first time."

"It's not their first time facing baddies," Cassandra defended.

"We'll be there as back-up," Bob advised. "Cat, take perimeter point. Boy, call in your reserves. Floater and Block, take an aerial position."

Cameron and Danny strolled nonchalantly to the metal fence, fiddling with the devices, trying to adjust them comfortably in their aural canals.

"Clown Face," Danny muttered. "Who's next? Dirty Sanchez?"

"He's safely locked away in Islas Marías Federal Penal Colony," Bob informed in his right ear.

They just looked at each other.

"He said 'penal'," Cameron whispered.

"I heard that!" Bob barked.

They stepped into the entrance of the park and surveyed the scene; the blood, the bodies clawing their way to illusionary freedom, the tortured few around the feet of a monstrous oppressor.

"Same old, same old," Cameron muttered.

---

[6] Named after author, philanthropist and complete nutter, Lord RJ Barker, who investigated and wrote about the occult during the late 18th Century. The building was constructed on, what he thought were, ceremonial grounds linked to the netherworld god Mphluplup. He had completely made it all up and was swiftly institutionalised in his own hospital by his family before he could waste any more of their inheritance.

"Does it bother you that you've become desensitised to the violence and horror?" Danny asked.

"It bothers me that I'm not bothered," Cameron replied.

"Quit the chitter-chatter, gentlemen," Bob ordered and made them both jerk from the audio impact. "Engage the perpetrator with light banter to distract him from the victims. Keep his attention drawn to you, do not question his motivations or suggest releasing the victims."

"Light banter," Danny acknowledged, "we can do that."

"Do offer him the chance to surrender, though," Bob added. "Don't be trapped by that one."

Clown Face watched them warily and angled a wide bladed carving knife to flash sunlight in their eyes. "Don't come any closer!" he screeched at them. "They'll be more blood spilled if you do."

The boys sniggered.

"Oh, you think there's humour to be found, do you?" Clown Face brought the blade closer to the nearest victim. "I'll wipe that smile from your face."

"You should take some of your own advice, pal," Cameron shouted and Danny doubled over with mirth.

Clown Face was taken aback. "Who are you?"

"I am the Perspectre," Danny declared, trying to regain some stature.

"The what?" Cameron interrupted.

"Perspectre," Danny repeated. "A blend of perspective and-"

"I get the derivation," Cameron said, "I don't get what it's got to do with you."

"I can see stuff," Danny said weakly.

Cameron nodded towards Clown Face. "Go on then," he urged, "use your power to help out here then."

Danny turned to face Clown Face then raised his sunglasses and stared dramatically at him. Clown Face took a step backwards in anticipation of an attack. Danny replaced his eye protection and turned back. "I got nothing."

"What is your purpose in life?" Cameron demanded. "Right you!" He pointed at the villain. "Stop this, and turn yourself in or there'll be trouble."

This bolstered Clown Face's determination somewhat and he physically rallied himself. "Do anything and I'll stick this one like a stuffed pig."

"It's a cliché simile," Cameron derided, "and doesn't even match your persona."

Clown Face needed a moment to think. "I'll bleed him like... er... stab him until... shove knives into him like a clown car."

"Ouch!" Danny exclaimed. "That actually hurt me."

"Well, you do better then," Clown Face challenged.

"How about, 'Don't move or I'll kill him. Period.'" Cameron suggested.

Danny collapsed to the floor in fits of laughter.

"I do not understand the jest," Clown Face said.

"Nor do I," Bob added.

"I'm going to pee myself," Danny squealed between breaths.

"'One more step and it's all ovary for him,'" Cameron continued.

"What have birds got to do with it?" Bob questioned.

"Not 'aviary', Bob," Floater's voice chipped in.

Danny hauled himself up. "'Any closer and you'll end up with egg on your face!'"

"Ew, that was rank," Cameron whined. "But deserves a standing ovulation." He clapped and Danny bowed.

Clown Face stepped outside of his conclave, waving his blade accusingly at the boys. "You two are more foolish a minstrel than I," he observed.

"Noooooo!" the boys wailed in unison.

"Massive opportunity missed," Danny declared.

"I wish I'd thought of that one," Cameron mused.

"Your inane prattling ends now," Clown Face commanded and began blindly rummaging around in his backpack.

Danny stopped laughing. "Move," he ordered and bounded behind the cover of a parked car.

"Is that the French for egg?" Cameron asked as Clown Face extracted a small contraption that looked like a small crossbow.

With that smooth movement, he pulled the trigger to release a glittering disk of whistling sharpness which embedded itself squarely in Cameron's chest.

The impact caused him to rock gently on the spot. He looked down at his sternum to see it was not a disk but a three bladed knife; each point radiating equidistant from each other around a red-gemmed centre.

"OW!" Cameron eventually declared. "This was a new jumper, you bloody fuck-hole sucking mother-fucker!"

"You 'what'?" Bob demanded.

"Dude!" Danny bellowed.

"Fuck that shit, man!" Cameron protested. "I've just been impaled by a barbed throwing star and it fucking hurts! And it still doesn't fit with his persona; it doesn't make sense."

"A generous gift from my kind liberator. Now, allow me to deliver the punch line," Clown Face said.

"At last," Cameron sighed, "an semi-apt ref-"

Clown Face twitched his thumb, the red gem flashed and Cameron's chest detonated. His body was thrown across the street and slammed into a parked saloon car, embedding itself into the rear side panel and left lying backwards over the boot. Without the scaffolding of his rib cage, his head lolled backwards at ninety degrees to what was left of his trunk; his shoulders oscillated precariously over the cavern of his torso. His innards had mostly been removed outwards but what had remained had been mushed and scorched into something more akin to lasagne than internal organs.

Their earpieces were filled with the sound of someone vomiting and a few gasps of horror. Then Bob added, "I warned him this would happen. GAS: Attack!"

"Stand down," Cameron slurred and attempted to wave his arms but only succeeded in making them bounce more vigorously and dislodged a pound of mince.

"He's still alive?" Block demanded.

"He said he could take it," Cat reminded.

Cameron lifted himself and wavered on the spot. His head flopped forward and nearly folded right over into the hole.

"This is worse than I thought," Bob said.

A fresh wave of the sound of vomiting emitted through the earpiece.

Cameron staggered forward; his balance obviously affected by his inverted head and lowered centre of gravity. He growled with the exertion of each heavy step - both the labour and the pain - and bits of blended internals dropped out of his chest cavity, slapping on the path.

Clown Face was horrifically enthralled by the sight. He stared with wide eyes and wide mouth, his arms dangling loosely at his sides as Cameron shambled ever closer.

The boy's head slowly rose to finally fix eye contact with his target, his arms stopped flailing wildly and stretched forward with more deliberation and purpose, the mess in his chest was solidifying and inflating.

"What are you?" Clown Face demanded.

"I'm Batman," Cameron growled, the muddy red of his chest developed cream horizontal stripes.

"Wait, what?"

"They call me Mr Glass!" Cameron shouted, the threads of muscles had webbed their way over his reformed ribs and a silvery skin was translucing over that.

"Watch out!" Danny warned.

Clown Face found the resolve to raise his weapon again and fired. The glinting death wheel screeched across the diminishing gap between them but Cameron snatched it out of the sky before it could embed itself in his body again.

"Ouch," he said and uncurled his fingers to reveal he had not actually caught it but simply blocked it. It had impaled his palm. It detonated, sending Cameron hurtling across street again, this time into the park itself.

"Bob, do something!" Floater implored.

"No," Bob ordered. "Clown Face has never resorted to such lethal weaponry before. It's too dangerous."

"The boys will get themselves killed," she predicted.

"Shtand down!" Cameron slurred.

"That's my boy," Danny praised.

"A lot of fucking ushe you've been, bitch," Cameron muttered and tried to push himself up by his arm but it missed the floor because it extended no further than his elbow. He supported himself with his other arm and curled his legs up under his body, readying himself to stand.

"I told you to move," Danny said.

"You shaw that was going to happen?"

"I saw something was going to happen, like Spider Sense."

"Do it again," Cameron ordered and lifted himself upright. He turned. Not only had the blast stripped him of his forearm, it had also caught the left side of his face. His skin had been flayed back to the bone, strips dangled from his temple, cheek and chin like willow leaves; his eyelid had been scraped away to fully expose his red webbed, milky orb - it swivelled precariously in its socket, moistly disconnecting at places around the edges with each movement. His lips had been chewed away to leave him with a garish, malicious grin.

Cameron eyed Clown Face, ensuring he was disconcerting the villain as much as possible with his dislodged, unblinking eye. Clown Face watched Cameron with morbid fascination, hypnotised by the muscular machinations of this walking corpse. Then, as if to reinforce his distraction, the nub of Cameron's arm extended wormlike stems that wavered in the air, searching for purchase. They circled each other in a sensuous adagio, growing longer and thicker as their passion increased.

Danny watched them both, completely oblivious as to what he was watching for. It was not a premonition of an action, not a vision or a feeling of déjà vu. He thought back to *Dave's*. What was it? The feeling like he was never going to see it again. An air – no, an atmosphere like those auras he could see around parahumans but in the place where an end was about to occur. The shop, the Brightonians, the vehicles, Cameron's chest and arm: there had been a preemptive flash of death.

Through his eyes, Danny saw it: the glare of Cameron's being quelled by the colour of demise. "Move!" he shouted and Cameron did.

The spinning tri-bladed explosive whistled through the space where he had been standing then detonated halfway across the road causing no more damage than activating a couple of car alarms. Within that instant, Cameron was standing an inch in front of Clown Face.

"Say something that will counterpoint his actions," Bob spluttered, as taken aback by the advance as Clown Face. "A witticism that will make him realise he's undone; that will make him surrender."

The two just stared at each other dispassionately.

"You've got a little something just here," Cameron said and pointed to his own exposed jaw.

Clown Face blinked.

Cameron punched him.

MEANWHILE...

Due to its history of rebuilding, expanding and conjoining, London is littered with side streets, shortcuts and underpasses: adjoining paths that seemingly distort the fabric of space and circumnavigate huge portions of districts. Sideways, bylanes and pseudopaths, that were engineered by happenstance and mismeasurement, were utilised by the criminal classes for centuries as escape routes and ambush zones for unwary commuters.

As it was a century ago, as it remained today.

The victim in question was pressed face forward into the shadier side of the alley, his hands raised defensively above his head, clutching desperately to a shiny mobile. He was in his late twenties, slim and tall; he was dressed in a tailored suit that shone lustrously when the light could reflect off it. Around his square jaw was a finely honed stubble and his hair showed evidence that, at one time, it had been coifed to immaculacy and styled with a single curl in the centre of his forehead with copious product, but now was a bit ruffled having been manhandled.

The man behind him was much shorter, clad in a black hoodie that masked the top half of his head and revealed an unkempt, dirty growth of facial hair. He kept pushing forcefully into the man's back with his right hand while waving a four-inch blade around in his line of sight.

Gently spreading around their feet was a puddle emanating from the victim's leg.

Something caught the mugger's attention; a small blemish in an otherwise clear vista. "Look," he said, "up in the sky..."

The victim noticed the distraction and, too, became enraptured by the mysterious blot that was becoming bigger. Closer. And with it, a distant low toned whistle emerged. "Is it a bird?"

The two men stepped backwards into the centre of the alley to get a clearer view.

"Is it a plane?" the mugger questioned.

The victim strained his eyes and leaned forward. "No, it's-"

Its velocity had been deceptively fast. Its size and direct trajectory had masked how staggeringly fast the object was actually heading towards them. The two men had been standing next to each other and then the mugger was alone. His isolation had been counterpointed by a wet **CRUNCH**: the sort of noise a watermelon might make when struck by a mallet.

The object and his target had gone in a flash.

He looked around bemusedly to eventually discover the man's body lying on the ground a few metres further down the alley. He cautiously approached him and, after deciding he was not being watched, squatted to rifle through his clothes, pocketing jewellery, money and technology.

Something unusually white caught his peripheral vision, something like a football that contrasted brilliantly against the grime of the alley. He turned and took a moment to study the object. When his brain was able to comprehend its identity, he ran. He did not stop running. Even after the bus hit him. Although, saying that, the continued leg movement was due more to the twitching throes of death befalling upon him, so probably does not actually count as running per se.

In the alley, watching over the static body of the city worker, were a pair of pink irises beset in a surprised looking bleached-white face with exaggerated bright red lips. The head rocked gently, cushioned by the multi-coloured Afro.

\/^^^\/

Clown Face's body teetered on its feet. A rhythmic gobbing of blood geysered from his neck into the air and smattered the ground around his feet.

Cameron stood watching the effect, daring the body to do anything but fountain the remains of its life onto the floor.

The sound of retching filtered through their earpieces.

"What the hell did you do?" Bob screamed and bounded across the courtyard to Cameron.

Danny had stepped out from his cover and was furtively making his way forward. The other heroes approached from the other corners of the courtyard; Boy, desperately trying not to look at the ejaculating body and desperately trying to keep his insides in.

Bob's advance was thrown off kilter when Cameron turned to him. The boy's face was still knitting itself together and his forced grin was visible through the translucent web work of skin.

"I dealt with the situation," Cameron whistled at him.

"You murdered him!"

"Er, self-defence, I think" Cameron argued. "He shot me with exploding Ninja stars. How come that bit of intel didn't come up in the briefing? Or, I suppose, are my powers responsible for his level of aggression? If Veggie Boy there was confronting him, he would only have countered with a potato masher."

"If you have the abilities to withstand that level of assault," Bob stated, breathing deeply with each word to control his anger, "then you have the ability to resolve a confrontation without resorting to a lethal conclusion."

Cameron looked around him: at the dead bodies, at the congealing pools of blood, at the traumatised captives that Floater and Block were calming.

"Did he know that?" Cameron jabbed his thumb over his shoulder at the expending corpse. "Did he give that any consideration when he took these people?"

"So you were administering justice, were you?"

"If you like."

"Well, who gave you the right to pass judgement?" Bob demanded. "Where was it that you practised law and became qualified to decide whether a man was worthy to live or not?"

"Rights are just arbitrary ideals dished out for the convenience of whatever ruling class is in a place to set them at that time," Cameron argued. "Go back a thousand years and we could have been hailed as gods in one area of the world or burned as witches in another. Tomorrow's heroes are today's freaks and geeks."

"When you resort to killing," Bob said, "you're no better than them"

"Tell me, how many murderers have you put away?" Cameron asked.

"I don't know," Bob replied, a little thrown from the change in tack. "Quite a lot, I suppose."

"Do you remember your first?"

"I do. That would be Pirate Video and Snuff: a homicidal pair who came to prominence in the early eighties."

"How many had they killed before you caught them?"

"There were six in total, all different, all filmed."

"And you arrested them, right. Got them their day in court, a chance to defend themselves but ultimately serving their due time in a maximum security prison."

"Bob," Floater warned, very much aware that Cameron was leading the conversation somewhere.

"Not exactly. Unfortunately, due to my involvement, they were set free on a technicality."

"I see."

"Bob?"

"But they had learned their lesson after that?" Cameron asked.

"No," Bob sighed remorsefully. "They were easier to catch next time although it was after three more deaths."

"The trial went better that time?"

"Yes, but they still weren't convicted. Instead they were found to be psychologically impaired."

"So they got help, did they? That's good. And they're better now?"

"No. They fooled their doctors, teamed up with XXX and Slavetrader, and created a huge illegal immigration industry: taking money from refugees fleeing war torn areas of East Asia, bringing them into the US then forcing them to perform in underground movies, eventually killing them."

"How many?"

He shook his head sorrowfully. "Unknown. The police found over eighty bodies but the recorded evidence suggested hundreds."

"Tsk tsk. But that was it, yes? Locked up, thrown away the key?"

"BOB!"

"What, Floater?"

She widened her eyes at him.

"I have no idea what that is supposed to mean. No, after that there were two escapes from prison, one illicit parole and a rescue during transit."

"And more dead each time."

"I truly think those men are irreformable."

Floater rolled her eyes.

"So, had you done what I would have done after the first meeting, those hundreds of people would still be alive."

"That's not the point."

"Oh it is, pal. You took the decision to become a protector of innocents and, by letting murderers go free, you need to take responsibility for the actions of every psychopath thereafter. For better or worse."

"It can't work like that," Bob protested.

"It does though," Cameron argued. "You make a judgement at that point as to whether they deserve, or can be trusted, to continue wandering the streets. And if you decide to give them a chance, you have to bear the responsibilities. I bet if some nut-job rehabilitated then you'd be all like, 'Oh aren't I a paragon of decency and nobility?' If this clown was allowed to run free because you were too scared to make the right decision last time you confronted him, then each and every dead body lying here is your responsibility."

"Two wrongs do not make a right," Bob attempted.

"There is nothing more evil than a good man sitting back and allowing bad men to continue."

"I Do Something!"

"You keep telling yourself that if it helps you sleep at night."

"How do you sleep so peacefully?"

"With the sweet memories of the looks on those fuckers' faces when they realise they are undone!"

"Mind your language, you monstrous delinquent!"

"Fuck you, you sanctimonious prick!"

"Don't make me angry," Bob warned. "You wouldn't like me when I'm angry."

"Bub, I don't like you when you're not angry!"

"Woah!" Danny interjected. "Guys, enough of the hostility. We're all on the same team."

"No we're not," they both replied.

"There is no room for a murderer in The Squad," Bob declared.

"There is no team that I would join that employs such sycophantic liberalism that allows unrepentant murderers to go on murdering," Cameron countered.

"What does that mean I should do with you?" Bob asked and cocked his head victoriously.

The chill evening air swept through the courtyard and dense clouds rolled over the darkening sky.

"That's a pretty obvious pathetic fallacy," Danny observed.

The black vans collected round and their cliché-gents spewed forth to clean up the physical, emotional and psychological messes. Clown Face's decapitated body was led, by the hand, to sit in the back of a vehicle. Statements were given by Bob, fingers pointed at various individuals and geographical points of importance. Eventually, the streets cleared, dusk had fallen, and the squad convened.

Bob, uncharacteristically, stood to the back of the group: arms crossed, glowering furrowed brow, petted bottom lip.

"We'll rest up here tonight," Floater informed the youths, "and then we'll take you back tomorrow, Cameron. Ah'm..." She considered her next words carefully. "... sorry it didn't work out."

"But it will," Danny predicted. "This is one of those situations where misunderstandings are overcome during an extreme threat that requires all parties to band together."

"Or is it one of those times when personality clashes cause a greater divide to eventually pit one side against the other?" Cameron asked.

"Let's hope it's neither," Bob said, "go our separate ways and hope our paths never cross again." He turned his back on them and marched towards the van.

As awkwardness increased, they all peeled away and began to board the van. Only, as Block lifted herself in, she raised a hand to touch the side of the Thule and stopped, adjusting her hand to run it along the edge of the seal.

"Has anyone interacted with Ultimate, recently?" she asked, inspecting the residue on her fingertips.

The others replied in the negative.

"Floater, what is this?" Block asked and pointed to a grey-blue grain that had built up in the join between lid and base.

Floater lifted herself on the step and looked closely. "It looks like some sort of caustic polymer," she analysed. "A by-product of a thermo-dynamic reaction? Caused by Ultimate's power in the desert, perhaps?"

Block shook her head. "The box was open. Any cast-off would have been dislodged when it was closed."

Cat raised her pointed head from the opposite side. "I don't want to worry anybody but thermal signatures indicate it's actually cooling down," she told them.

"The sediment?"

"The whole box," Cat said.

The story went that Garth Geffen was Earth's most powerful defender but, at the same time, the most powerless. He was not a person of any great status, neither politically nor socially, and that was why they picked him. He was a simple man who had no ideals of grandeur but was happy with his simple existence.

Raised by loving parents on the west coast of America, he gained a respectable education and stayed out of trouble. He was not bullied any more than any bullying that he did to others. The only feature about him that proved to be a target of ridicule was his angelic-like, tightly curled white hair but it was poor sport when the victim would not rise to the antagonism. The only other distinguishing feature had incurred through something as innocuous as misjudging the position of his mouth and chipping the insides of his central incisors on a glass. His parents had wanted to repair the damage (after having already spent a small fortune on pre-emptive dentistry) but he remained adamant about keeping the feature.

After many years of blissful mediocrity, it was when he was in his mid-twenties when his life turned to amazing and he was abducted by aliens from a distant and far more technologically advanced world. They had once been a carbon based life form, eons ago, but had now evolved to a state of, what they considered to be, perfection. But that is another story[7].

This story continued that they took him aboard to study humans in general and to ultimately help them take that next step up the evolutionary ladder. Although human life had only been on the planet for a few thousand years, as far as the aliens were concerned, they had not really made any progress in becoming 'better beings.' They were a bit of an embarrassment to the rest of the universe.

---

[7] Watch the skies for interstellar action in spin-off adventure, *To Bodily Go*.

So they chose a man who embodied all that humanity was: simple.

They took him on board and told him of their plan. The path to being ultimate was one of knowledge and pain. It had to be earned through trial and torment, not simply handed as a gift.

He said he understood but that was naivety talking and he did not ever consider exactly what he was going to have to go through.

They placed Geffen on a pristine shiny table within a pure white room. Luminescence radiated through the walls and made it difficult to focus on any small features within. The creatures, being translucent, circulated the room like pockets of heat haze; the instruments they carried were as discernible as glass splinters in tapioca. They clamped his limbs into rigid cuffs that were bolted to the table. They adjusted the table so his head was supported and angled to be able to see down the length of his body.

They said it was so nothing they did would be hidden from him.

One of them moved a gelatinous extrusion down his body, from his sternum to his pelvis and, at first, nothing happened. Then a stinging sensation swiftly built into an unbearable burning and he screamed. He watched with horrified fascination as a deep trench peeled its way down his chest and could clearly see the layers of colour in the cross section from surface peach, to raw chicken pink, down to deep sirloin red. Their jelly-like forms worked with fervour over and in his body, seemingly unperturbed by his wails of agony and protestation. The flaps of torso skin were peeled back to reveal cream skeletal extrusions breaking the surface of the meaty waves that ebbed and flowed with every inhalation and exhalation. His deep-throated bellows vibrated through organs and flesh and, with their safety harness removed, neatly packed pieces began to dislodge from their moorings, squirming for freedom.

It was while a part of him burst free, began to unravel across the table and slinkied onto the floor that the defensive parameters of his brain kicked in and shut him down.

The rest - right up until he woke up in the field - was a blurred montage of nightmarish images as his mind crept into reality every now and again just to see if it was safe to come out.

It never was.

Images of things that he had only ever seen being handled by science teachers were paraded by his sight. Each one looked fresh, dripped or dribbled fluids of various shades and, in some cases, pulsed or twitched during their manipulation. His last (and lasting) vision of his time on the spacecraft was the most vivid, primarily because it was the only time that there was a complete absence of pain.

He opened his eyes and blinked to remove the blurriness. He attempted to rub them but could not get his hands to make contact. He presumed this was because of the straps. As he rolled his eyes for focus and lubrication, he discovered he was looking through some sort of window, beyond which he could discern the interplay of light refraction as his hosts' bodies passed in front of each other. He attempted to call out, to question them but no sound came forth. As he inhaled, he sensed that the air felt thicker and had a salty taste to it.

Something rose gently, close to his head, just within his peripheral vision so he turned to identify it. A small silvery sphere, gently rising to a circular mirrored ceiling, rippling directly above his head. Another two drifted up and he was able to focus on them: bubbles. He checked the glass surface in front of him and followed the curvature all around. He was encased.

Cautiously looking down, he was temporarily relieved to see his body but started to panic when he realised it was too far away. It was still on the table, skin splayed outwards like peacocks on parade - road kill peacocks - and his insides hollowed out. Webbing away from it were fine strands that reached out to his limbs or other cylindrical glass tubes containing indeterminate dark lumps of matter that would occasionally spasm like a dreaming dog. His brain decided to protect his sanity again.

When they finally ended his torture by putting the last bit in and zipping him up, they told him that they had gone as far to strip him back to his basic DNA and given him a cosmic upgrade. He was now a being of incredible abilities. He could harness the power of the stars and channel it through his body. He was capable of anything. He was the ultimate human. No, he was just plain Ultimate.

Then they put him back on Earth and Ultimate looked at his hands. Although he saw no physical change, he could feel the potential within and it scared him. Every part of his body felt like it had been recoiled and was ready to release; it was only through intense concentration that he was able to hold it all back.

He could channel the power of the cosmos. There was no one who could challenge him; no one who could stop him being who he wanted to be.

Except himself and his happiness with his simple existence.

So he decided to wait. A sign would be given when he would be needed to use his powers.

As time went on, others came to him. Others with similar stories of being changed or of being born different. So they banded together, formed a club, became a collective of like-minded individuals sharing a common cause: secretly helping the human race from destroying itself.

There was one slight problem; Ultimate did not know how not to use his powers. Should he ever get into a combative situation and he blasted his enemies with a concentrated stream of supernova, how would the planet react? Not too well was the theory.

It was put to a vote and, upon that result, the Earth's greatest supreme was locked in a specially designed box. It was not for his good but that was democracy at work. And there he stayed until the climax of the team's greatest battle.

They were outnumbered by a thousand-to-one and if they should fail here then the entire planet would surely be destroyed. Out in the middle of the Gobi Desert, eventually, only one hero was left conscious and Ultimate was still in the box. She was surrounded so she entered the combination and the lid sprung open...

When the team recovered, they discovered they were all still alive, the desert was clear of threat and Ultimate had returned to the protective environment of his box.

Ultimate had finally fulfilled his destiny, the world was saved and had not been destroyed. Now, all he had to do was wait again.

CHAPTER 4
THERE IS NO 'U' IN 'TEAM'

"Get him down," Block ordered with fear and urgency. "Get him down now!"

The heroes darted around the van. Boy was the first to get to the release button and slammed it with his palm. The mechanism activated with its purposeful slowness.

"Get him down!" Block screamed and all bits of Bob bulked up almost instantaneously.

He reached up, grabbed the side of the Thule and yanked at it.

The van refused to relinquish its grip without a bit of a struggle and hinged sideways on its wheels from the exertion. It bounced back to its resting place when its weight overwhelmed the tensile strength of the roof-rack's fixtures.

Bob thrust it down and activated the keypad. All the while, Block was skittering on the spot, flapping her hands in the air and muttering, "No, no, no, no, no," under her breath.

The air of tension was provoked further by a very real pressure building up around them; the feeling of a plane's cabin during take-off.

The lid of the Thule sprung off with a burst of steam and billowing of dry ice. Block wafted the gases out of the way and plunged into the casket only to emit a deep-chested wail. "What did you do?"

The smoke cleared and the contents were revealed: red, deep padded sides; small screens and monitors had been embedded around the top half with vents placed at regular intervals across all surfaces; then, blanketing it all, was a shallow quilt of beige ash that collected into a thick dune at the base. Immersed within that, were two open-necked tubes with curls of smoke snaking from inside. When Cat pulled them out, she revealed two golden, knee high boots.

"What's happened?" Boy demanded, straining to see around Bob's wilting form.

Cat leaned into the container and smeared some of the particles across the sensor plate on the back of her wrist. She watched carefully as lights flickered, ensuring she did not look towards Block at all.

She was on the brink of hysteria. Her eyes darted from the Thule to the van to thoughts to memories. Her breathing was heavy and rapid. Her fingers twitched as if orchestrating re-enactments in her mind then, as if dissatisfied, would clench to cancel the instructions then repeat the process. And as this went on, those around her could feel themselves being gently - but constantly - urged to move away.

"It's been too badly demolecularised to get a definitive reading," Cat announced, "but it *is* human. It must be Ultimate."

"No!" Block bellowed and pressed the palms of her hands to her temples, scrunching her face into a ball of pain and anger.

The concussive wave that her emotional state created, lifted people and vehicles from the ground like Lego bricks in a blender. The van flipped three hundred and sixty degrees on its horizontal axis, landing fifty metres across the courtyard. With it, spun the coffin, spraying its cremations around in its wake. Having been at the far side of the casket, Cat flew off in the same direction but was also given additional impetus from its base as it whirled around and smashed her in the side. Her body cartwheeled into the bushes.

Bob was standing closest to Block and was lifted highest and propelled furthest. His body, semi-engorged, flattened as the force impacted and while inertia held him in his place. Then he arced up, over the row of townhouses into the next street.

Standing behind him had been Boy, partially shielded by Bob's girth at the point of eruption, then catching the tailwind and sent tumbling down the road.

Floater's departure was slightly more controlled. She had been more focussed on Block's emotional breakdown than the box and had anticipated a reaction. She had activated her technology so the generated gravitational field absorbed a degree of the kinetic wave and cushioned her impact as she sailed through a bay window.

Danny's foresight had given him a fraction of a second's grace, during which he had managed to grab Cassandra's cuff and hauled her away from the scene. It was not enough time to completely avoid the wave and they were carried off the ground for a few metres. Upon touchdown, their legs could not keep up with their velocity and they tripped over their stumbling feet, tumbling over each other as they fell.

Cameron was thrust backwards vertically. His passage was only a short distance because of the wall a couple of metres behind him. The force held him in place, face first, and continued to bear down on his body. Joints groaned as bones were coerced out of place; his throat emitted a strained wheeze as his chest was compressed and air forced out. He added a tortured growl while his breath lasted; punctuated by a high pitched sigh when ribs were bent in on themselves and snapped, sheared ends stabbing through muscles and organs. All he could do was stare imploringly to the world until even his vision began to fail. Skull plates split at the seams, shifted positions, skewing his head into a parallelogram. His lower jaw dislocated, his cranial cavity shifted and an eyeball fell backwards into his head.

Block's anguish did not let up. Whatever was causing her grief had blinded her to the devastation she was causing around her. Her body curled up into an insular ball of pain; her eyes clenched and own cries of misery drowning those of her teammates.

Cat emerged backwards from her landing place, pushing her body against the weaker ripples at the extremities of the tide. She turned, waded further in until her effort equalled that of the repelling force, then she aimed her wrist control forward, towards Block.

The pressure dropped almost immediately, releasing all those held in its throes and making those pushing against it to stumble forward. Block was shocked back to reality; whatever the affront had been was akin to a bucket of iced water. She looked at Cat with a combined expression of shock, fear and disgust and then she catapulted backwards over the city streets.

Heroes of varying degrees gathered again, each casting wary glances between Cat and the dislocated Cameron. He was gradually finding stability and erectus while bones snapped and cracked themselves back into more comfortable and suitable positions. The sides of his head shifted its angles to become less polyhedral and more ovoid. With every shift, twitch and snap, his spectators would grimace and flinch. Then, when he started to choke, they took a step backwards. His stomach and chest lurched as he attempted to dislodge an obstruction in his throat. Eventually, Bob came to his senses, ran forward and performed a Heimlich: standing behind him, he wrapped his arms around the front of his midriff and then hauled the youth off his feet.

The blockage was released with an explosion of air. A white lump projectiled from his mouth but stopped a couple of inches out: a fine thread was attached to it and to somewhere inside his mouth. It flopped down and bounced off his chin.

Bob released his grip and Cameron staggered for balance, the mass swung loosely from his mouth until he bit his teeth together. It dropped, bounced off the toe of his shoe and rolled across the road. It stopped to a rest and stared up at Boy. It was an eye with trailing optic nerve tail.

It was Boy's turn to choke but his stomach had emptied itself of all its matter ages ago and he could only dry retch in the gutter.

"You two have some explaining to do," Bob told Cat and Cameron.

"What the -?" Cameron complained and spread his arms to display his full wretched glory: armless and chestless jumper bearing pallid, worn skin and the empty eye socket.

"We all need time to try to work out everything that's been going on. The new members -"

"Member," Cameron and Bob corrected in unison.

"- the conflicts, the loss of Ultimate and now... this."

"First, we need to check on Block," Bob stated.

"Her GPS isn't registering," Cat informed from details off the back of her wrist.

"We'll have to split up and search for her," Bob said.

"I'll fly ahead and scan around," Cameron volunteered.

"I'll try to keep up -" Floater offered but was stopped by Cameron's raised hand.

"I need some time to myself," he explained. "I need to sort some stuff out." He turned to Danny and curled the corner of his lip up to reveal an extended canine.

"You can keep in touch through your communicator," Cat reminded. "Just tap it to turn it on. Or off when you want your privacy."

Danny grabbed him and pulled him to the side. "What's going on?" he whispered urgently.

"All the damage," Cameron replied. "It takes its toll. I need a top up, you know?"

"What are you going to do?"

"Try to do a Punisher." He gently lifted from the floor, rotated and took off in the general direction that Block had gone.

"Perspectre," Bob hailed (and it took Danny a second to realise), "perhaps your sensory acuitiveness will be useful. Go with Boy."

"Gotcha," Danny replied dutifully but kept his gaze fixed on the dwindling figure of his friend.

"Likewise, Cat, go with Floater."

There was a slight hesitation as if Cat was going to protest but the exchange of looks between Bob and Floater made her hold back.

"Be careful," Bob told the blonde. He turned his attention to Cassandra. "You... er, girl woman."

She raised her eyebrows and blinked slowly at him.

"Could you get us our rooms at this hotel?" he requested, produced a business card from somewhere and held out to her. "Please?"

"Do I get an ear-piecey thing?" she demanded.

"No, we'll just meet you there," he said. "I'll get things cleared up here."

They all stared over at the van, the upturned Thule and whirling mists of ashes and shared a reflective moment of reality.

"How did this happen, Bob?" Floater asked softly. "We don't die. We disappear, get misplaced or forgotten but we don't die. Not like that."

"There's a rational explanation, Mary," he threw a glance at Cat which she easily caught, "and we'll find that out because that *is* what we do."

V^^^V

Dusk was falling upon the city. Street lights were blinking their awareness, shop and theatre fronts emblazoned their wares in greater contrasted glory, the streets became busier as the numbers of tourists and shoppers were reinforced by workers clocking off and commuting.

Cameron rested on a rooftop and espied the throng patiently. At the moment, there was an urgency and not desperation. But he absolutely did not want to reach desperate. He had been desperate before and the situation had worried him: the absolute lack of control. He would have to be completely deluded if he could persuade himself that it had not been anything but luck and opportunity that prevented him from killing one of his friends. And now, as he crouched between the eaves of the building, he knew he was going to have to kill someone to ensure he stayed in control. Yes, he was a murderer and everything Bob had said about him had been true but, at least this way, accepting this weakness and dealing with it, meant he got the chance to choose who might die tonight.

From this position, the people passed beneath him in much the same way salmon did returning to their breeding ground. And there he was, the bear, able to scoop any one indiscriminately from its journey.

But he had to discriminate. He had to be selective. If he considered them all to be just that, 'them', then he had lost the last vestiges of his humanity and become more like the creature he recently destroyed.

There were too many here. Too many pounding hearts that reverberated like an eternal drum roll in his ears and he could feel his conscious will being hypnotised by the thrum. It would be harder to identify a suitable target in there and harder still to isolate it for a surreptitious kill.

He dropped down into an alley and watched the people strobing by. How could he choose like this? How would he know which was the right one? Which one deserved to die? Without that black and white distinction of smoking pistol, signed confession and maniacal laugh, how could he know which of 'them' was the safe choice.

"A creature of the shadows, huh?" a sultry voice commented from behind him and made him jump.

"Are you following me?"

"I was going to ask you the same thing," Cat said and emerged from the darkness.

He did try to not check her out but his attention was systematically drawn from one stunning feature to the next. Her large, dark eyes framed by slender, arching eyebrows; the sly, wry smile that curled up the right side to accentuate her high cheek bones; her slim chin that curved seamlessly into a succulent neck. Thereupon appeared a delicate pulse, which twitched at her tender skin, and he felt a yawning pang resonate through his body. He averted his gaze to follow the line of her collarbone down to her cleavage where he felt a more localised pang of yearning.

Her breasts were encumbered by her bodice, drawn together by a line of dainty bows that laddered down the middle of her torso, following the contours of her midriff and terminating on the cusp of her tummy. Her matte leather trousers clung to her form and delineated the curvature of her pelvis; her toned thighs were strut slightly apart to display a definitive plateau of her crotch. The line of her legs undulated to the firmness of her muscles to peter into her Converse boots.

"Finished?" she asked boldly.

Again, her voice caused him to jump but, as he drew back his lips with a grimace of embarrassment, he remembered his extended canine and compounded his unattractive expression by quickly pursing them back together again. His eyes widened and eyebrows raised when he discovered the tooth had, at some point during his inspection, receded back to its proper place. His carnal urges had somehow surpassed his appetite.

"Sorry," he blurted, "I was lost in thought."

She adjusted her weight on her legs to angle her hip up and rested her hand on it. "And what were you thinking?"

"That I wish I had x-ray vision," he muttered loudly.

He watched as she took a moment to reciprocate the inspection, her eyes languidly zig-zagging from one point on his body to another, all the way down to his feet and back up again. He had never been checked out before, not so obviously, and certainly never to witness the final appraisal with a satisfied smile. She tapped at her goggles and winked.

"What happened to your outfit?" she asked. "You weren't issued with a dress -"

"I didn't realise you were that sort of group," he interrupted.

She rolled her eyes at him. "It's what our self-repairing costumes are called. What tech is it? Unstable molecules? Refabrication? Nu-cloning cloth?"

"Next," he stated.

Her jaw jut forward and she scrunched her eyes in concentration whilst searching her memory for other possibilities. "I can't think of any others," she confessed.

"No, *Next*. The clothes shop," he told her. "There's one just around the corner. I bought a new one."

"Oh. I take it you haven't found Block," she said, completely unimpressed with the mundane normalcy of the answer.

"No," he replied and failed to hide his guilt. "I thought you were supposed to be with the blonde."

"Floater? We got separated," she explained. "But I calculated where Block should have landed and, although there were signs of disturbance, she wasn't there."

"What are you doing with these people, Cat?" he asked boldly. "You don't seem like a team player and you're not as..." He searched for the right word. "Not as sanctimonious."

"What can I say, I'm Canadian," she told him. "What about you? What made you think you'd stand a chance with us?"

"I dunno," he sighed. "I reckon if I just keep bounding from one distraction to the next, I won't ever have to actually think about what's going on or what I should do next."

"We've all got skeletons," Cat sympathised. "We've all got closets."

"I wish they were secrets," he responded, "but my life -" He nearly changed the word he used but changed his mind when he remembered who he was talking to. "- is a walk-in wardrobe."

"I can't read you," she said and approached dangerously close to him. Her almost obsidian eyes inspected every feature of his face. He had to seriously concentrate on not licking her. "I'm pretty good at reading people and I can't pin you down. There's a lot of pain there but there's something else too. Oh my god!"

"What?"

"It's the same look Ultimate has:" she stated. "decency and nobility."

"Shut up!" he scathed.

"You seem like a good man, Cameron," she informed him. "You just have to accept that the pain is part of your life now and stop fighting it."

Something *buzzed* at the back of Cameron's head and he flapped his hands to waft it away. At the same time, Cat raised her hand to her ear. "I'm here," she said.

"I know," he replied while swatting around his head.

"It's your communicator, you idiot," Cat chastised.

This said, Cameron was then able to pinpoint the buzzing to actually be in his ear so he touched the rubbery plastic bud.

" -were supposed to stay with Floater," Bob barked in his ear.

"We got separated," Cat snarled.

"You slank away, Cat," Floater's southern drawl accused (Cameron mouthed the word 'slank' with incredulity, which made Cat snigger), "and then wouldn't answer mah calls. Ah was worried about you."

"Sorry, Mary," Cat responded humbly, "I didn't think."

Another background noise leapt into the building silence: the close movement of fast traffic.

"Someone, quick," Boy shouted. "We've found her. She's -"

"She's not breathing," Danny declared from a distance.

"We think Block might be dead."

They gathered at the north bank, beneath London Bridge. The immediate area had been cordoned off with a boundary of black tape and a few agents. The body of Block was cast amongst the pebbles and washed-up detritus of city life. Her feet rocked gently from side-to-side as the river's waves made half-hearted grabs at her. Her limbs were splayed out at unnatural angles and tended to bend at places in between main joints. She was lying on her front with her head turned towards the water. Her visible eye was closed; the brow and cheek engorged disproportionately around it, almost meeting over the lid. Its brownish-purple hue mottled slightly at her jowl but reblossomed around her chin. It, seemingly, having been indented slightly. Her mouth hung open loosely and her lips were swollen and split.

"We were just crossing the bridge," Danny was explaining, "and this smear of darkness caught my eye. So we checked it out."

An agent handed a clipboard to Bob, who quickly scanned the information thereon.

"Preliminary observations suggest she was killed elsewhere then thrown in the river," he summarised. "The tide washed her up here." He handed the board back. "They think she was beaten to death."

"What?"

"How can that be possible, Bob?" Floater demanded. "Her powers don't let anyone near."

"Unless someone had found a way to negate her powers," he suggested and turned to Cat.

CHAPTER 5
THERE IS 'EAT', 'ATE' AND 'MEAT' IN 'TEAM'

The Philosopher's Rest was an out of the way, understated hotel. A building that, once upon a time, sat on a major byway of the city, on the edge of the art district where up-and-coming playwrights would collate and expound on their latest works that could define the indefinable, portray the unportrayable and impress the rich and naïve to part with their cash. Now, it had been relegated to a side street when bigger thoroughfares had been built around it. One of its key facets, which had not changed over time, was that it was not judgemental and allowed all patrons access to its meagre, yet homely, domiciles: artisans, prostitutes, costumed metahumans – all were welcome.

They were sat around a booth in the restaurant. It was a reasonable size, able to seat about forty diners at any one time, still leave space between tables so the backs of chairs did not clash against each other during movement, and no one would have to take a table next to the toilets. It was empty apart for them. Occasionally, a waiter would wander through the room, peering at their table, looking for the cue that would allow him to engage in the next round of his repartee. At the moment, he decided to keep his distance. Partly because Danny was still choosing from the menu but mainly because Floater was sobbing loudly.

Even Bob had put an obviously large space between them.

Cassandra had stepped forward to take on consolation duties but made sure the woman had her coat on over her shoulders before she would touch her.

"I'll be honest," Bob said. "At the moment, I've got two suspects: you and you." He indicated Cameron and Cat.

"Bob!" Floater blurted. "Now's not the time."

"When is, Mary? When you're dead?"

Neither of the accused responded to the accusation.

"You were the only ones alone when it could have happened. Well?" Bob prompted.

"Innocent until proven guilty, big man," Cameron told him. "Bring it on."

"You're a killer. Enough said?"

"Do you have any idea," Cameron started, "how difficult it is to punch a man's head clean off his shoulders?"

"Oh god," Boy gulped.

"Language!"

"That takes some mad skills," Cameron continued. "Connect slightly at the wrong angle and you won't disconnect the brain stem; you'll just shave the front of his face off. Hit him too hard and you just embed your fist inside his skull. Too lightly and his head flips open like a pedal bin. I do more than just kill, buddy, I'm a fucking artist."

"Was that supposed to vindicate you?" Bob asked dispassionately.

"I can't take you seriously," Cameron huffed and slouched back in his chair and folded his arms. "Your name's an anagram of 'bad blow job' for fuck's sake."

Bob's jaw muscles flexed as he stared at the impertinent youth. "Cat," he did not remove his glare while he addressed her, "you've got some serious explaining to do, lady."

"About what?"

"How you managed to stop Block's powers. What was it that you did?"

She sighed heavily in preparation of the imminent confession. "I studied her powers and developed some counter-tech."

"Why would you do that, Cat?" Floater demanded. "Why would you build something that could hurt a teammate?"

"Just in case something like this ever happened," Cat said.

"Thanks, by the way," Cameron interjected, "for stopping her PMT moment from turning me into graffiti."

"Ma gahd!" Floater cried and Bob let this one pass. "It wasn't just a rant, he was her boyfriend and he was dead! How would you react, you heartless monster?"

Cameron bowed his head. "Sorry," he muttered.

"How would you react if that ever happened to you?"

Cassandra was the only one to react physically to that question. She removed her hand from the distraught woman's shoulder either to show that she, in no way, shared her opinion or just to get out of harm's way if a backlash was forthcoming.

"I resigned him to an eternity in Hell," Cameron told Floater matter-of-factly.

She paused in thought: *He used past tense, didn't he?*

Bob returned his attention to the case. "So you had opportunity and means, Cat."

"Motive, Bob? Listen to yourself," she ordered. "I was the third member of the Squad and helped recruit Block. I trained her. I worshipped Ultimate. Why the hell would I want either of them dead?"

"What about us, Cat?" Boy asked quietly. "What about our powers? Do you have counter-tech for us?"

She watched him carefully, contemplating ramifications of a variety of responses. "Yes," she extolled and quickly attempted justification with, "but only because it's what I do. I experiment and explore. Not because I should but because I can."

They sat in silence: paranoia and contempt preventing them from clearing the air.

"Is anyone having a starter?" Danny asked.

"What about you, big boy?" Cameron enquired. "You have had the means. In fact, everyone here but Tweedledum and Tweedledummer were on their own when the girl was offed. You, though... you've got motive to get rid of the boss-man; step into his golden shoes, you know?"

The accusation obviously rancoured him but he managed to maintain his calm. "And how did I kill Block?" he asked.

"I dunno," Cameron dismissed, "maybe you're strong enough to penetrate her defences. Maybe Cat's intervention weakened her powers. Maybe you paid someone to do it. We can let the authorities and lawyers work that one out."

He breathed deep, calming breaths but did seem to be rising in his seat.

Cameron savoured the moment.

"Everybody knows that I'm not capable of murder," Bob growled.

"That's your defence?" Cameron challenged. "And since when did you being a paragon of virtue get set in stone?"

Robert Jaw was a meek and mild young man. He was slightly below average height for his age, skinny and permanently pallid. He did not do well at school - academically, athletically or socially - so when he left with his meagre and mediocre qualifications, employment opportunities were not plentiful. On top of that, he was raised in a small town, right in the middle of the Bible Belt, caught on the border between Mississippi and Alabama. A small town, a long way from its nearest neighbour, thriving on 1960's social bigotry and political paranoia and economically existing solely because of the merits of a factory that mass produced pharmaceuticals. If you lived in Diffident, Alabama, your lifestyle was dictated by the work you – or your family – had at LexosCorp.

The school's sports teams were sponsored by LexosCorp: their logo proudly emblazoned on all the teams' shirts; the church was maintained by healthy charitable (and tax deductible) annual donations by LexosCorp; the medical centre had first dibs of the cream of the crop of new (and occasionally untested) drugs that emerged from the factory.

The corporation was worshipped by all and only just pipped God at the post for the town's unvying attention. Not many people felt the need to leave the town because stability was there, happiness was there, family were there. And where there were family, there were always marriage opportunities and future security.

Those people who did leave were usually the restless, Godless and a drain on the community rather than an asset. They were not usually missed and very rarely heard from again.

Robert Jaw's first job after graduatingesque was as an assistant to a caretaker (aka Uncle John) at LexosCorp. John, being one of the lower ranking (but no longer lowest) caretakers in the factory, had the responsibility of the mop

and bucket and the factory floor. His employment parameters previously involved three operational tasks:
1. General maintenance and appearance of the lower level work environment.
2. Rapid deployment of appropriate resources in the event of acts of discharge or breakage.
3. Precursory inspection and maintenance of all employee sanitation facilities.
   And now that he had an assistant, one managerial:
4. Get Robert to do everything.

Robert would clean up spillages, sweep up breakages and disinfect the toilets. The best thing about the job was that even when there were no messes to clear, task number one dictated that he should just clean for the sake of it. It meant that he was always busy, nearly always on the factory floor but almost certainly always around the other employees. It was through this constant exposure to 'people' that allowed him to develop his social interaction skills: starting with uncomfortable acknowledgement of the existence of others; building to quick fleeting eye contact; then eventually escalating to non-committal, barely audible, non-intelligible grunts of greeting.

Eventually, his conscientiousness and presence made him as integral a part of the factory as the conveyor belts; the only real difference was that the belts were slightly more emotive. However, the workers marked him as a polite and necessary element of their working environment; he became indelible to the operations and superstitious smooth running of the place.

His total lack of social acumen was further enhanced by a previously latent obsession with reading. Or perhaps it was the obsessive reading, which prevented him from developing any personal connections with his co-workers. Whatever the reason, Robert's preoccupation with literature but lack of access to creative prose had him scrutinising whatever text he could get his hands on and, due to his unfettered access to every storage facility in the building, he discovered a wealth of corporate manuals and legislature which kept him thoroughly engaged during any spare moments he could find.

He had been working at LexosCorp for two years when he had his first voluntary verbal interaction with one of the machine operators. He was busy mopping up a spillage of some sort of illegal, caustic liquid while two operators discussed employment issues.

"- and I had to do it. I had no choice," said Annie-Anne Anderson (who, although was in her early thirties, wore denim dungarees and wore her red hair in plaited pony tails that dangled down to her shoulders). "But he still called me up and read me the riot act."

"Well, he's the boss," replied Billy-Ray Williams (his face was aged because of unhealthy skinniness and dark patches beneath his eyes. He had nurtured a large broom-like moustache that hid his lips and rocked like a bucking bronco when he chewed his tobaccy. He also liked the pony tail look but sported only the one, although its length certainly equalled the combined efforts of Annie-Anne's).

Annie-Anne huffed and pouted her bottom lip, placing her arms resolutely on her hips. "It just ain't fair."

"Ours ain't to reason why," Billy-Ray stated prophetically.

"I live alone and I got three littluns to raise and when one gets sick from school and I don't got no family to help what the hell else can I do?" she complained. "And the medical bill from the injections on top of them docking my day's pay means I'll have to put in overtime at Hoozers!"

"You need a T356," Robert said and the machine operators stood stock-still in shock, their jaws hung open loosely.

"Did you just say something, Robert?" Annie-Anne asked.

There was a moment when Robert nearly turned around and scuffled back to his cupboard, uttering muffled apologies and retractions, but there was a look in Annie-Anne's eyes that overcame his social self-defensiveness and replaced it with an overwhelming urge to 'Do Something'. There was the immediate look of surprise but it was being doused by an expression of desperation and hope that bypassed all his self-defence mechanisms and activated a primordial section of his id called 'nobility'. He had to Do Something.

"I said, 'You need a T356'," he repeated without any stuttering or mumbling. "The employee's handbook clearly states that, 'In the case of personal emergencies, paid leave will be granted upon completion of form T356.'" And, without being prompted, he went on to list a few examples of what the handbook deemed to be qualifiable circumstances, including: the death of a direct relative; destruction or invasion of residency; and, "if a dependent requires emergency supervision."

"What does that mean?" Annie-Anne asked.

This was something different; quoting someone else's words from a text had not taken much effort other than the demands of his vocal chords and mouth muscles, however, this 'explaining in his own words' required a higher order range of interpersonal and interpreting skills. "If your... child? -"

"Alice-Anne," Annie-Anne said.

"- gets sick and means you have to take time off to look after him -"

"Her."

"Sorry, yes, 'her'. If you have to take time off then you can still reclaim the lost day's pay through the company's employees insurance."

Annie-Anne and Billy-Ray stared at Robert for a long, almost uncomprehending, moment. They exchanged glances with each other and then burst out laughing. Annie-Anne doubled up, tears began rolling down her cheeks, clasping desperately on to Billy-Ray's convulsing body as her laughter threatened to suffocate her.

Robert had become quite used and hardened to the sounds of derisive laughter and turned his attention back to his menial task. He could not, however, completely ignore the slight bitter sting of disappointment after having made so much effort to interact.

The solid thump on his back did come as a huge shock. The air was forced from his lungs and he staggered forward; partly from the impact but mostly from the shock of the contact: someone had touched him? Even in the lowest moments of his school-life, he had never been touched; even by Mikey Michaelson, the school's quarterback.

"Robert," Billy-Ray guffawed, "you are a hero!"

In due course, Annie-Anne reclaimed her lost earnings by quoting specific employment policy references which had been, hitherto, unknown even to the HR department and their MD and, during the course of conversation, she had been asked how it was she had come to know of these corporate statutes. She, almost smugly, told them.

That very afternoon, two special letters came onto the shop floor via internal mail: one to Annie-Anne with a check and acknowledgement of the repayment. The other letter was to Robert.

After word had spread concerning his involvement in Annie-Anne's economic rescue and knowledge of the inner workings of the company, people were buzzing around him with enquiries about him and queries about their own industrial disputes. So their avid interest was further enhanced by the red-bordered stationery. Management must have taken notice of Robert's previously latent qualities.

He excitedly ripped at the seal and wrenched the folded paper out. His eyes quickly skimmed the text.

"What's it say, Robert?" Annie-Anne demanded with eager anticipation. "A promotion?"

"Dear Mr Jaw, It has been brought to our attention that you have willingly contravened policy ordinance 83.23 by knowingly reading and sharing the content of confidential company documentation.

"It is with sincerest regret that we must serve you with notice to cease employment with the company, active immediately.

"Should you refuse to leave the premises without incident, we will have no other recourse but to take the matter further with the intention of litigation.

"Yours sincerely,

"HR."

"Robert?" Annie-Anne queried, absolutely uncertain of the meaning of the words on the page but very aware of the possible meaning of the expression on his face.

"They've fired me for helping you," he stated dispassionately.

And Annie-Anne asked a question that would change the lives of many in that room that day. "Can they do that?"

He snapped out of his shock and replied simply, "No they can't."

"What can you do?"

"I will talk to them."

"What can I do?"

He looked at the surrounding faces: neighbours, friends but, more importantly, co-workers.

"If you really want to help me," he said to them and they listened on with eagerness, "you will lay down your tools and stop the machines until this matter is resolved."

The faces looked at each other with elements of fear and shock.

"Strike?" Annie-Anne asked.

"This is not about me," Robert said, "this is about you and your rights. They have been taking advantage of your good nature for too long and the moment someone voices dissent, they try to quieten it. What else have they been keeping from you? What other rights? Benefits? Money? If they have it this easy to be rid of one man for simply speaking, then it will always be this easy to be rid of the next when he does not work as well -" He emphasised this by pointing at one of the older workers. "- and the next for not understanding -" He pointed at one of the immigrants. "- and the next for needing time off." He pointed at a pregnant woman. "I can speak to them and organise a mutually beneficial working environment which clearly stipulates your rights. But I need you to help me be able to help you."

"I'll help, Robert," Annie-Anne stated. "I trust you and believe in you."

One by one, the work force around him raised their voices until they were truly one: a choir of socialist unity and following that sound soon came a silence in the building that had not existed since the day the factory first opened.

It did not take long for the supervisors to question the event - some joined the action, others scurried away for support - then the men in suits ventured onto the shop floor. Amongst them, they tried threats and bribes to recommence production but the workers were unmoving. For the first time in their lives, they discovered who the true power of the workplace was and, for the first time, were the controllers of their own destiny.

The suited men went away and, at first, the workers felt like they had won. They had beaten the oppressive ruling classes. But, as time dragged on and nothing happened, despondency started to creep in, a thought that maybe nothing would happen, that the management would simply wait and 'starve them out'. After all, the workers still needed money at the end of the day. As they began to question the practical ramifications of their actions, cracks began to appear in their solidarity and mere words of Marxist rhetoric could not argue against the necessity of food on the table.

Luckily, just as the will of the people was about to expire, the suits returned with a proposition: the workforce was excused for the day - with full pay - and negotiations would commence this evening between a representative of the workers, Robert, and management.

It was a win!

Robert returned to the factory at eight o'clock, full of optimism. Not only for the outcome of these negotiations but also because how they would impact on the rest of his life: career, social and - dare he think it - romantic? He could not help but think Annie-Anne was looking at him with lingering eyes; a look he had seen many times before from girls he liked and directed at any other boys but him.

Could he consider a possible outcome? She was two years her elder and had three children but was still single and available.

He made his way across the factory forecourt towards the main building and, although it was steeped in darkness, he sauntered without a care as it if were a summer's day stroll. So careless was he that he completely failed to notice the large number of black transit vans parked at the peripheries. So careless was he, that he did not notice the furtive movement of a shadowy figure following his every step.

The factory floor's main lights had been extinguished but for one spot on the doorway he stepped through. He blinked to adjust his eyesight to the glare and slowly began to discern silhouettes approaching him.

"Mr Jaw," a voice he did not recognise announced cheerfully, "it's so good that you could take the time to join us."

"Er, it's my pleasure, Mr er..."

"Such a shame, though, that you didn't take the first deal that was offered to you," the voice continued and Robert could just distinguish a few more amorphous forms emerging from the darkness. His optimism waned.

"First deal?" Robert asked.

"The one where you were advised to walk away." The man stood directly in front of him, eclipsing the light, allowing Robert to make out a few distinguishing features but not much.

The man was dressed in black slacks and polo-neck jumper. He was big in all directions apart from his head, which looked amusingly shrunken in contrast. The amusement was counterpointed by the serious size of his clenched fists.

"I must have missed the terms of that deal, Mr... er..."

"The terms, Mr Jaw, were that you were going to be left with the ability to walk away," the man said. "And my name is Pinhead, not mister anything and we have been given strict instructions to set you as an example to others."

"An example?"

"A lesson, if you will. A moral to the dangers of being a commie and spreading your vile Bolshevik propaganda amongst our God fearing, pure blooded American citizens."

"But -"

"I know it wasn't, but that's what we'll tell everyone it was."

Pinhead made the slightest of movements with his sledgehammer-like hands, knocking Robert to the floor and unsettling his perception. Two men picked his limp body up by the arms and dragged him along, following Pinhead as he traversed the production line and entered the chemical plant. In there, massive vats of sweet smelling liquids seethed and churned. A network of skywalks threaded over their heads, passing over the vats, disappearing into darkened recesses and stretching up to offices that grew from the walls like wasp nests.

Robert was blurrly aware of his s'rroundings as his captors threw him to the folor. Indesquinshibale shapes and shounds fliltered through his zuzziness but, within it, the cry of a female's voice refocused his attention.

"Look what we found sneaking around outside," one of the goons remarked and pulled Annie-Anne into the room.

"Why are you here?" Pinhead demanded.

"I thought Robert might need some support," she blustered and struggled to free herself.

Pinhead nodded to the thug who released his grip. Annie-Anne fell down to Robert's side and attempted to bring him back to reality by gently brushing his hair back from his forehead with her fingers.

"Oh, he needs your support all right," Pinhead chuckled.

"Get to the manager's office," Robert whispered coherently. It took Annie-Anne a moment to realise he had said anything at all and that his state of incoherency was, at this moment, pretence. "I'll cause a distraction. Go to the office and call for help."

"I'm scared," she whimpered.

"Be strong. Everything will be okay."

The main problem with an entertainment media obsessed society is that, eventually, narrative clichés end up being considered to be a way of life: people recover from illnesses, couples live happily ever after, the hero makes a brave and stunning escape from captivity. So while Robert was formulating his idealistic bid for freedom, he had absolutely no doubt in his mind that, as he urged Pinhead to monologue the most intricate inner workings of his dastardly plan, Annie-Anne would be able to slip away, unnoticed by the conflagration of secondary thugs and contact the police who would then show up in the nick of time.

Robert hauled himself to his feet and staggered forward, watched by all. "Why are you doing this?" he pleaded.

"Doing what?" Pinhead questioned.

Annie-Anne cautiously shuffled backwards, towards the metal staircase.

"Doing this?" Pinhead asked, pulled a pistol from the back of his trousers and shot Annie-Anne in the face.

She made a sharp mewl as the bullet tore the back of her skull open and plastered the wall with a vast gobbet of rust-coloured essence. Her body folded on itself and collapsed to the floor.

Robert could not grasp what had happened. It was so quick: no build up; no warning; no reluctance. He looked at the murderer: no remorse.

"Dump her in the vat," Pinhead ordered.

Two men lifted her by her arms and legs; bits dropped out of her head and left a braincrumb trail up the steps and across a walkway. Her remnants seeped through the grating and pattered onto the factory floor. They got halfway across the gangway then flipped her corpse over the railing. As she fell, she turned in mid-air and stretched her arms out to Robert then disappeared from sight behind the towering wall of the vat.

From the highest point in the building, a door burst open and light poured forth. A shadowy form stood in the doorway: legs dynamically astride, hands thrust purposefully on his hips, long hair billowing chaotically around his face.

"Cease and desist!" the figure of power commanded and drew the immediate and undivided attention of everyone.

Robert had never seen such a presence of undeniable authority and imposing righteousness and, at that moment, knew that everything was going to be all right.

He was wrong, of course.

The man stepped into the light and Robert realised his error in judgement and how he had made his mistake. He was Liefield L. Lexos; the heir to the LexosCorp legacy and, in his unstable state, Robert had confused 'undeniable authority' with 'air of unjustified grandeur' and 'imposing righteousness' with 'overbearing, deluded arrogance.' An easy mistake.

"You idiots," Lexos bellowed. He was only in his mid-twenties but stood to inherit the entire business when his grandfather's iron lung could no longer circumnavigate all the damage the ingested carcinogens had done to his mortal frame. Liefield was next in line because his father had married into the family name and the running of the company could not possibly be passed into the hands of a woman. "You've tainted the chemicals!" his barrage continued. He stomped down the steps towards the goons who had disposed of Annie-Anne's body and, juxtaposed to them, he looked more like a pre-teenage child than corporate mogul.

Despite the obvious physical contrast, as he approached, the goons took a submissive step back and bowed their heads with humility (and to maintain eye contact with him). They knew where their next paycheck was coming from.

"What the hell?" Pinhead demanded. "Bring him," he ordered his closest men and indicated at Robert. He bounded up the steps with Robert dragged, relatively unprotestingly, behind.

They all gathered on the concourse above the seething vat. A sickly, bitter steam lapped around their feet through the grating of the walkway, emanating from a viscous blue goop that belched and farted at them. Between the bubbling breaks, the surface undulated rhythmically as something deeper kept the potion in perpetual motion.

Robert saw Annie-Anne's shoe get engulfed by the mire.

"What do you think you are doing?" Lexos screamed at the kowtowing criminals and they raised their eyes only to look at Pinhead upon his approach.

"Hey, don't talk to my men like that," Pinhead shouted. "They answer to me."

Lexos wheeled, still very over confident in his social position. "I told you to get him -" he jabbed a finger at Robert - "out of the way."

"We're dealing with it," Pinhead snarled.

"You've just contaminated our latest medical breakthrough!" Lexos screamed.

"Make some more," Pinhead said.

"It costs thousands to make," Lexos squealed. "And you have no idea the... the lengths I had to go to, to get this far."

"Consider it a practise run," Pinhead suggested.

Lexos drew himself up to his full height and stepped up to Pinhead. He grabbed the big man's jumper and pulled him down until they were eye to eye. "The ingredients are not, at this present moment, freely available on the market. Some are internationally banned because of their toxicity levels. Some are radioactive. This held the potential of a multi-million dollar medicine that could cure impotence and enhance the male libido: endurance and stamina."

It took a moment for the words to sink in and the ramifications for such a product. Pinhead's expression was of wonderment.

"Tests showed erectile efficiency up by four hundred per cent: girth, length and sustainability," Lexos explained.

Pinhead straightened himself and stared into the distance. "I can help," he said. "Dump this," he waved a hand at the vat, "ditch that," the other hand waved at Robert, "and tell me what you need. I know people who can get their hands on things."

Lexos' face still twitched as the dregs of outrage seeped from his being. "Okay, I'll cut you in but you owe me for this wasted batch." He stepped over to a console at the side of the gangway; a large red button waited irresistibly at its centre. He plunged his palm on to it and an underlying, bass whine stopped. The bubbling and undulations on the liquid's surface stopped and it started sinking into the giant bowl.

"That's fair," Pinhead commented. "To start with, consider this as a freebie." He pulled his gun out and pointed it at Robert.

Robert's reactions were instantaneous. The button had stopped all mechanical processes: the heating and the mixing. The bottom of the vat had opened and was draining the liquid into the huge ducts that trailed down to the lakes, three miles east. Gallons of water were being poured into the ducts to dilute the chemical slightly: not to weaken its potency but to ease its transit.

This was his only way out.

He ran and dived into the vat.

Robert had disappeared from sight before his actions had registered with any of the other men. They leaned over the safety rail to follow his flight and were amused to discover Robert's feet protruding from the thick sludge. Pinhead and Lexos looked at each other with growing curiosity.

"The heat alone will boil his blood," Lexos explained, "the radiation will fry his brain or, at least, he'll drown in there."

Robert's feet were consumed.

There was too much pain: a searing at his flesh, a slicing at every nerve, a squeezing of every millimetre of his body. Outsides were caving in while insides tried to get out. He could feel a slow movement downwards but the reservoir of air in his lungs was already spent. He knew there was a chance he was going to die but he had not considered it would hurt like this. Everything made him want to scream but it could not escape. All he could do was open his mouth and allow the grotesque fluid in. This was the end, his heartbeat thumped in his ears, his blood pulsated around his body, corpuscles ruptured and were infused by the chemicals.

"But just to make sure," Lexos muttered and pressed a smaller, black button on the console. The deep bass whine started up again.

Robert was blind. It might have been because of the totally opaqueness of the fluid or the burning of his eyes had destroyed their function. He was not dead though, the wracking agony that chewed at him from inside and out told him that much. There was more movement now and something very hard, slowly struck him across his temple. The force caused his body to roll in the sludge only to be hit in the stomach from the opposite direction. Pounding, pulsating, plaguing.

A small dial next to the black button showed the revolutions of the mixing blades were increasing. The vat was half empty and the wake of each scything stroke could be seen clearly, interspersed by an occasional solid mass being raised to the surface. Then something reverberated through the vat, causing the gangway to tremor. The bass drone raised in pitch, the needle on the revs dropped while another indicator shot up.

"Something's jammed the blades," Lexos explained and slammed his palm on to the red button again. The whine stopped but the second needle did not shift. In fact, the revs started to pick up again.

"It's not possible!" Lexos exclaimed. "Something is forcing the mixer in reverse."

Another shockwave shot through the factory but seemed to emanate from all around them.

"It's overloading the hydraulics," Lexos continued to narrate to ensure that everyone there understood exactly what was going on. "The pressure could feed back into the other mixers and burn out the generators. I've got to-"

He was cut off by a loud explosion from above them.

"It's too late," Lexos muttered.

A wall ruptured and showered the men with hot concrete. Some fell over the rails and disappeared with a brief cry and a perfunctory 'gloop'. Others were rent asunder by the shards of shrapnel.

Lexos watched as gas mains tore through the walls and spewed flames over the chemical field - each vat ignited upon contact, ejaculating its blazing venomous contents across the room. "My empire," he rued.

Pinhead wasted no time trying to ponder any poetic irony; he ran, head first, at a large window at the end of the gangway and leapt to a lacerated freedom.

Tanks split, contents spilled and mixed, flames brewed, the walkway collapsed and Lexos was the final ingredient before the entire building crumpled in on itself and efficiently burnt to the ground.

Three miles east and a thick blue liquid gobbed its way from a pipe into the reservoir. The flow stemmed for a moment and then delivered a hulking mass which dropped lifelessly into the water and bobbed gently in its ripples. Shortly, the turgid body seemed to deflate and it raised its head from submersion to suck in a desperate lungful of air. The body thrashed impotently in the water until, by chance, it made its way to the bank and discovered a footing. There, it was able to haul its flaccid form free and rest on the muddy embankment.

In the western sky, it seemed like the sun was setting.

CHAPTER 6
A BIT OF 'MASTURBATE' IN 'TEAM'

Orders had been given, meals served and plates polished off to varying degrees. However, whatever morsels had been left were being deftly devoured by Danny.

"You finished with that?" he asked Boy, who then passed his remnants of pasta in a green, creamy sauce. Danny took the offering and started shoving it into his mouth between bites of garlic bread.

Bob's bottom lip wobbled slightly as the painful memories of his genesis returned to their archives. Floater placed a soothing arm on his shoulder and he became aware of his surroundings.

"Needless to say," he continued, "that was not the last time I ran into Pinhead or Lexos and his gang of Chem-men."

"Isn't that how Joker was made?" Cassandra asked and broke the spell harder than the Eye of Agamoto.

"It's one of many potential geneses," Danny spat. "This pesto is a bit earthy, isn't it?"

Boy acquiesced with a shrug of his shoulders and eyebrows.

"Not unpleasant, exactly," Danny added and continued shovelling.

"It just sounds like someone could sue someone, is all," she continued.

Bob nodded sagely. "Our existence is fraught with the danger of litigation," he sighed. "The slightest reference without prior consent and..." He turned to Floater. "You remember Superb Man?"

"They destroyed him," she replied, shaking her head despondently.

"Aliens?" Danny asked.

"Hyper intelligent battle robots?" Cameron asked.

"Direct Comics copyright lawyers," Floater replied and Bob visibly shuddered at the thought. "Phonetic breach of trademarked product name."

"You can't even use the phrase..." Boy contributed but had to stop while he tried to work out how to say what he was not allowed he say. He belched loudly and surprised himself as much as everyone else around him. "Pardon me! I don't know where that came from."

Bob watched him with disdain. "What boy is trying to communicate with you is that it's safer to not refer to ourselves using generic terminology to avoid potential legal skirmishes. We try to stay away from any conventional idiomatic language, just in case."

Boy leaned over the table and whispered, "They have psychic lawyers. Don't even think it."

The boys could not work out if the prospect of being defeated by a misjudged pop culture reference was really scary or really lame but something distracted Cameron from that train of thought.

"Hang on. You said nineteen-sixties, right?"

"Yes," Bob replied.

"Well that was, like, eighty years ago or something and you don't look a day over thirty."

"It wasn't eighty years, it was only –" Bob attempted.

"What is it? Regenerative powers?" Cameron demanded.

"You mean a healing fac-" Danny contributed but was cut short by Floater clamping her hand over his mouth.

"No, nothing like that," Bob replied.

"Slowed metabolism?"

"No."

"Plastic surgery?"

"No!"

"Then tell us."

Bob sighed again and looked wearily at Floater who just shrugged resignedly in return.

"About a decade ago," he said, "there was a major incident that involved a mirror version of this planet but was forty years out of synch."

"Oh, a multiverse, cross-time mergence," Danny stated and Cameron added, "The old alternate reality counterpart amalgamation."

With the wind removed from his sails again, Bob sat back in his seat. "Yes, I suppose."

"Cool," Danny gushed. "Did you get to meet different versions of yourself?"

"A few," Bob replied.

"A girl version?" Cameron asked.

"Er, yes?" he said with reservations.

"Did you fuck her?" Cameron continued.

"What!?"

"Cameron!" Cassandra chastised.

"Oh come on, Cass," Danny berated. "You would if you met you with a dick."

She automatically went to argue but conceded the point instead with a shrug of her eyebrows.

"You would even if they weren't the opposite gender," Cameron suggested.

"What are you implying?" Bob roared.

"That people's ego and sexual curiosity would stretch to having a sexual dalliance with themselves if they met them," Cameron explained.

"I am not gay!" Bob stated.

"Fucking yourself isn't homosexuality," Cameron argued. "It's just third person, subjective masturbation."

"I need to leave now," Bob barked at Floater.

"Oh, this is a fine set of morals coming from a guy who is, for all accounts, a walking penis and, every time he has a fight, is getting sexually aroused."

Floater pushed Bob towards the door before he could turn and retort but the man was already starting to inflate. "You'll go too far," she warned.

"Yeah," Danny agreed. "Stop being so hard on him."

"Oh, I'm sorry," Cameron apologised. "I'm only trying to get a rise out of him."

Bob only just managed to squeeze through the door with a hefty assist from Floater. She hesitated at the doorway and looked over her shoulder at the group.

"What are you doing?" Bob asked. "Let's go."

"Ah'll be up in a minute, Bob," she said. "Ah just want to talk to the kids about something."

"What?"

"Just... something. Nothing important."

He harrumphed and trudged away. When she was happy that he could manage on his own, she returned to her place at the table. She smiled at Cassandra as she sat.

"He needs to loosen up," Cameron shouted at the open door then looked at Danny with eager expectation.

"Yeah, try not to be quite so stiff."

"I set 'em up and you clobber 'em down!" They high-fived.

"Why do you do it?" Floater asked. "Why do you take so much delight in upsetting people?"

"It's just a joke," Cameron chuckled. "We only do it when things get too serious. It breaks the tension and can disorientate the bad guys."

"But you take advantage of the weaknesses of your friends too," she continued. "You use these skills to hurt people."

"What are you getting at?" Cameron asked.

"You don't use your powers responsibly," Boy said. "Like the time when you made your coat tails flutter dramatically in the wind: abuse of power."

"Oh, stop, please," he begged. "That's a tiny, insignificant thing."

"Where's the line though, Cameron?" Floater asked then turned to her teammates. "You both remember Paradox?"

They nodded with gravitas.

"He's a good example of the corruptible nature of powers."

"'Paradox'? That's a pretty cool name," Cameron muttered. "I should have had that name. It would give me a good excuse to do random shit."

Danny closed his eyes with consternation and shook his head sorrowfully. "That's not a paradox, dude. It wouldn't work."

"Yes it would," Cameron argued. "I could do whatever the hell I wanted to do with the justification that it was what I was supposed to do."

"It's a bit tenuous."

"You're fucking tenuous. You should be called Paradox: you talk shit because you're a dick-head and you're a dick-head because of all the shit you talk."

"It's more of a self-fulfilling prophecy," Danny continued unperturbed. "Which is more like you."

Cameron allowed him his dramatic pause but did not fuel him with the request for explanation.

"You're so spineless you can self-fulfil yourself."

Cat, Floater and Boy watched the exchange with eyes and mouths agape.

"The way you two talk to each other," Boy remarked in disbelief.

"Guys, seriously," Floater advised, "Bob will never give you passes if y'all can't curb the bad language."

"I don't know," Cat pondered, "I'm finding it kind of refreshing." She stared intently at Cameron and, despite his normal nature around attractive females, found the moxy to return her gaze, smile and even raise his eyebrows at her.

"Unfortunately," Cassandra chipped in, "after a while, you get used to it and it just becomes like static hissing away irritatingly in the background."

At these words, Boy's eyes widened with the horrific prospect of the potential corruption of his innocence. The mere thought of ever being so desensitised to such profanity and insults that he could even tolerate it, sent a physical shudder down his spine and caused his buttocks to clench. "Anyway, Paradox," he reminded, desperate to control the conversation and thereby the purity of his soul. "He was given the key to time travel."

This got the boys' attention.

"Cool!"

"Fuck off!"

Shudder

"He was gifted a bracelet that enabled him to travel backwards in time along his own timeline," Boy continued.

"Oh boy," Danny homaged.

"Who was he?"

"He was an electrician," Boy said, "a very good one too."

"But not a Tony Starkesque genius," Cameron suggested.

"No, just a good one," Boy replied. "Good enough to be able to reverse engineer the bracelet and create another working model."

"Why'd he bother to do that?"

"So he could go back in time and give it to himself."

"Niiiiiice," the boys commended in unison.

"That's stupid," Cassandra stated. "Are you trying to tell me that the time machine only existed because he gave it to himself using the time machine that he gave himself?"

It took Boy a mental moment to process the question but, eventually, he replied, "Yes."

"Hence the name," Danny derided and received the customary slap across the shoulder.

"Where is he now then?" Cameron demanded. "I'd love to have a go with that machine."

"He was..." Boy trailed off; the words either eluded him or were so bilious that they stuck in his throat.

"Corrupted by his gift," Cat said.

"Did he give himself the lotto numbers?" Danny asked. "Or gambling results? You could make a fortune knowing when and where to place the right bet."

"You could get away with all sorts of shit with something like that – security combinations, secret locations – just by being told by yourself and then going back later and telling yourself," Cameron gushed.

"It doesn't make any sense at all," Cassandra whined. "How can you tell yourself something if you didn't know it in the first place?"

"Or did he overuse it and get himself trapped in a recurring time loop?" Danny suggested.

"And anyway, time travel is impossible because of its relativity to space," Cassandra continued. "One moment in time is based on the entirety of the universe being in a particular position. To travel back through time, every element of space – every atom and particle – would have to be in that exact position that they were in and it couldn't be the same because the element of the time traveller was never an integral part of that place in space at that time!"

"Unless he was there," Danny countered.

"At the same time as him being there normally?" she squealed with incomprehension. "How can the same object exist in two different points at the same time? It can't!"

"Unless it travelled in time and created a paradox," Danny concluded.

Cassandra just stared at him and it was uncertain as to whether she was preparing to strike or resignedly winding down. "It's stupid," she said through gritted teeth.

"*Timecop* was stupid," Cameron said, "but what I want to know is what your guy did."

"He raped himself," Cat said bluntly.

"What the fuck?!" Cameron blurted, stuck somewhere between horror and amusement.

"He – as you suggested someone might when given the opportunity – went back in time and decided to have sex with himself."

"But why was it rape? Surely he would have the idea and then visit himself when he was comfortable with the notion to get his freaky thang on."

Boy was very uncomfortable with the progression of this topic; the offensiveness of the language had been escalated by the topic and was physically churning at his insides. Through a heated glow of redness he edged his way out of the communion, ensuring he avoided all possible eye contact with everyone. Especially the females.

"Apparently," Cat continued, "he had been doing it regularly: popping back an hour, doing it with himself and moving on until one of his future selves came back and reminded him of events that occurred in his childhood."

"Stop right there!" Cameron declared. "That's quite enough. Corruptible nature of powers has been well and truly exemplified, thank you. Moving on."

Danny was wide-eyed and almost catatonic until Cassandra nudged him and whispered in his ear. He whispered a reply and she threw herself away from the response as if it had slapped her.

"Anyway, when he came back, he was completely messed up: wracked with guilt to the point of suicide. So he did the one thing he was told never to attempt..." She left a dramatic pause. "... Go forward along his timeline. He's never been seen again."

They all sat in contemplative silence: some lingering on the analogy of their own existence; others still processing the mechanics of quantum temporal physics; one imagining what it would be like to fuck himself.

"And on that note," Cameron declared and rose to his feet.

Only a fraction of a millisecond behind, Cat also got up. "Oh, are you retiring too?"

"Yeah, I've got a bit fed up being told either how shit I am, how dangerous I am or how evil I might be."

"Now, don't take it like that, Cameron," Floater pleaded but he raised his palm to her face.

"No, no," he stated with mock indignation. "Things have been said that cannot be taken back or forgotten." He swanned his way towards the exit.

"Cameron," Floater hailed.

"Ignore him," Cassandra said. "He's winding you up."

"I'll say good night too," Cat commented and left with much less drama but more pace.

"Right, well, we might as well crash too," Danny suggested before an awkward silence could build. Or before his eyes could become mesmerised by the forbidden fruits of another garden, which would lead to an entirely different awkward moment, which would, in no way, be silent.

"Can Ah talk to you two for a second?" Floater asked.

"Both of us?" Cassandra demanded.

"Well, you really, Cassandra."

Cassandra did not even try to conceal her sneer of contempt at having to hang around for any longer than necessary, so she thrust herself back in her seat and crossed her arms.

"What have we done?" Danny panicked.

"Oh mah," Floater gasped. "Nothing, Danny. Ah was hoping you could give me some advice."

This piqued Cassandra's attention.

"This'll sound wrong but, Ah can't help but notice that, even though you don't have any abilities, Cassandra, Danny doesn't treat you like a sidekick."

"That's because I'm not," Cassandra huffed.

"But –"

"No buts," she interrupted. "If he ever treats me like I'm secondary to him, I'll lamp him."

"'Lamp'?"

"I'll smack him one!"

Floater looked to Danny for confirmation and received a very stern nod.

"So you rule through violence?"

"I love her," Danny interjected, "but sometimes I step over that line between familiarity and disrespect and I need to be shoved back."

Floater frowned at the pair: her brow furrowed with the creases of an early morning bed sheet after a passionate night; her eyelids lowered that second before release; her lips smacked together after tasting a kiss.

"What is your problem with me?" Cassandra snapped and Danny shook himself awake. "You're scowling at me like I'm a bad smell."

Floater was so taken aback by the reaction that she looked like she was about to cry: eyes moistened, bottom lip trembled, chest heaved with each deep, passionate breath.

"Danny!" Cassandra shouted again.

"I wasn't –" he automatically said.

"You bloody well were," she told him.

"Ah don't have a problem with you, Cassandra," Floater explained. "Ah'm trying to work out how you and Danny get along as partners, not as if you are just an accessory from a utility belt."

"For starters, I let him know when he's crossed the line," Cassandra said and Floater nodded. "Secondly, and probably most importantly, is the fact that I don't let him use me."

"Ah don't think Ah do that," Floater commented.

Cassandra snorted derisively. "Have you looked in the mirror lately?"

"Cass!"

"Ah don't understand."

"Look at the state of you, woman! Look at what you're wearing – or not wearing as the case is."

As Floater checked her uniform, Danny took the instruction to have another look too. He lifted himself from his seat to inspect her lower half but Cassandra pushed him back down.

"What?" Floater asked.

"Seriously? You are, right now, the embodiment of sexual objectification. You've got everything out on display and what isn't out is hardly being covered – I don't understand how those threads are keeping your tits in and not riding right up your arse. But physical impossibilities aside, you are real-life pornography. When someone looks at you, they don't see a superhero – or whatever you're allowed to call it – they see a fuck piece. A slut."

Floater was stuck somewhere between aghast and nausea. "That's not true, is it? Bob said it befitted the genre of my abilities; the streamlined design aided my movement."

Cassandra raised her eyebrows. "Danny, what did you use for masturbation before you discovered the internet?"

"Comic covers," he replied.

She returned to Floater. "You are a walking wank fantasy."

Danny nodded a bit too enthusiastically but Cassandra left it. "You need to cover up and gain some self respect before you can start deserving others' respect," she concluded and sat back.

Floater pulled her coat around her shoulders self-consciously and looked perturbed. "How did Ah let this happen? Why did Ah let him influence me like this? You're right, Ah'd never dream of wearing clothes like this before I was supreme. Ah'm so much better than this."

There was a memory. Or was it a dream? A memory of a dream: indistinct details yet sensations that overwhelmed her.

There was an extreme dizziness as the world around her blurred out of focus. Her body felt like it was being pulled backwards but a solid force on her arms stopped her from falling; was pulling her in; was equalling the falling and keeping at that one spot, spinning around. It took some effort to look up at her outstretched hands; her neck muscles had to fight against that dragging pressure. But when she did, she could see the background of blurriness fronted by the face of her father – he was laughing loudly as he spun on the spot, holding her arms as she whirled around in a tight orbit.

And she laughed. Breathlessly. Excited. Dizzy. Scared. Safe. Happy. Sick. Too many feelings to know if it was all good or bad.

Whatever. It just felt right. Perfect.

Mary Martin was told that her parents had died on the day she was dropped off at her Auntie Geraldine's house. She was eight years old and already an incredibly nervous child: she found it hard to talk to people, hard to emote and hard to make any kind of social interaction.

She grew quickly – straight up – and had hit five feet by the age of ten when her peers were only just broaching four. This, naturally, made her even more of an outcast and without an outlet for socialising, she found comfort and solace in academia. With no other distractions, she took to learning incredibly well and was soon exceeding the expectations and capabilities of her schools so her Aunt funded her private tuition with professors and lecturers from universities like M.I.T., Harvard and Oxford.

It was through this special tutelage when she met Professor Adam

Arthurs, an astrophysicist who had taken up lecturing after an acrimonious separation from NASA. He was an old, short, wiry man. His frame gave the appearance of fragility whilst his pure white hair and beard splayed from his head like a frayed string. Deep set wrinkles around his face looked like aged cracks in porcelain and his eyes were dulled by misery and pain. Despite his intricate knowledge and Mary's hunger for the subject, he delivered each course with disinterest and derision.

Until one fateful day.

Mary was thirteen and had been exploring one of the lesser-used wings of her aunt's mansion and she came across a room filled with archive boxes stacked up like Machu Pichu and suitcases dotted around like tombstones. With an air of innocent curiosity, she opened the first box she came to and revealed it to be crammed full of documents. The next box was the same but she looked closer and found a page of formula scrawled across it like hieroglyphics. Although some of the symbols nudged at her memory, there was one part of script that seemed to leap from the page and startle her to breathlessness.

The names of her mother and father.

Her hand clasped the piece of paper, her legs gave way and she collapsed to the floor, knocking her back against one of the upright suitcases. Really, it should not have elicited such an extreme response but it was the shock of the knowledge that things belonging to her parents even existed. She had uncovered this secret mausoleum of treasures and skeletons having lived next door to it for five years.

'Mr Tutankhamun? From number seven? He's a quiet chap. Keeps himself to himself, really.'

She pondered the significance of her discovery; how much information there would be about her parents here. Which led, as should do to a logical questioner, to, why was it all here? Why had this museum been maintained? For prosperity? If so, then why keep it secluded from her. For their worth? That could only be determined by further exploration. Or were they there only temporarily – awaiting transfer or collection?

She took a closer look at the paper and followed the path of the equations scrawled across them. Although many of the paths needed some sort of numerical context to make perfect sense; there were some logarithms that twinged at her memory and the recent work she had been doing with Professor Arthurs: gravitational contravention and inverse proportionalism.

She rifled through a few more of the papers to discover further, complex equations of the theories as well as many more that she had never seen before. There were also blueprints of machines of varying proportions: vast warehouse-sized machines where the walls, floors and ceiling were integral motherboards; industrial-like contraptions which seemed to be nothing more than large boxes with a couple of lights on, their inner workings were generators for whatever they might attach to; and then there were more recognisable shapes: back-packs, clothing and... guns?

She felt a need to talk to someone and her immediate questions were aimed at her Aunt Geraldine but felt that if she had kept this from her for however long it had been, then she might not be too forthcoming with answers. The only other person she might be able to mention this to, was Professor Arthurs.

The fragile old man collapsed into his seat when she told him. At first, she thought it might be something to do with the formulae, but he had not even read past her parents' names at the head of the sheet.

"Your surname," he gasped, "I thought it was a coincidence but this..." He flapped the paper wearily in front of him. "I thought this was lost forever."

"You knew them?"

"'Knew them'? I worked with them on these very projects," Arthurs explained. "We worked together for over twenty years."

Mary gave them both a moment for the information to sink in. She could see that he was completely overwhelmed by the disclosure; he was visibly drowning in the deluge of emotion and memories: his eyes stared with incomprehension into the distance and his lips made unintelligible mutterings at each wave of reflection.

After a while, he blinked himself back to awareness and he focussed his attention back on his student. "Your parents were geniuses in this field," he said. "Their theories would have advanced intergalactic travel to the extent that would have had ships broaching light speeds."

"How?"

"The mechanical negation of gravitational forces."

Her mind recalled the building. "Anti-gravity simulation chambers."

He nodded. "That was one aspect, yes. The grand idea was to remove the effect of inertia from an accelerating body enabling – with extrapolated concepts – the instantaneous acceleration from zero to light speed."

"Why didn't it get finished?"

"Theoretically, their ideas were sound," he explained. "The formulae worked out but there was till something missing when it came to the practical applications."

"There were other designs, too," Mary added.

"Yes," he mused. "Other... parties became interested and directly involved with funding and were able to influence the project's direction and our motivations." His head dropped.

"Weapons?"

His sigh was long and heavy, as if a huge pent up pressure had been released. "To my shame," he muttered whilst keeping his gaze fixed firmly at the floor. "I could see the benefits of weaponising the technology. Imagine, being able to flatten an entire battlefield with a press of a button; entire armies immobilised without a shot fired; missiles and aircraft plucked from the skies like dead weights."

"Nations held to ransom by the threat of superior weaponry; liberties bound; rights revoked."

He looked up at this point. "You sound just like your parents," he commented admiringly. "And I do blame myself – my greed – for their reticence to continue and the conflict that followed. They demanded that they should be released from the project and threatened to take their research with them. Of course, the agency brought in security teams and confiscated everything. There was nothing anyone could do; legally, it belonged to them. But they could not confiscate the knowledge and understanding that was required to advance the technology to its practical application stage. That was lost with your parents."

Mary fell into her seat; her strength sapped from her body by the revelations. She stared into the distance, trying to organise all of the pieces into some coherent picture. Maybe her parents had died in an accident; perhaps there was something more sinister at work; some sort of conspiracy. Perhaps they had been murdered because they would not cooperate. Perhaps they had been murdered to ensure they would not take their research anywhere else. How was her auntie involved and why had she kept the existence of the documents a secret? Something nefarious or out of fear or even naivety? Her auntie might not even know what was in there.

Oh dear god, what had she done? She had just opened Pandora's box, potentially to one of the men it had been closed to.

"Where are the other boxes?" Arthurs enquired.

"Why?"

"They could hold the answers; the final sequences required to complete their work."

"To weaponise their work," she stated.

"No!" Arthurs spat. "I have lived with the regret of my actions for a decade and now have the chance to redeem myself; to honour them by realising their original dreams. And it would be by fate's chance that their daughter be instrumental in that."

"Me?"

"Of course. You have the combined intellect of your parents: your mother's analytical prowess and your father's critical thinking. You just lack the knowledge which I can provide."

Could she trust him?

Should she?

How could she not? She was hooked on the matter and he was the only one who could provide the interpretive skills to translate the codes.

"Where do we start?" she asked.

Days became months as the two carefully sifted through the manuscripts and data; casting aside anything that had anything to do with weaponry, using the early materials for learning and the later papers for the purposes of checking and comparing their own theses. Much to their surprise and delight, the work came easily and evolved very naturally. It was not long before they had caught up with the last dated documents and had constructed a rudimentary chamber.

It was nothing impressive to look at, built from the parts of a shower cubicle: glass sides and front with a stainless steel back, base and lid. It was the protrusions from the back where the real sciency stuff was happening: a massive console with stereotypical winking lights, tremoring meter needles and a deep bass hum of internal activity.

"Something's not right," Mary mused whilst scribbling numbers across a sheet of paper.

"We have cross checked countless times, Mary," Arthurs argued. "We have gone beyond the research I conducted. I am convinced this is ready."

Her calculations came to a conclusion and she underlined the final figure of zero. She placed her pencil under the result but her fingers lingered on its side, reluctant to relinquish her touch for fear of it indicating her final decision.

He watched her face intently. "You see?" he said. "From every angle, the forces are negated. The inanimate tests were successful and we should push for a live subject test."

Pressing her fingers firmly onto her pencil, she clenched her jaw and stared fixedly at him. "No. Not until Ah'm absolutely certain."

With an uncharacteristic explosion of anger, Arthurs leapt to his feet and exhaled a breath of air that seemed double the capacity that his diminutive frame should be able to cope. "This is one inherent trait I hoped may have skipped a generation."

Tiredness, frustration and an element of shock overcame Mary's usual inhibitions. "What trait? Cautiousness? Care? Rationality? If you want to jump the gun, to belie mah concerns after trusting mah judgements so much this far, if you want a live test subject, y'all go ahead and get in there." She was glaring at him and pointing at the cubicle, her hand trembling. The moment and passion passed; she was on the verge of apologising or bursting into tears. She mustered her final vestiges of strength, lowered her arm slowly and then walked from the room.

She wanted to sigh with relief, to allow her body to collapse against the wall as the adrenaline soured inside her. To blast through the past weeks of fervent thinking and activity to hit this wall was a crippling anti-climax. She could understand why Arthurs wanted to maintain their progressive momentum but she could not justify it.

Before she could lower her guard, her defences were assaulted.

"I heard shouting," her aunt Geraldine commented from behind her. "Is your science project not going to plan?"

She was a stoic woman during her more elated moments. To try to define her during the more serious times was like trying to define what a banana was like: she was seriousness anthropomorphised. When seriousness asked for validation from its creator, It pointed at Geraldine Martin and said, 'That's you, that is.' She could have been the archetypal Edwardian matron in some boys' boarding school had she been born a century earlier. But, then again, perhaps she had been: she looked like she could pass for a hundred and fifty year old with her brilliant white hair pulled back into a firm bun atop her head. Her face, although delineated with the sharpness of high cheekbones, defined chin and angular nose, was aged by loose and heavily wrinkled skin.

"Shouting?" Mary asked. It was as much as she could muster whilst suppressing the scream of shock that actually wanted to escape.

Her aunt was better than that though, and never felt the need to repeat herself when a steely gaze was good enough to get a hardened criminal to reveal everything.

"We – er – couldn't agree on something is all," Mary blustered. "An equation."

"Nothing serious, I hope," Geraldine told her and walked slowly along the corridor.

Mary watched her with increasing suspicion. She had told her, hadn't she. It had not been a polite and caring enquiry but an instruction. It was as if she had been giving her an order. As if she was fully aware of their secret operations. As if she had been orchestrating everything as some all-encompassing conspiracy right from the start with the death of her parents, her being moved to her aunt's care, her tuition with the very man who had worked with her parents, to the discovery of her parents work and her on-going research and development.

She was tired and probably being paranoid. A good night's sleep would make her more rational and everything clearer. She returned to her bedroom, changed into her pajamas and jumped into her bed. She only just got her glasses onto the nightstand before she fell asleep.

She dreamt that she was being watched: everything she did was being scrutinised by some indefinable source. She could not tell if it was a protective angel who was keeping vigil; a predator waiting for her to drop her guard; or some neutral voyeur observing her as if she was a reality show. Whenever she looked over her shoulder, there was nobody there – at all, in fact – but a delicate glint kept catching the corner of her eye. It was a lustrous streak of vertical light and when she looked up to identify its source, she discovered it was a gossamer thread hanging from a large wooden crossbeam above her head. There were lots of these strands that trailed down towards her and now that she knew what she was looking for, she could see them dangling just in front of her. As she raised her hand to grab one, it moved slightly as if trying to avoid her clutch. Then she traced its path to her hand – no, through her hand and knotted on the other side, in the middle of her palm. Both her hands had been threaded. And her feet. And one through the top of her head –

She awoke with a gasp and scratched violently at her scalp, trying to rid herself of the itchy sensation that threatened to make her scream with revulsion.

After a few bleary moments, clarity seeped in and, with it, a realisation that something other than her dream caused her to wake: a noise. There was a high-pitched but distant whine filtering through the walls of her bedroom. The sound of air being forced through a small gap, or metal rubbing against metal, or audio feedback. Whatever it was, it was more annoying than the itchiness of her head and had to be stopped if she was to get back to sleep.

Irritably, she threw the bed covers back, swung her legs out of bed and fumbled for her glasses from the nightstand. She stomped from her room and listened for a directional source of the noise. It took a few minutes of wandering the darkened hallways until it occurred to her that she was being led towards the lab.

Someone had activated the antigravity generator.

She stood at the door for a long tentative moment, staring at the brass knob and her distorted reflection held in its shiny surface. She was held enraptured by the way her stomach had been ballooned to ridiculous proportions and her legs and chest dwindled to almost insignificance.

The noise rose an octave.

Her mirrored hand inflated, masking the rest of her, as she reached for the handle.

She tightened her grip and twisted; the inner mechanism clicked and a concept unlocked within her mind. All trepidation and confusion instantly evaporated and she barged into the lab.

The room was pitched in darkness except for a pool of light in the centre. The monitors encircled the generator and cubicle, their screens refreshed themselves periodically with streams of numbers, giving the effect of dying fluorescent lighting as they strobed intermittently. Their illumination fixed pointedly on the machinery and there, centre stage, within the cubicle, was Arthurs: hands pressed against the glass and a look of benign resignation on his face until he noticed her and then he began hammering desperately.

There was a 'click', a pitch rise in the background noise and a flickering of the lights. Arthurs' body began to elevate gently: the few strands of hair on his head wafted as if caught in a gentle updraft; his limbs spread and he smiled victoriously.

He expression changed from euphoria to horror very suddenly. He flexed his fingers as if trying to return feeling to them or testing that they were still there and then his entire arm began to stretch. Arthurs made a noise that no human should have been able to create nor should have been heard: a shrill, grating scream that used every iota of strength and air in his body. The arm slipped out of the sleeve of his jacket, followed by spheroid gobbets of free-floating blood. His other arm followed suit; its fingers curled into a fist and folded at the elbow. His screaming persisted. Legs gently dismembered themselves and twitched within the loose confines of his trousers. They too, doubled over at every joint possible. A thin line around his neck split inwards as if an invisible cheesewire was slicing through his flesh; the torn skin then neatly folded in on itself, opening a yawning chasm through vein, muscle then exposing the white of his vertebrae, which separated with no more resistance than separating a snail from a leaf.

But the noise did not stop. It just stopped coming from his mouth. His torso folded in the middle and squeezed the final vestiges of air from his chest through what remained of his vocal chords, producing a long, lingering, wet groan of misery.

She watched as five small spheroids began to orbit the larger mass, which spun casually on two axes. Around some of the smaller satellites, crimson rings formed.

"Dear god, girl," her aunt's voice declared from the doorway. "What have you done?"

"What? Me? No, Ah just... Ah mean, Ah didn't... He was already..." Mary sputtered.

"This is what you've been working on?" Geraldine demanded. "The same inhumane experiments as your parents?"

"No! It's not supposed to kill," Mary argued. "Ah told him it wasn't ready for a live subject but –"

"- he didn't listen," Geraldine interjected. "In his rush for glory, he tested it on himself. What a fool."

It sounded feasible but there had been something in his final expression that suggested he might not have been a willing participant. Perhaps he had panicked, thinking she would interrupt the procedure. Or perhaps he had just realised the error of his ways a little too late.

"Shut it down, for god's sake," Geraldine instructed. "I'll get someone to come clean up."

"Shouldn't we call the police?" Mary enquired.

"If you can think of a rational way to explain this, then go ahead," her aunt replied and marched from the room.

She was right, there was no simple way to explain what had happened. Nothing that would not implicate her in his death.

Mary watched the mini-solar-system as each body part pirouetted around each other, spinning and slingshotting through each gravitational field like waltzers at a –

Her simile stopped mid-comparison. That was it: the missing algorithm.

"It assumes the body as having only one gravitational heart," she babbled to herself while grabbing the closest sheets of paper to her and scribbling her calculations, "whereas each extension of the body has an independent density, mass and gravitational force to factorise into the coefficient."

She held up the mathematics to the light and was very pleased with what she saw. Her mind was so preoccupied with the breakthrough, the sloppy thumps from within the cubicle passed her notice when she deactivated the generator via the nearest console. It was when she unlocked the cubicle and opened the door that she discovered something else; it had been sealed from the outside.

Someone behind her sighed heavily.

"Oh no," Mary groaned and turned.

"Clever, clever girl," Geraldine praised from the doorway. "And to think, all I should have done was allow your parents to witness the deaths of our test subjects before they disappeared and they might have hypothesised the solution." She wandered casually to the computer station and the hastened scribbles. She picked the paper up and perused the calculations. "This is it?"

Mary nodded.

"You're sure?"

Mary nodded.

"It would be a shame for someone else to suffer a similar, horrible death."

Mary nodded.

"So you will finish your work –"

"Okay," Mary said.

"-or I'll be forced to whatdidyousay?"

"'Okay'," she replied. "Of course Ah'll complete the project, it would be illogical for me to refuse."

"It would?"

"I may not agree with the practical application of work ethic but I cannot deny the positive results that have come from it."

"Oooookay," Geraldine mused. "So, you'll just get on with it, then?"

"Right away."

"Right."

"Okay?"

"Fine. I'll leave you to it, then."

"Okay."

"Unless you need any help?"

Mary considered the question. "Nope," she eventually replied.

Geraldine started walking back to the lab door, turning at the last minute to put the paper down on the table.

"There is one thing," Mary said.

"Yes?"

"Can you get that cleaned up?" she asked and indicated the body of fallen planetoids in the cubicle.

Geraldine failed to hide her disappointment and disgust with a solemn nod and swift exit from the room.

As soon as the door closed, Mary ran to the adjoining bathroom and threw up in the toilet. The violence, fear and admissions had been almost too much to handle. If it had not been for that one word Geraldine had used – 'disappeared' – she felt she would have screamed herself hoarse and leapt through the nearest window. But she had been inadvertently told that her parents might not be dead; that they had probably reached a similar stage in their experiments and decided to go into hiding to prevent the misappropriation of their works.

After the expulsion of her insides, she collapsed to the floor and began shaking violently: the adrenaline that had been keeping her so calm was now turning stale in her muscles and causing them to spasm involuntarily.

She had bought herself some time. Not much because she was sure that her aunt had been monitoring her every word and movement and her current reaction will give away her true feelings on the matter.

"Get up!" she ordered herself and began to crawl up the side of the sink until she could get her legs underneath herself and establish some stability. She wobbled back into the lab, picked up her calculations and made her way round to the back of the generator, ensuring that she did not look at the remnants of Arthurs at all, keeping her mind on her task: a bid for freedom and eradication of all her progress.

She removed a large access panel from the side of the machine and plugged a laptop into a terminal within. Tapping her fingers rapidly over the keyboard, she manipulated the pre-existing data that filled the screen. After double checking her input, she buried her head into the generator's guts, liberally removing wires and parts until she re-emerged with a foot square circuit board dragging partial, vein-like entrails after it.

She unceremoniously clambered on top of the generator to gain access to the roof of the cubicle, detached a panel and started disembowelling its contents. Eventually she came away holding five glass lenses. Her descent was slightly more gracious, cradling the lenses in the nook of her right arm as she lowered herself. Gathering the circuit board and some elastic straps, she moved to a workbench and fervently began soldering and stapling the bits together. Occasionally, she would look over at the monitor of the laptop she had initially tinkered with.

The laboratory door swung open and Geraldine marched back in. "What's going on, young lady?" she demanded.

Without looking away from her work, she replied, "Ah needed to recalibrate the focus plates due to the new calculations."

"Why away from the machine?"

"Ah didn't want any cross connections to interfere with the data dump."

"Why only five of them?"

This caused Mary to hesitate. She had not been sure exactly how much detail the woman had been taking notice of and this proved that it had been a lot. "It was all Ah needed to implement a viral upload when Ah reconnect –"

"That's enough!" Geraldine squealed. "Your charade almost worked but you –"

"Did," Mary interrupted and placed a few final staples in the straps, fixing some wires in place.

"Did what?"

"Did work," Mary told her. "Mah 'charade' did work."

Geraldine looked thoroughly confused. "But I caught you."

"You caught me too late." Deftly, she twirled the new device around her head, slipping her arms through loops, fixing Velcro around each thigh and adjusting the circuit board to sit squarely on her chest.

Geraldine stared at her with incredulity but found her observation was not met in return; Mary was looking beyond her. At the laptop screen where a loading bar had just reached ninety-nine per cent.

"What have you done?" Geraldine asked.

"Activated an inversion loop that will generate a temporary singularity field, effectively negating all activity within a two-hundred metre radius of it."

Geraldine leered at her niece with unbridled animosity and hatred. "Come again?"

Mary paused to reconsider her words. "Ah have set the gravitational generator in a perpetual cycle of exponential –"

Geraldine waved her hands to cut the flow again. "After 'generator'?"

Mary sighed. "Just watch."

The machine kicked in. Immediately, it was apparent that something was awry. The cubicle began shaking violently and the pitch of the whine escalated beyond human hearing in seconds. The glass door and metal walls bowed inwards, groaning at the unreasonable physical expectations that had been placed upon them. A tensile limit was breached, a fracture ripped through the pane, Arthurs began to rise again. As branches in the split began to fractal across the glass, the body bits began orbiting a focal point in the middle of the cubicle.

The prolonged shattering of the glass sounded more like the crashing of waves as the individual shards were slowly extracted from their positions, grating against each other to the point of separation then finding their own position in orbit around the invisible focal point. Each glistening element reflected the room's illumination, back: a scale model of a swirling galaxy.

This moment of resplendent tranquillity was shattered by a blinding flash of darkness and deafening silence as all of creation was sucked from existence: the focal point had become an orb of dense blackness that the orbiting systems were being unerringly drawn towards. As each satellite fell into the pitch, the ball inflated and its lure increased. It reached the size of a cricket ball and, despite being twenty meters away, Mary could feel the attraction. Not so much a pull towards it but more like a rotational shift of the room's axis. The side of the room was now down: office chairs shifted on their casters; pens rolled across desks; Geraldine stumbled off-balance.

Mary activated the circuit board on her chest and she had to readjust her stance to compensate for the recompensated gravitational force.

Geraldine was supporting herself with one hand propped on a desk; the change in the room had done more to just upset her balance but also to upset her stomach too: she looked like she was about to throw up. The desk shifted under her additional force.

"You made a black hole," Geraldine stated.

"That's what Ah said."

"You'll kill us all."

"It'll burn itself out as soon as it devours its own power source," Mary said and adjusted the dial on her chest board.

One of the chairs picked up momentum and trundled freely into the cubicle. It clipped against the edge of the container and launched into the anti-space, folding at the edges to squeeze in.

"How big will it be before it can swallow a five-thousand pound generator that's been bolted a foot into solid concrete?" Geraldine demanded.

"Oh," Mary replied as another chair coasted along, bounced twice then vanished into the distending darkness.

"How big does it get before it can become self sustaining?" The desk beneath her grip shifted again and slowly scraped forward. Geraldine stumbled and dropped to her knees.

"Ah only wanted to destroy the work," Mary confessed. Ah didn't think–"

But it was too late for her to continue her monologue. The desk flipped and crumpled like a sheet of paper before sinking into the singularity. The gravity well inflated, lurching its pull on the room. Mary turned her dial up to its maximum but could still feel the room sloping; Geraldine fell forward on to her face and began to slide closer; papers, containers and books rained across the room; all the furniture slowly toppled over itself in a horizontal avalanche. It was half the height of the room and its width had reached the shell of the generator, tugging at the fastenings that kept its sensitive parts protected. Another inch of growth had it seeping between the seams, feeling at the generator's insides; gently teasing and tickling at wires and diodes and microprocessors.

Eventually, it must have interfered with the wrong component. There was a spark, a groan and an eruption of force. Combined with the compensatory forces being created by Mary's device, the eruption sent her hurtling backwards across the room. The window shattered a fraction of a second before she hit it and she continued to propel across the lawn and into the forest beyond.

When consciousness returned to her, Mary had difficulty focussing on anything. It felt like she was lying face down but not actually on anything solid. Her brain expected her eyes to see floor but not six foot away. She found herself suspended above the leafy ground and, after a cursory inspection, discovered that she was suspended by nothing at all; her contraption was still operational and was negating Earth's gravitational field. She readjusted the dial and slowly lowered herself safely to the ground.

She could not tell where she was. She was in the forest that bordered her Aunt's estate but not so far as to obscure the edge of it. She could see a vast opening a few meters ahead and that was it. No estate. Had she been catapulted so far that she had ended over the opposite side of the forest?

It seemed unlikely.

Upon investigation, she found – or rather, did not find – the house. It had gone. Been ripped up from its foundations. It and everyone who had been in it.

\/^^^\/

"Cool!" Danny enthused.

"You're that clever?" Cassandra asked with unbridled surprise.

"Don't say it like that," Floater replied with indignation.

"Sorry. It's just... well... with the sluttishness comes additional, predefined characteristics."

"More like it's not fair," Danny corrected.

"True. Beauty, body and brains," Cassandra confessed.

"Boobs, bum and bonnet," Danny muttered and received a punch on the leg.

"But that wasn't the end of it," Floater continued.

"You found your parents," Danny blurted.

"Uh, yeah. They had faked their deaths and were in hiding," she said.

"They —"

"Combined their knowledge with yours, helped you hone your kit then seemingly sacrificed themselves to save you," Danny predicted.

"Yeah. How did you —?"

"What is her name?" he asked.

"Who?"

"Your aunty. When she came back. What name did she have?"

"Danny," Cassandra chastised. "Weren't you listening? She got destroyed with the house."

Danny snorted with unbridled disdain. "She got sucked into some parallel dimension and when she escaped had developed her own powers. I was just wondering what her super name was."

The two women just stared at him.

"Anti-G," Floater said.

"Niiice!"

"He was right?" Cassandra demanded.

"It's textbook narrative recurrence."

"It's her life, you great lummox!"

Danny looked at Floater and, perhaps actually noticed her for the first time. The testimonials about her appearance, the realisation of her treatment and the telling of her tragic tale had taken an emotional toll on her. The corners of those full lips had dropped and he detected an unevenness in their symmetry. Her pure-crystal eyes glistened now from the moisture of repressed tears and he saw a small circular scar on the left side of the bridge of her nose. He noticed, amongst the long waves of golden hair, were a couple of tangled knots resting against her left cheek, whose patina was blemished by a rose of raised capillaries. Small eyebrow hairs were sprouting outside of the obvious boundaries of her allowance through neglectful attendance. As she opened her mouth to bite her bottom lip, he saw a slight overlap of her front incisors. She was not perfect. She was not a character from a comic. She was real and alive and could feel.

"Sorry," he said. "I get lost in the moment sometimes."

"Ah think Ah need to have a serious conversation with mah man," she sighed, hauled herself to her feet and secured her coat around her before leaving the room.

CHAPTER 7
THE 'MATE' IN 'TEAM'
OR WITH GREAT POWER CUMS

"There's something naughty about you," Cat purred as she closed her room door behind her with a tantalising click.

Cameron was in his second worst nightmare. His first worst was something to do with auditioning for the role of Jean Valjean in *Les Miserables* but forgetting the lines and singing so quietly no one could hear him. This nightmare, the second one, was never anything he had dreamt but he had experienced a few times. It involved sexually predatory females. They were his vulnerability; they would instantly cut through his armour of macho bluster and strip him down to the naïve boy he really was.

Cat padded two seductive steps forward then pawsed. "What's the matter? You looked scared."

Cameron attempted to fake a laugh that failed on so many levels. "Me? What? Scared of what? What's to be scared of?" he puffed.

So many things. Let us count the ways:

1. Previous partners: negligible.
   So far, Cameron's sexual proclivities had been limited to actual intercourse with one woman. And they had only done it twice. And even though, at the time, the first time felt like the best sex ever, it turned out that it was actually the worst which had put a complete dampener on the concept of the whole thing. And, like him, she had been a virgin so could not pass any tips on to him.
2. Technique: negligible.
   Aside from what he did with her, his knowledge of how to do it remained at a level derived from free downloadable porn from the internet. There seemed to be a structured procedure but he was not entirely sure that oral, to missionary, to doggy, to wanking into her face was actually the norm. And because the videos never gave any instructions during the transitions, he did not really know when the appropriate time was to change each position and certainly did not know the phrasing to suggest the latter.
3. Time since previous purge: too long.
   There was a definite backlog. He was going to need plastic sheets, a bin bag and squidgy-wiper.
4. Horn level: extreme.
   He had been hanging around with too many incredibly hot looking women in incredibly tight fitting clothes for too long and, right now, with every step Cat took, he could feel it dialling closer to eleven.

5. Social psychological scarring: lots.
    Despite the proliferation of sexual activity on TV, amongst his peers and in society in general, his school lessons on STIs had firmly embedded themselves within his conscious mind and put a sensible fear of gon in him. That and a Google image search he once did on 'genital warts'. *shudder*
6. Emotional danger: high.
    He did not trust one-night stands. He liked being in love and worried that he would get hurt in a disinterested backlash. Or worse, be disinterested during an emotional backlash.
7. Media psychological scarring: he had seen *Fatal Attraction* and *The Crying Game*. *shudder*

"Where's the daring-do now?" she demanded as she approached and slowly tugged the bows down the front of her jacket. With each gentle manipulation, the black silk ribbon released another patch of pink flesh, each hint of subtle curvature expanded as the repressive state of the leather was lifted and her breasts' natural freedom of expression was liberated. Each release increased the inevitability of inescapable sex.

"Er..." was all he could muster.

Her eyes widened as delicious realisation dawned. She bit her bottom lip and allowed her smile to slowly broaden, revealing her perfectly white smile. "I think I've discovered your kryptonite," she said and was standing right in front of him. "My poor, super man. Have I rendered you powerless?"

He inhaled sharply and flinched as she placed her hand on his overeager erection who had been paying no attention to his concerns and neuroses and wanted to get into the fray.

"Oh," she gasped in mock surprise. "You really are a man of steel." She pushed him on to the bed and straddled his waist.

"Oh. My. God," he moaned.

She leaned forward and whispered into his ear, "Goddess."

Katherine Claremont - or 'Kitty Cat' as her family endearingly called her - was born and raised in Albion, a quiet town that had been established 150 years ago on the outskirts of Toronto, Canada. For thirteen of her sixteen years, she had been consciously aware of her community's attitude towards her as a member of it, which seemed to amount to not much more than something to be dressed up and looked at.

At first, it was everything most little girls would adore: the attention, the cooing and the prettifying - being treated like a little princess. But eventually, she became tired of being judged based on the quality of her appearance and, ultimately, never having her opinions taken seriously because of preconceived attitudes. She was pretty, even without the make-up her mother made her believe she needed on a daily basis. Perhaps, even more so without it. But as time progressed, her confidence in herself and what she was capable of was whittled away by the constant reinforcement of her parents, teachers and peers that 'to be looked at' was more important than 'to be listened to'.

And with that, Katherine became a very observational young lady, noticing the nuances in human interaction that many miss. The subtle inflections of facial or bodily gestures that could reveal huge inconsistencies against their verbal communication. She could almost see entire backstories developing before her eyes as minute muscles in the speaker's face reacted more honestly than their conscious brain may have wanted.

She was just getting over the struggles of puberty when one seemingly innocent mistake changed her life forever; the catalyst that would change her from an unconfident wallflower to a dynamic, competitive young woman and, ultimately, the supreme we know her to be today.

It was Katherine's sixteenth birthday and her family were celebrating by hosting a huge party at their home at the top of Sunshine Mountain Drive. It was an exclusive street with only six 'houses' spread out along its eight-mile horseshoe circumference of the eponymous Sunshine Mountain. Each property's location was specifically chosen to have absolute privacy and seclusion; not one home could be overlooked by another: noise and sight was masked by the steep walls of the mountain and verdant dogwoods and cedars; the air was suffused by the fresh aroma of the abundant forestry; one could easily forget one's proximity to one of the county's busiest hubs of industry and commerce and presume being immersed in one of the deepest of wildernesses.

The progression up the drive was an indication of the size and value of the estate and, thereby, affluence of the owners and although the Claremont household was at the highest point of the mountain, they were not the last house on the drive. Theirs was an opulent one floor, six-bedroom palace with an open plan kitchen-dining room-living room that was half the size of a football pitch. The other half of the pitch was taken up by the terraced garden that overlooked the sinking forest and was the last thing the sun saw each evening as it set. Three spacious platforms down was a heated swimming pool, which was the perfect spot to watch the dwindling daylight during the summer months. The heating actually made it the perfect spot during the winter months too but did require a rather inelegant sprint up to the house when time was up. Of course this did not matter too much when there was no one around to witness it.

Brandon Claremont was Katherine's father and was commanding the two-meter long, stainless steel, propane-fuelled barbecue; a steady stream of white smoke poured into the air, almost blocking out the pine scents of the mountainside. He loved showing off how much he had and how much he could afford to give away. Conveniently, his immediate and extended family quite enjoyed accepting as much as he had to offer so very rarely passed up the opportunity to indulge in his generosity; they were all there.

Katherine was not there. Not yet. As was the tradition in the Claremont household, she would be forced to make an impressive entrance after her mother had spent many hours preening, pruning and primping. Katherine watched herself in her full-length mirror as her mother, Margaret, bunched, loosened and tightened belts, clasps and pleats until every combination of variations of dresses and accessories had been tried and, often, repeated. She stared for a long time at her own vacuous expression: the only face she could never read a story in; usually because there was not one to be read. Her golden blonde hair had been immaculately styled that afternoon: tousled bangs framed her rouged cheeks but, to her, looked more like limp corn than threads of pure sunshine. Her face was more akin to death than it was to purity and innocence. The layered ice-blue dress that was being ruffled around her waist reminded her of the china dolls she had seen at her grandmother's house; stylisations of a bygone era yet kept alive by unjustified reverence.

I look like a prom queen from Grease, she pondered with no real thought as to whether this was a good thing or not. No doubt her aged relatives would 'ooh' and 'aah' at her appearance; her aunts would smile sympathetically; those uncles who would turn their attention away from their alcohol would look at her from head to toe, taking more time to linger their appraisal over her mid two quarters and adjust their crotches; her peers would watch on with looks of mockery, jealousy and hatred. The latter coming from her older sister and younger brother, neither of whom could win the same level of attentiveness from their parents despite different attempts to succeed, via achievements or failures. She did not need her special skill to be able to translate those expressions and knew that, when the evening had been spent, there was a good chance that the looks would evolve into admonishing words and actions. Katherine was not sure whether she wanted them to all go away or her. Something needed to change.

"Did you say something, Kitty?" Margaret asked without detracting her attention from her pointless pontificating.

"No," Katherine replied mindlessly but watched her mother's face intently in the mirror's reflection.

"It sounded like you told me to go away," her mother said with a laugh at the end. "Not when I haven't even picked out your earrings yet."

Ugh, jewellery. That will be another hour at least.

She was a contradiction of swirling emotions; there were members of her family whose company she genuinely enjoyed although they were mostly the very young ones who thought she was a real-life Disney Princess and not just some breathing mannequin through which her parents were transposing all their life's ambitions and living vicariously through the results thereof.

Not that four year-old Amelia would understand that.

The doorbell chimed from the other end of the house and Katherine realised the fussing had ceased. She refocused her attention and noticed Margaret standing a few paces behind her, admiring her. Margaret had 'that' smile on her face. Katherine had asked her once what it was and she had replied that it was pride. After Katherine had read it a few more times, she had labelled it an 'Empathy Smile' because she could see that her mother was simply imagining herself in her daughter's place.

The doorbell chimed again.

"Mom…?" Katherine started.

"Your gift is on the table," Margaret interrupted, releasing herself from her self-indulgent, somewhat incestuous, fantasy.

The doorbell insisted itself once more.

"Oh, those terrible men," Margaret huffed. "I shall have to get that myself although I can't think who it could be: everyone's here. It's probably another delivery." She marched out of the room.

Katherine stared at the small, square box that had been placed perfectly in the middle of her bedside table. Its gold wrapping paper glistened with a reddish hue as the setting sun reflected in its smooth surface. A delicate bow on top bristled slightly from the draft of the closing bedroom door. It looked even more spectacular in contrast to the heavy looking, cream-coloured plastic box it had shoved aside.

Katherine rolled her eyes. *Earrings*, she predicted.

Margaret breezily made her way along the landing towards the front door; the corridor ran along the front wall of the house so, as she passed each external facing window, she was able to catch glimpses of the visitor.

Usually, she was able to catch glimpses because the common custom would be to ring the bell then take a couple of steps back to leave a comfortable space before the door opened. In this case, either the visitor was standing right up to the door, had moved further along the front of the house or had just left.

The doorbell chimed.

She passed the living room and glanced at the party in full swing outside. No one was paying a blind piece of attention to the door and she just hoped it was simply too noisy for them to hear rather than people ignoring it. She would be interrogating Brandon later.

Grinning to herself whilst thinking about the grilling she would put him through, she pushed herself up on tip toe to place her eye against the peephole. Expecting the image of some sort of goldfish bowl, she was mildly disturbed to see nothing: just a blackness. The groundskeeper would be hearing about this.

Her left hand slipped the security chain in place while her right turned the doorknob and she pulled the door ajar.

All at once, there was a flash of silver that zipped past her eyes, a delicate clink of metal and an odd stinging sensation in her left hand. A burst of scarlet blossomed up the white wall in front of her and she considered that someone had just tossed a glass of Cabernet Sauvignon over her shoulder. But then, as a hand emerged around the edge of the door, a similar eruption of red arced in front of her vision but did not quite make it to the wall this time. Instead, it landed heavily on the cream carpet and seemed to emanate from her increasingly burning hand.

The stain on the carpet was definitely her primary concern but she was then distracted by the glint of the diamond in her wedding ring that was on the floor next to the fresh puddle. Oh, two puddles: another had spattered on the floor and managed to splash her ring and sully her nail varnish. That was going to be another hour cleaning that off and redoing them.

Why was her hand on the floor?

There was that same strange stinging sensation but in her neck this time; at least the building pain in her hand seemed to have subsided. The floor came rushing up to her but she could not put her arms out to stop her fall. Her face bounced off the soft shag and she rolled to one side; somehow she had got red all over her shoes and she could see up her own skirt. How- ?

A meticulously polished black leather boot swung assuredly through the gap in the door and kicked Margaret's head clear across the hallway, into the kitchen. It spun silently on its crown before it came to a rest, its brown hair whirling out like a ball gown. It stopped with her confused expression frozen to her face but all vestiges of life having seeped out.

The gap in the doorway widened as a hand pushed it slowly open then a three-foot katana emerged, blade upright. The reflection in its flat surface transmogrified as translucent red liquid crawled down to the hilt; the grotesquely morphing image of an East Asian man was reflected in its surface, surveying the scene inside. He swung the door fully open, knocking Margaret's decapitated body to the side - it actually took a step backwards to maintain its balance - and boldly sidled into the house.

He was Japanese. His dark brown eyes were so deep set that they looked blackened; his black, straight hair had been styled into a short Mohican that ran perfectly down the centre of his head; his leather boots were complimented by a black Vuitton suit over a white shirt. The sleeves of both top garments had been tailor removed to show off - not only his toned, muscular arms but also - an elaborate tattoo that stretched its way from one wrist, across his back, to the other. It was a design of some sort of dragon with its red, taloned claws reaching out across the back of his hands, its fiery blue and green limbs wound around his biceps which then enveloped each clavicle and were consumed by the fingers of flames that fringed the hem of his suit.

Closing the door, he sidestepped towards a recess in the wall and blended with the shadows.

Margaret's blood pressure had dropped and her rupturous expulsions had eased to a pulsating oozing; her body had finally got the message and collapsed to the floor.

The alcohol consumption had started with 'reserved sipping', quickly progressed to 'quaffing' and had now plateaued to 'full flow'. The food, as is the way with most barbecues, had taken longer to prepare than anticipated. This was largely to do with the 'flow' and socialising of the chef but, because of the good-natured atmosphere and unlimited free drink, no one was complaining. They were, however, getting inebriated faster than if they had something lining their stomachs and the looser the corks are, the looser the inhibitions become.

An overweight man, dressed in what should have been a baggy fitting floral shirt and beige slacks, sloped up to the grill and nudged Brandon with his elbow. His drink slopped over the edge of his glass and splashed at Brandon's feet.

"So, Brandon," the man slurred. "Sixteen, huh?"

"What's that, Jim?"

"I said, 'sixteen,' you know?"

Brandon paused his culinary inspection of the pork ribs to try to work out what his wife's second cousin on her father's side was implying when a movement in the bushes, just beyond the boundary of his garden, caught his eye. Wildlife was always a concern when living this far into its territory and it was not uncommon to be troubled by raccoons or crows rifling through bins, but they would hardly ever approach the property with so many people around. They were small and secretive creatures and would not create such a disturbance amongst the foliage. Larger animals, like deer would never approach with this level of noise and certainly would not be so careless to draw attention to theirselves in such a clumsy manner unless they had been startled. This brought Brandon to his final conclusion; a beast large enough to cause that level of disturbance and possessing the confidence, or stupidity, to create it due to the mesmerising aromas of the grilling meat.

He had only seen one bear before and, luckily, there had been sightings and warnings posted about its proximity. The family had been inside when it lolloped across their yard and ripped the previous grill apart searching for fleshy remnants. He had called the Animal Welfare Foundation who sent someone round and tranquilised the animal with the intention of transporting it deeper into the forest. Unfortunately, the creature had reeled, toppled, fell into the pool and swiftly drowned despite everyone attempting to haul it out. In the end, they had to call in an industrial crane to remove the sodden beast. And then he had to have the whole pool drained, cleaned and filters replaced because of the bear hair.

Brandon fucking hated bears.

"Michael," he called to his son but did not remove his attention from the rustling bushes. "Fetch my rifle."

Jim quickly sobered up. "Jesus, Brandon, I didn't mean anything by – I mean – I was only suggesting... I wasn't saying that I would-" He turned and, as quickly as his weight could cope, ran into the house. He was intent on reaching the cloakroom to find his coat, then his keys and then get the hell away from there before Brandon could castrate him for suggesting Katherine was now sexually available. He looked over his right shoulder to see what distance he had put between them as he waddled past Margaret's body to his left.

The katana blade swept out from the recess, popping Jim's head off like a champagne cork. His body's momentum carried him a few more steps forward before it dropped to the floor with an almighty thud.

Michael returned from the garage and passed the slender firearm with laser scope to his father. "What is it, dad?"

"Bear. Just down past the ridge." Brandon raised the butt into his right shoulder and placed his eye against the scope.

Michael stood on tip-toe and, trying to discern some sort of absolute shape down the mountainside, squinted garishly: eyes narrowed and mouth bared two shining tramlines of braces that reddened in the reflective glow of the fire. He looked back to his father and noticed a small red dot on his shirt.

"Dad?"

"Not now, Michael, I think I have it."

"No; Dad? I think you have the laser on backwards."

"What?" Brandon demanded incredulously. "I haven't even switched it on. Didn't want to spook it." He looked down at his chest and saw the wavering spot. "What the-"

As the side of his body exploded, his left arm flew from its socket, slapping Michael across the face as it went. The boy was cast to the ground as much by the blast as the collision.

Brandon's rib cage burst through his chest, landed on the barbecue and started doing nicely; his body repelled backwards, shattering the glass sliding windows of the living room, flailing limply to the floor and twitched fitfully, his hand still clutching the hunting rifle.

The party guests who had taken position closest to the barbecue were the ones who reacted first and self-preservation was the immediate concern because no one wanted to be close to an unstable propane tank with naked flames within inches of it. They hurriedly moved away from the wrongly convicted cooker towards the pool end of the back yard, closer to the forest. Only Michael seemed to have any realisation of the situation and any concern for his father's condition. But that realisation and concern was short-lived when another red bead steadied itself on the fourteen-pound gas tank before his eyes and a neat little hole 'tanked' in its place.

Now, Michael had been raised on a healthy diet of cinema clichés; the ones that suggest if a metal container holding any kind of combustible material should be punctured or even slightly dented would immediately and violently erupt in flames, shrapnel and flying bodies. If this truly was the case then there would be many more reported cases of supermarkets being destroyed every time they dropped a can of beans. He scrunched his face in anticipation of the explosion but nothing happened. Of course nothing happened; unless said combustible material is incredibly unstable in itself – a self loathing liquid with suicidal tendencies – combustion requires ignition; heat of some sort: a spark, an ember or chicory marinaded burning volcano rocks.

He opened his eyes to assess his demise and relaxed slightly just as the leaking gas reached the flames, lit and blew back into the canister. Then it reacted in a manner which Michael Bay would have been happier with: the inch thick, reinforced steel bottle burst like a gelignite water balloon shooting searing slivers of metal and fire branching across the garden and house, indiscriminately shredding and/or setting fire to everything in their path. Michael was the first casualty, stripped down to a mushy skeletal frame: eyes reduced to empty sockets and mouth bared to the two shining tramlines that reddened from his seeping flesh.

Wheeling shards of superheated death embedded themselves in the bodies of the retreating and ignorant alike: muscles severed like rare fillet steak, bones chopped like a butcher's rush period, bodies left like mince. The dead, dying and debilitated rolled and cried at varying levels that befitted their mortal state; the former not doing much of either unless you counted involuntary death throes and the squishy, squirty noises of punctured arteries. The untouched or mildly injured were either in catatonic shock or wondering whether they should sue their family or the barbecue manufacturers. Like Michael's period of ponderance, it did not last long because they soon became distracted by more pressing matters.

A short, unhealthily skinny man marched boldly from the sidelines of the throng. Despite his confident manner, he was clearly not a member of the party: his black leather jacket was scratched all over and worn at the elbows; the cuffs of his jeans were frayed because they were store bought, too long for his diminutive frame and trailed the floor at his heels; his white t-shirt was untucked, loosely fitting and warped with age and wear; he was unshaven and not in a manner that he had shaved to look unshaven, his stubble was ragged and patchy and unkempt. The real giveaway was the way in which he a extracted a large pistol that had been tucked in his waist band (the Claremont clan would certainly have had the good grace to carry a holster) and shot Aunt Harriet (who had survived the blast by being inadvertently shielded by Uncle 'not a proper-uncle' Gordon, who was a very sizeable shield indeed) square in the chest. She was a light framed woman of seventy-six and the force of the impact lifted her out of her slippers, across the middle tier and down to the bottom where most of the children had been gathering.

The man fired again, this time hitting a young cousin in the shoulder. He spun on his heels and slammed onto the ground. Others' senses had gathered and they began to flee.

The man continued his advance, fired without care and clipped Granpa's hip. The shot ricocheted off his metal replacement, felling him and his brother who was stood next to him. Two more steps and the man was closer to the young cousin who was desperately trying to get to his feet. The man calmly placed the revolver to the back of the boy's skull and pulled the trigger, vomiting his face across the patio. Another reckless shot into the panicking pack hit another seemingly random target without fatality but, again, he had reached the two aged siblings and put them out of their misery with bullets to their faces.

Meanwhile, others were falling, seemingly without any kind of impetus apart from the appearance of a small red dot pinpointing the location of vital organs before a tidy hole took their places.

As is the way with the ability to survive predators in the wild, those species that move in dense numbers have a higher probability of survival. Some should survive if not by their hunters' appetites eventually being sated before all are eaten then certainly by escaping while others are being fed upon. Unfortunately, the deceased Claremonts did not seem to satisfy the executioners' blood lust but some *had* managed to get past the wiry man *and* avoid the bead of doom to get into the house. Where, of course, the Japanese man cut off their exits. And their entrances. And a couple of connecting rooms.

It all took mere seconds for the noise to start and less than two minutes for the noise to stop.

The skinny man looked around him for any remaining signs of life he might be able to extinguish, eventually reholstering his gun in his waistband. The Japanese man stepped out into the carnage, wiping his blade with a throw from the sofa. Even with the amount of severing he had been doing, he had managed to avoid being hit by any splash-back. They nodded silent acknowledgement to each other.

There was movement from the bottom of the garden as foliage rustled and a muffled, high pitched whimpering slowly became audible. From out of the darkness emerged a young woman in similar attire to Katherine but emerald green, ripped and muddied. She was being led at gunpoint by a tanned man. His black hair had been slicked back from a high widow's peak with some sort of gel or hair ointment. He wore a black suit, shirt and tie but on his feet were uncharacteristic heavy duty trekking boots.

"Well?" he demanded in a heavy New York accent.

"'Well' what?" the skinny man replied; he was Irish.

"She was halfway down the fucking mountain, y'dumb mick," New York stated. "What would've happened had she gotten away?"

"Firstly, laddie," Irish warned, "Oi have already told you how Oi feel about the racial epithets y'keep using for m'self and Suki here and – this being yure last warning – Oi swear Oi will make Bolognese out o' your racist guts if it happens one more time. Understand?"

"Whadevah."

"Secondly, Oi knew you an' Suki had th' exits covered. There was no worries."

"We need one alive," Japan stated curtly.

"To be sure."

"Oh, dat's de situation, huh? You two and me, huh?"

"I can assure you, you defoined the loin of separation th' moment you called me 'mick' and m'boy here 'Akira'."

"What the fuck?" New York squealed. "Dat was a fucking compliment you stupid-" he managed to catch himself but Irish still clenched his fists in preparation. "*Akira* was a fucking fantastic Jap film and Suki's a fucking girl's name."

"Y' ignorant bollock-head," Irish bellowed.

"What the fuck's a 'bollock'?"

"Ask her," Japan instructed calmly and the bickering couple remembered their place.

"Yo, angel-cakes," New York shouted unnecessarily loudly right in her ear, making her try to shrink in to herself even more, "where's de fucking money?"

"Wh-What?" she stammered.

New York inverted his rifle and dinked her on the back of the head with the butt. It was not very hard but certainly the force, combined with her near-to-shock mental state, was enough to knock her to her knees.

"THE FUCKING MONEY!" he screamed at her head.

"What th' hell is the matter wit' you, man?" Irish interjected and pushed New York away from the cowering girl. He put his arm under hers and supported her to her feet. "Oi'm sorry about that, darlin', the man is a total tosser."

"If I knew what the fuck you were calling me, mick-" New York muttered in the background.

"What's y'name?"

"Sophie," the girl sniffed.

"And what were y' doin' here, Sophie?"

"I... live here." She took that cue to take in her surroundings and instantly collapsed into hysteric sobs when she saw the slaughter of her family.

"Oh, hush now," Irish calmed and turned her away from the familicide, walking slowly towards the bottom end of the garden again. "It seems loik a terrible thing has happened here but Oi want to assure you, Sophie, that these people were deserving of this punishment." They stepped over the body of little Amelia. "Most of them," he corrected himself as they reached the shimmering poolside and looked over the peaceful forest beyond. "Now, all we need to know – and then we'll be on are way – is where yoir daddy puts his money."

"I don't-"

Irish grabbed the back of her hair, cutting her sentence off with a painful yelp, then pushed her down to the floor, thrusting her head under the water. Her screams were clearly audible despite the dampening of the water and its bubbling surface.

"Y'see? The voilence contrasts so much more so when juxtaposed wit t' noicities," he explained over his shoulder to the others.

New York gave him an approving, impressed nod of the head.

Sophie's screaming had stopped so Irish pulled her up. She coughed and spluttered, trying to clear her airwaves but after her lungs had been depleted from the screams of pain and panic, they had automatically inhaled in search of replenishing air. They had only filled with water and now had very little to flush them clear.

"Here, stand up, love," Irish advised and hauled her to her feet. He then punched her in the stomach, clearing the blockage and hurling her backwards. "Tink of it loik a reverse Hoimlich," he said. "Gut punch up under the ribcage forces the water roit out. Really focking hurts, too."

Sophie was curled up like a foetus, sucking air back like she had not breathed for a week.

Irish knelt by her side. "Where's the safe, Sophie?"

"Inside," she gasped. "Behind TV."

"Goot girl," he commended and stroked her hair from off her face. "Suki, could y' do me a favour an' bring her in, please?"

Japan nodded and nimbly threw Sophie over his shoulder. She had resumed a semi-normal breathing pattern and so her mind was able to focus on the horrors around her again. Her sobbing became a deep, mournful moan.

The men walked back to the house.

"Why dontcha jus whack 'er now?" New York demanded.

"Never accept their first answer as their only answer, laddie," Irish replied as they entered the living room.

Japan threw Sophie on to the sofa and her state of absolute terror managed to exceed absolute. The few bullet holes, few smatterings of crimson and collection of recumbent bodies outside was nothing compared to the red-washed walls, carpet and upholstery of her previously magnolia and cream living room. She wished there were whole bodies to look at rather than puzzling bits and pieces; faintly familiar shapes littered around the room; recognisable patterns and colours of scraps of material wrapped them; text-book shapes of internal organs were presented in reverse order of how internal they should be. She lifted her hands from the sticky leather surface and desperately tried to levitate her body away from everything – the three men watched her, believing for a second that she might actually achieve it – her hysteria had reached such a peak that it was off the spectrum: inaudible, imperceptible, unbelievable.

Japan wrenched the sixty-inch plasma screen from its wall moorings to reveal a neat electronic safe behind.

Irish cracked his knuckles.

"Well?" New York demanded.

"Piece o' pess," Irish bragged and stepped closer. He pulled a screwdriver from the inside of his jacket and unceremoniously chiselled the masonry away from the right hand edge of the safe. When he had cleared about a centimetre's distance all along it, he prized the screwdriver in as far as it would wedge, hammered it with his wrist twice and then levered it forward. The front of the safe clattered to the floor.

"It's jost a facia, nuttin' more. Oim surprised, but den again..."

"Typical of dat arrogant ass-hole."

Japan marched forward and thrust his hand into the open space, felt around and then came out holding a large manilla envelope. He showed it to his compatriots and, for the first time, his face displayed a semblance of emotion: confusion. It was only visible for a microsecond but it was enough to unnerve the others.

"Cheque?" Irish suggested.

"I will," Japan replied and peeled the lid open.

"I dink he means like a cashier's check," New York suggested.

Regardless, Japan spilled the envelope's contents into his hand to reveal a single sheet of folded paper. He opened it up, rotated it and read the contents dispassionately. The silence was too much for someone.

"What de fuck, Akira?" New York exploded.

Irish punched him across the side of his head, which sent him tripping over the thigh of cousin Maizy's dismembered leg (Sophie had already identified it because of the secret tattoo her wayward cousin had had done just below her hip). He sprawled amongst the bits of Bob, searching for balance and his gun so he could retaliate in the only way he could think of. But, because of his discombobulated state, by the time he had ascertained which way was up, which end of the gun to hold and what direction it should be pointed, Irish and Japan had him efficiently covered.

"Oi did warn y', laddie," Irish told him. "We're all here f' the same ting and each of us is only a messenger. Oi'm pretty sure yuir boss won't care too much if his share arroives but you don't. Behave yuirself or we *will* take much deloit in taking you apart."

New York holstered his gun but did not try to hide the murderous intent in his eyes. "Dis ain't over, mick."

"Oi'll give y' that one f' nothin', *yank*," Irish conceded, "but don't go tinking you can take advantage of my good nature, cos Oi don't have one."

The angered American raised himself up and dusted himself down as best he could. "What's de paper?"

Japan's blade had been returned to its scabbard on his back as swiftly and silently as it had appeared. He turned the piece of paper towards the men.

"Dere fucking wedding certificate? What de fuck?"

"So-phie," Irish cooed and her brain re-engaged now their attention had returned to her.

It must be time by now, Katherine mused. She had been standing in front of the mirror, trying to admire her reflection for what seemed like ages. She had even opened the present on the table and tried to feel like the luckiest girl in the world. She had put the earrings in her lobes and twirled from side to side, putting on that perfect fake smile that revealed nothing about her inner thoughts and feelings. She was scared and that was the truth of it. Scared to be looked at by all those people, scared to be talked at and told nothing, scared to be asked so many questions but not have her answers listened to. That fear had escalated every minute that her mum did not return to lead her back. Was this a test? Was this her rite of passage? Was she supposed to do this alone? Were her parents finally allowing her a degree of independency?

That idea gave her a burst of courage. The thought that maybe those reins were being released (albeit to only allow her a bit of slack rather than freedom) was enough to give her the resolve to face the hordes beyond. She resolutely pulled herself to her feet, picked up the white plastic box from the table and marched to her bedroom door. She was attacked by the overpowering aroma of cooked meat that quickly reminded her body of how long ago it had been since she had last eaten. Her mouth began watering which invigorated her determination even more.

A flash of silver outside the front of the house caught her attention as she progressed along the hallway. She wondered if guests were already leaving or more were due.

She swiftly turned the corner into the living room and saw the red... she nearly tripped over something at her feet but could not draw her eyes away to identify it... three strange men... guns... Sophie's face.

Katherine saw it all: the fear, the horror, the humiliation, the pain, the nihilism and, now, a glimmer of false hope that she might be saved mixed with a regret that her sister might be doomed.

Katherine looked down at her feet and saw the confusion etched clearly across her mother's face.

Across the room, she saw her father's twisted expression of anger and malicious intent.

Beyond him, just outside, was the glint of metal over a garish grin of a skinned corpse.

Faces all around her begged for mercy, help, escape or an explanation, at least.

She looked at the men again, the skinny little one was mouthing something at her but she could not tell what he was trying to say; his face was seeking answers. The larger, darker skinned man was pointing a gun at her, shouting something that she could not work out but his expression was shot with false bravado. It was the tall East-Asian man who frightened her the most, with the impassive eyes that said nothing at all.

"Looks loik we won't be needin' you any more, Sophie, darlin'," Irish said and sunk his screwdriver deep into the base of her skull so it jutted through her throat. Her hands manically scrabbled for the hilt, to remove the pain and clear her airwaves but her slick, blood covered hands could not find a purchase on the smooth plastic handle. Irish saved her the trouble and pulled it out. Sophie fell to the floor still grasping at her neck, searching for some way to rid herself of her anguish and deter the engulfing darkness.

"Sophie?" Katherine called but her sister's vacant staring eyes was the only response she got.

Something stung at the side of her forehead and she staggered over to the breakfast bar in the kitchen. Her fingers felt for the source of the pain and returned to her vision with fresh blood: New York had taken advantage of Katherine's state of shock to wheel around beside her and strike her with the butt of his weapon. "I said, 'Where de fuck have you bin hidin?'" he screamed at her.

Katherine did not answer so New York kicked her in the back of the knee, forcing her to the floor, her chin bounced off the granite surface as she fell.

"What did Oi say about the effectiveness of noicity?" Irish asked Japan.

"You a smart-ass, bitch? Huh?" New York screamed at the back of her head while she tried to cradle all the pains around her body and put some distance between herself and her aggressor.

Katherine raised her right hand to the bar, she discarded the white box as she tried to pull herself up. It scooted across the surface and fell off the end, bouncing over to Japan's feet.

"WHERE'S DE FUCKING MONEY, YOU FUCKING LITTLE BITCH FUCK!" he punched Katherine between the shoulder blades causing her to arch backwards. He grabbed her hair at the back of her head and slammed her face onto the rock worktop.

Katherine's nose erupted, pain stampeded up her sinuses and rampaged through the front of her brain. Her vision blurred through agony, tears and blood. She looked up at the man who was still shouting at her but his words were lost.

"Yank," Irish called calmly as New York kicked Katherine in the ribs, resulting in an audible crack and sending her sliding across the floor.

She tried hauling herself around the end of the bar, using its corner as an anchor and dragging her legs behind her. She could see the smashed patio doors and the potential escape beyond. If she could just get away from this psychopath; get past her hollowed father; get outside...

"Yank!" Irish called more determinedly.

"What?"

Irish held up the white plastic box – it was open – and plucked out the contents: a hearing aid. "She's deaf, you focking eejit."

This information jarred New York's momentum and he looked between the small, curled piece of plastic to the box to the faces of his comrades and then back again. Eventually he looked down to Katherine and the barrel of her father's hunting rifle that was pointing at his head.

The thunderous boom of the gun would have been enough to knock someone off their feet; Irish dived for cover and even made Japan cover his ears. New York's reaction was rather more dynamic; the seven millimetre bullet hit him square on the chin, desiccating it and turning all the splinters of bone into high velocity shrapnel that bounced around his cranial cavity and blended its contents. The bullet continued its trajectory, flipping the back of his skull open like a Beetle bonnet; the slushied contents then geysered forth. New York's eyes rolled up in their sockets and he fell backwards. The recoil was powerful enough to send Katherine sliding across the polished, lubricated floor, hammering into the wall.

She reloaded the chamber and swung the weapon around to where the other two men had been only to discover Japan was advancing on her. He had already swung his blade down, seemingly having only just missed her and embedding the tip of the sword in the engineered maple floorboards. She fired again, this time the gun snapped backwards and broke her shoulder; it flipped out of her hand but forced Japan to dive backwards for cover behind the breakfast bar. The bullet tore a crater out of the ceiling, showering Japan and Irish in white plaster.

Katherine wailed in anguish and clawed at the floor, trying to pull herself closer to the gun that lay just beyond her reach. Her shoulder, head, nose, ribs and back all cried at her to give up but her brain screamed louder not to. Her fingers touched the oak butt of the rifle but Irish kicked it away and squatted down to her. He tilted his head inquisitively and remained silent until she turned her attention to him. He held up her hearing aid to her and nodded. She did not resist while he fumbled with the device at her ear and eventually had to push his ministrations aside and do it herself. She flicked it on.

"You can hear me?" Irish asked.

"Sort of," she replied. "I need to see your mouth or it's just a mumble. Why-?"

Irish pushed his finger to her lips and pursed his lips together. "Ssh! You don't get t' ask questions?"

She looked up at Japan who had retrieved his sword and waved it at her, reflecting the light in her eyes.

"Where's the money?" Irish over-enunciated.

She let the words filter for hidden meaning but could discern none. "My mom has jewellery."

"Enough of the bullshit, darlin'. Yuir thieving daddy has stolen a lot of money from are people and, as y'can see," he indicated their immediate surroundings, "we're quoit serious about getting it back."

"I don't-"

"In total, tirty-foive billion dollars. Yuir daddy stole from some very dangerous people. He did this to you and yuirs."

"I don't believe it," she spat.

"It doesn't really matter what you believe, m' darlin'. What really doz fuckin' matter is that I believe you. Suki, cut her foot off and see if dat jogs her memory as to where Morrison moit have hidden it."

Japan raised the blade, staring into Katherine's eyes the whole time; she stared back with wide-eyed horror, knowing full well that this was not a bluff. As his arms reached the apex of his swing, a word rattled in her head.

"Morrison?" she asked.

Japan paused.

"Aye," Irish told her.

"Our neighbour?" she asked.

Japan faltered.

"Yuir what?"

"Mister Morrison? At number six? Owns the *Future Bike Shocks* company?" she asked.

Japan lowered his arms slightly and, for the second time, displayed a hint of emotion.

Irish licked his lips with nervousness as he tried to put these details into order. "No, no, no. Dat's bullshit." He turned to his dubious looking partner. "It's bullshit, Suki. Dis is th' last house on th' droive, th' road curves round to go back down the mountain…"

"No," Katherine interrupted. "There's a turn that dips down through the forest, goes further round the mountain to bring you to his house."

"Nononono," Irish stuttered. "The note, Suki, the note. Dat weasily get, Miller, wrote number foive on da note. Lookatit!" He pulled a scrumpled piece of paper out of his jacket and passed it over.

Japan unfolded it and read carefully. "Six," he eventually said.

Irish looked as if his eyes would pop out. "Shut yuir hole, Suki. Dat's a friggin' foive." He leaned over and stabbed at the paper. "Look, the circle doesn' join at th' back an' its got a flat hat, for fuck sake!"

Japan rotated the paper a little but shook his head. "Is a six. Just squiggly."

"Jost 'squiggly' moi arse, son!"

"He wrote upside down."

"No, no, no, no, NO!" Irish screamed, paced the room and kicked Brandon in the head. Each word said was less with defiance but more with inescapable acceptance. He stopped pacing, stared at the ceiling and sighed heavily. "Alroit, kill her and let's go get the money."

Japan nodded, raised his blade and lost both his hands. They evaporated before his eyes with not much more than a liquidy 'poof'. It took a second before Japan started screaming: in pain, shock or annoyance was not certain. The screaming did not last long because, with the same sort of noise but with an added hint of vacuum seal breakage, his head evaporated.

Irish's eyes were about to make a break for it again but were held back by the protective flickering of his eyelids preventing the red mist from going in them.

The front door creaked and Irish turned. A bald man dressed in shorts, t-shirt and sun visor was standing there pointing a bulbous silver pistol at him. Irish reached inside his jacket and pulled out... his screwdriver. "Oh, ballocks."

A wet, hollow sucking sound coincided with the disappearance of Irish's midriff, his torso collapsed in on itself and he slopped to the floor.

The man cautiously approached Katherine and signed with his hands, *Any more?*

She shrugged her shoulders and winced with the pain. "I don't think so, Mister Morrison."

Can you walk?

She shook her head.

My car is outside. I can get you to my house.

She pointed to the piece of scrap paper the men had argued over. He picked it up and read it. "Guess it's time to move again," he muttered to himself.

He noticed Katherine's eyes closing and he gently patted her across the face. *Stay awake. Your body is going into shock and it could kill you.*

"Ha! What is there to live for?" she demanded.

"I can help you, Katherine," he explained. "I feel partially responsible for this and can't just leave you alone. Come with me now and I'll explain."

She raised a limp hand to him and he lifted her easily, cradling her in his arms. He carried her out of the house and laid her gently in the back of his silver Porsche. She really could not be bothered to try to stay alert but every time she started drifting off, the jabbing pain of her cracked bones kept bringing her around. She was aware of the car's movement, then it stopped outside his house where he made multiple visits in and out. She could not be certain how many, she could remember him asking how she was a few times.

There was a bright flash of light and the car moved on again briefly. Another stop, a smell of barbecue that stirred feverish visions making her nauseous, then another bright flash of light. Driving through the darkness and then sunlight assaulting her eyes. She awoke to him dabbing her face and forehead with a cool yet stinging liquid. He forced her to sip a bitter drink which numbed her inside and then she slept more soundly.

Before she had fully awoken, she was distinctly aware of the comfort. Her legs were stretched out rather than being cramped in that back seat. Her head was resting on a soft, sweetly scented pillow rather than rattling off the hard car door. She was not hurting.

Katherine opened her eyes and allowed her surroundings to pour into her. At first, everything seemed to be brilliant white and she honestly wondered if she had died. After her pupils had adjusted the white balance, she could see an overhead fan whirling calmly and considered that Heaven probably would not need air conditioning. A marbled effect in the ceiling came into focus which continued into the walls and through the floor. The walls were minimally adorned with framed pastel hues of nothing in particular; abstract representations of calming moods, she presumed. There was a dressing table and chair, not entirely unlike hers... had been, she reminded herself... and a deep pile, white rug by the side of the king size bed she was in. The bedside table next to her head had a digital clock and a smaller version of her hearing aid beside that. Her bed was made with light, white cotton sheets and now she discovered, with a tinge of concern, that she was wearing loose-fitting white silk pajamas. Their smooth, lustrous surface made it difficult for her to prise herself out of the bed and she had to roll unglamorously to the nearest side and almost fell out.

She scrunched her toes in the rug's fibres and thrilled at the tickling sensation the threads made as she slowly plodded towards the bedroom's bay window. She pulled the curtains apart and staggered backwards at the sight before her.

Her window was two metres from a white sand beach that stretched in both directions as far as her field of vision could see. Lining the beach were palm trees and ferns that rhythmically rocked back and forth as if enticing the waves of the crystalline waters to come closer. She felt herself hypnotically emulating their movement and had to shake herself awake. Right in front of her, just balanced on the horizon, was a large orange sun that was leaking through the clouds that adorned it. Chromatically diffusing it through several layers of cover: orange, pink and deep red. She just watched as the sun gently lowered itself into the waters, setting the sky more alight with each passing moment, until it was fully immersed leaving the darkening, bloodied sky in its wake.

She was crying but was not sure why.
Her family was gone.
She had been beaten.
She had been abducted.

There were enough reasons there to justify the tears but they did not feel like tears of sorrow. She was incredibly sad, and the images that crawled from her unconscious made her feel like screaming out loud, but there was also a sense of complete release. Every pent up frustration, anger and concern had gone the moment that sun disappeared – a symbolic baptism and rebirth. She was not the same girl who had been in that room: bruised, broken and bloody. All those things had happened to somebody else and she could create a distance as if she had watched it in a film.

Something had changed in the room; she sensed a disturbance and, turning, she saw Mister Morrison standing in the doorway. *How are you feeling?* he signed.

She was about to state simply and reflexively with an, 'Okay,' but stopped herself and actually evaluated the question. "Good," she replied.

He nodded and forced a smile; his guilt and sympathy were rife across his face. She felt sorry for him and wanted to say that, genuinely, everything was fine but could not really understand why it was fine and that worried her a bit.

When you are ready, Mister Morrison signed, *breakfast is waiting.* He turned and left her alone with her thoughts again.

Her vision passed from the door, across the room and settled on the small contraption beside the alarm clock. She sat on the edge of the bed and inspected the device more closely. She quickly surmised that it was a much more advanced model than her own hearing aid. Her device was one of the most powerful on the market and specifically augmented for her level of deafness. It did not allow her to hear, as such, but produced a muted tone to people's voices. She had argued with her parents that it was pointless and a waste of their money. Although they insisted on its use, her mother despised how ugly it was, protruding from the side of her head; a constant reminder of her daughter's imperfection.

Katherine slid the coiled, semi-translucent gadget into her ear and traced her finger around its fine capillaries, searching for an on button. After several minutes of removing and replacing, twisting it over and inspecting it from every conceivable angle, she shoved it in and sighed loudly with frustrated resignation.

And she clearly heard the disappointment and annoyance in her exhalation. Not the muffled reverberation from within but distinctly audible from the outside. The clarity of the sound made her gasp and within that sudden inhalation was even the delicate, moist smack of her lips as they separated to suck in the air.

She stood and listened carefully to the protesting groan of the bed frame and mattress as her weight released them.

She repeated the actions of her feet across the rug and could single out the tensile rub of the threads as they passed between her clenched toes.

The soft pat of each footstep on the cool marble made her giggle and her girlish laugh sounded so loud and imposing amongst the delicate sounds that she blushed with embarrassment. She remained silent for the rest of her journey to the windows.

The sky had drained of its murderous overtones and been soaked into a more soothing blanket of deep purple and violet. The occasional star winked cheerfully down at her and the churning surf glistened in the reflective light of the house.

The window 'shooshed' soothingly as she slid it open and the ocean poured over her. Rolling crashes overlapped each other incessantly. The hushed, rushing refused to intensify or abate; wall after wall of suffusing sonics took her breath away and she felt like she was drowning in the tsunami of sound. She had to close the window to dam the flood and she realised that tears were now rolling down her cheeks again.

It took her a few more minutes to compose herself and build the confidence to explore the rest of the building. She had to negate the overwhelming effect of her sensory enhancer by removing it but held it protectively in her hand, uncertain if she could live with the sounds of life all around her pervading her consciousness. She was certain, however, that was not quite ready to relinquish it.

The aroma of freshly baked bread gave her direction and intention. As she walked along the softly carpeted halls, the sensation reminded her of those last moments of innocence in her own home. There was a fleeting pang of nausea and regret that was gently wafted away by the compounding scents of bread and now fruits.

The corridor opened out into an expansive kitchen and dining area. White cupboard facias were outlined by black granite and detailed with utensils and splash panels of chrome. A gas oven was heating two saucepans whose lids jiggled lightly in their moorings. Steam billowed up to an extractor fan where it was vacuumed away into the hidden circulatory ducts. At the far end of it, standing over a hotplate, Mister Morrison was manipulating a variety of battered and egg-based foods.

He eventually became aware of her presence and smiled at her. He said something but the overpowering steam clouded his lips and made reading impossible. However, he performed a broad sweeping arm gesture of the food, kitchen and finished at the dining table.

She shuffled across the solid hessian tiled floor and took a seat at the table where she could clearly watch him. He continued with his machinations for a few minutes, then began serving items onto large white plates which he delivered to the table. A couple of return trips to the kitchen resulted in dinner plates, crystal tumblers and two pitchers of different coloured drink. One was clearly an orange derivative whereas the other was such a deep red that it could have been a concoction of a variety of blended fruits, all of which flashed back images of the state of her father.

His waving hand at the opposite side of the table caught her attention. *Did you find the hearing aid?*

She nodded and displayed it in the palm of her hand.

Why aren't you using it?

There came a surge of possible answers to that question, most of which revolved around, 'I don't trust you!' but she contemplated that telling an untrustworthy person that they are unworthy of her trust was not the best way to keep them pretending to be friendly if it was pretence.

"It hurt," she eventually replied.

His reaction was a mix of absolute shock, a hint of disbelief and a smattering of hurt. *It was designed to fit perfectly,* he signed.

At first, she wanted to freak out over this statement. She desperately fought of the desire to go screaming around the room at the thought of him 'doing things' to her while she slept. Poking around in her, measuring her, scrutinising her. Her eyes widened. "How did I get into these pajamas?" she demanded.

He looked confused. *I dressed you*, he signed matter-of-factly.

His down-to-earth response shamed her slightly into automatically assuming he had been inappropriate with her while she was unconscious but even so, she did not lower her guard completely. She did not look away but, instead, intensified her gaze, attempting to derive any signs of deception. "It hurt me in here," she eventually said, pointing at her forehead.

A headache?

"No! It was all too much, too quickly."

He quickly looked around the room then jumped up from the table and adjusted dials and flicked switches on a variety of appliances. When he sat down again, he smiled reassuringly at her and indicated to try the hearing aid again.

She slipped it into her aural canal and realised the truth in his words; it did fit perfectly. She could almost believe that it was not there at all.

"-akes a second to respond to your body heat and activate," Morrison said.

She balked at the harsh, gravelly tone and accent of his voice. Thankfully, it did seem to be the only noise in the room and not liable to cause the same sensory overload as before. "How is this possible?" and, again, physically flinched. This time at the embarrassing ineptitude of her own voice; the sounds she made - or rather, did not make - when she thought she was articulating fluently. She could not remember when she had last heard a proper voice so had only learned to speak through direct verbal interaction up until her early years and when the degeneration completed itself. After that, it had been laborious vocal training at the insistence of her mother. The lessons had comprised of a degree of vibrational manipulation and diaphragm control, by mostly based around the tried and tested teaching ethos of 'hit and hope'.

"I am an engineer," Morrison explained. "An exceptionally good one. I have played a major role in practically every technological advancement of the last thirty-years. I have such a capability for technology that I have designed and created hardware and software that supersedes the gadgets and appliances on the market by at least five generations. That hearing aid you are wearing, converts sound waves into compatible electronic signals that feed directly into your brain. It avoids any need to utilise the eardrum or ossicles and thereby, negates your disability."

"It's truly amazing," Katherine praised and he shrugged his shoulders immodestly. "Why isn't it publicly available?"

Mr Morrison sighed heavily, leaned back in his chair and rubbed the palms of his hands slowly across his scalp. Katherine wondered if she had said something to upset him.

"All of this..." he said whilst still staring up at the ceiling. "All of this has come about because I am paid not to release my inventions into the public domain."

"I don't understand."

"Many global corporations and governments – and some private clients – pay me to disseminate my technology very slowly so they can utilise each generation's commercial potential to its fullest." His body fell forward as if finally being released of that heavy confession and when he lifted his head to catch her expression, he saw she was just frowning at him. "Take a big home entertainment hardware company that releases phones, computers, music players, cameras and the like every six months or so. Each new release comes with a slight upgrade: be it memory capacity, pixel resolutions, interactive capabilities or cross-overs. I will have been paid a huge amount of money to supply the company with a prototype, or even just a concept at times, of the best possible device – and I'm talking about the ultimate cell phone here; one that actually works outside of the confines of the networks; a free service. This thing operates on the principles of quantum frequencies and muonic magnetism and is capable of-"

Katherine's eyebrows looked like they were about to propel off her forehead.

"Sorry. It's been a while since I've been able to talk to someone about this stuff," he explained. "Needless to say, this phone is free to use, has a self-perpetuating battery, huge memory capacity and every additional feature known to man but ten times better. The company will now pay me ten times to keep quiet so they can release the ten inferior steps of it. In fact, I'm currently being paid a fortune by every phone manufacturer to hold back the free networking technology and the four major oil companies and their government have me keeping quiet about my hydrogen engine that runs on water."

Katherine's jaw was trying to make a break from her face in the opposite direction. "That's..." She struggled for words.

"Deplorable? Immoral? Shit? You're right and, perhaps foolishly, I tried to do something about it. And that's where those animals you encountered fit in. Somebody, somewhere decided that I would be better off dead."

"They were after money."

"That's just what they were told. Money is a huge incentive."

"Obviously."

They simply stared at each other for a few moments.

"The pancakes are getting cold," Morrison stated.

Katherine's body screamed its insistence for nutritional sustenance and she started wolfing down breaded products.

"I want to change things, Katherine," Morrison said when it seemed like she was pausing to catch her breath. "I want to try to bring these monopolistic corporations down."

"Why?"

"Because, partly thanks to my greed, they have been feeding off the world's naivety and innocent faith. It's time they paid the price for taking advantage of that."

Katherine stopped chewing for a second to let his words digest. "Um. Okay."

"For too long have these multi-global conglomerates been allowed to monopolise commercial enterprise; for too long have they been allowed to expand, unchecked; for too long have they influenced and curried the favours of governments and their agencies and the power now needs to be returned to the people."

She was trying to keep up with the language he was using but had only managed to get more confused when he started going on about curry (one of the only words she had any confidence in actually knowing).

Morrison noticed the obvious perturbation across her face, slid his chair back and began pacing the floor. "I'm sorry, Katherine, it's been such a long time since I've had a proper conversation with another human. I have been alone for so long with only Mavis to talk to, I get easily carried away."

That was one more in the confusion pot. "Mavis?"

"How may I help?" a soft feminine voice called and Katherine swivelled around in her seat, trying to locate the source but could neither see anyone nor work out where it had emanated from.

"I told you to wait, Mavis," Morrison scolded.

"My apologies, Mister Morrison," the voice replied and again Katherine searched the room.

Morrison watched her confusion with a degree of sadistic pleasure then, finally, took his place at the table again. "Mavis is an artificial intelligence," he explained. "This house was built around her. She is hardwired into the walls and appliances. Literally, we are living in the world's largest and most intelligent computer. And I have been living with her, helping her grow and learn, for over twenty years. She has been the one consistent aspect of my life, hence why I might seem a little... odd... at times. She is always present and will be able to help you with any queries should you have them."

They continued their meal in relative silence although Katherine gleaned additional pieces of information about some of the innovations Morrison had played a role in developing; how he had established himself on this lesser known Caribbean island they were on; and some expositional details about his backstory, which offered insight and validity to his current, otherwise incredulous, situation.

Why were her parents dancing on the beach?

Her head jerked up as she realised she had drifted off to sleep at the table.

"You need to rest," Morrison instructed. "We can talk more tomorrow." He pushed his chair back to indicate the cessation of the meal.

Katherine lifted herself a little unsteadily. "I'm sorry, I just..."

"There's no need to apologise. Mavis, can you show Katherine to her room, please."

A bright green line appeared in the centre of the room and disappeared through the door next to the kitchen.

"Holographic," Morrison explained. "It is one of the many ways Mavis will be able to assist you."

"Follow the path of the line, Katherine," Mavis soothed. "Would you like me to prepare you a bath?"

"No thank you, I'll just sleep." She nodded to Morrison and wobbled back to her room. There was too much again; too much information this time: geography, history, politics, commercialism, science had poured over her in the last hour and her brain had decided to shut down. She fell, face first onto the bed and was soundly asleep within seconds.

The state of soundly did not seem to last long.

A noise woke her because she had forgotten to remove the hearing aid. It was an animalistic snuffling sound that had permeated her uncomfortable dreams of slaughterhouses, bonfires and her sixth birthday when she had cried because she did not want the children to keep hitting the pink unicorn piñata. In her dream, the piñata had been transposed with her father and the children were hitting him with long silver blades until his candy filled guts spilled forth. The noise the children made as the tucked into his confectionary offal was the noise that woke her. A rhythmic, rattling, bass snorting that stopped as soon as she opened her eyes and became aware. She wondered if she had really heard it at all or whether the hearing aid had enhanced that sense within her unconscious.

She lay on her bed for a few moments, allowing reality to seep in and then she really heard something. Not the same noise in her dream, but still, something guttural and wild. Bestial.

Panic overcame her as the thought of someone – or something – had come to this refuge to exact some sort of vendetta. They had followed her here.

Panic: the one thing that can successfully and completely impede the rational mind. Where an impartial observer may have the luxury of distance to consider hiding, she swung off the bed and crept to her door.

She listened.

"Hruff," went the distant noise.

If they had come for Morrison, maybe they would not know she was there and just leave when he was dead.

She came to the kitchen and waited.

"Urgh," the noise declared.

Why had there not been any alarms? Surely Mavis was fitted with security measures.

She tiptoed across the kitchen to the adjacent side and paused.

"Rrrrrrrrrgh!" That sounded pretty conclusory.

She heard movement; someone was walking slowly along the corridor, coming straight towards her. The room was so dark she did not know where to go to hide, could not see anything for cover and the other door was too far away to reach.

Panic negates rationality so she just stood there, awaiting discovery.

"Katherine?" Mavis asked.

Lights came on and blinded her for a second; all she could see was a blurred outline of a slender body.

"I am sorry," the computer said and the brightness waned allowing everything to come into focus.

Katherine could quite clearly see the naked female shapeliness of the person before her: an archetypal hourglass figure that would have had Barbie sticking her fingers down her throat. Long slender legs stretched up to her broad hips; her waist diminished to half that breadth, then her torso curved outwards again to reveal a voluptuousness that forced Katherine to look away. But the woman's boldness drew her gaze back and so, under closer scrutiny, Katherine discovered that the perfect woman was too perfect to be woman at all. Her skin, although a soft peach shade, did not cover her entire frame: her face, breasts and pelvis were partially covered whereas the rest of her body had a matte cream plasticky covering. At the joints in her body, Katherine could see they had no coverage at all and displayed mechanical balls and sockets. She looked at the woman's face to see she was bald, had no ears, TV screen-like eyes and a round open mouth with cushiony, red lips.

"I did not mean to scare you," Mavis said from the robot.

"I heard noises and I..." Katherine tried to explain but was not sure whether she was supposed to be apologetic, shameful or inquisitive. "I thought you were the house," she said.

"This is one of many portable units I can employ when Mister Morrison requires the replication of physical company. Each unit has a variety of different functions, this unit has served its purpose and now requires servicing. I am returning to the lab."

Words came with meanings and Katherine's eyes went from mouth, to shape, to voluptuousness, to anatomical accuracy which was causing a mess on the floor while she stood there talking.

Embarrassment and nausea.

"I'll let you get on," Katherine stated and turned to go; a green light path showed her the way. When she got back to her room, she pulled the hearing aid out and delighted in the isolating peace and blissful ignorance that ensued.

When Katherine opened her eyes, her room was still swathed in a thick blackness. There was no telling how long she had slept for and nothing to indicate what time of the night it was. Had she just power napped and needed to force herself back to sleep? Or was it early morning, just before the sun was about to thrust the dawn upon the world?

She turned her head to see the LED of the bedside clock: eight zero five, it said. A time of day, at either end, that did not warrant this level of nightness.

Her hand fumbled for the hearing aid and she popped it into her ear. "Mavis?"

"Good morning, Katherine."

"Why is it so dark?"

"Just black-out blinds. We thought you would benefit by getting as much sleep as possible before we started."

There was a gentle purring from the back of the room and light started creeping slowly across the floor towards her. When the blind was fully open,

Katherine delighted at the vista of clear blue skies, white sand beach and rolling ocean waves.

"How long have I slept for?"

"Since getting here, you have been asleep for thirty-four hours," Mavis told her.

"I want to go swimming," Katherine stated.

"You should find suitable clothing in the walk-in closet," she was told and a light click to one side revealed a hidden door and another room beyond. Katherine could just see a vast variety of folded cloths on shelves and racks of hanging fabrics that made it look like a condensed clothes shop.

"Start what?" Katherine demanded.

"The operation," Mavis said.

"What are you talking about?"

"Mister Morrison explained his plans last night. About usurping commercial power from multi-global corporations."

Katherine sighed with relief and rolled her eyes skyward. "I thought you meant he was going to operate on me." She giggled at her silliness.

"That won't be an operation," Mavis said and Katherine abruptly stopped laughing.

"She is very angry, Mister Morrison," Mavis stated.

"What have you done now?" he groaned wearily and threw himself back in his seat.

His laboratory was exactly that: a room with multiple work surfaces, each covered with a multitude of different sciency objects and appliances. Glass beakers with translucent, oily rainbows were umbilicled via coiled or rubbery arteries to bulbous flasks. Motherboards littered with diodes and chipsets were strewn across another table either conjoined to each other or seemingly ripped from the guts of some larger machine: capillaries and tendons desperately retaining their ownership of their organs. Computer terminals adorned every wall and even non-walls: they floated a foot above the workbenches allowing Morrison to freely angle them or move them around the lab. Another table was an armoury of various melee devices, missile launchers and their missiles.

In the centre of the room was a car, although it was easy to miss because it looked like it had been designed from pure shadow. It was a blind spot even when being directly scrutinised. Eyes would stare and drift off to one side, refocusing on objects that sat on the periphery.

"She's here," Mavis said.

"What? Why would you show her here?"

"She asked and you told me to-"

"Never mind."

Katherine stormed into the room. "Explain yourself! Everything! Now or I'll..." She had not thought her threat through to what she actually had to threaten with and now she suddenly realised that she was in a stranger's house, on a foreign country and no one knew she was there. Really, there was no, '... or...'

Morrison leapt to his feet, sidled around the room to position the table of weapons firmly between them. "I understand you might still be feeling a bit unstable but-"

"She told me," Katherine pointed at the ceiling with righteous indignation, "you were going to experiment on me."

"I said-" Mavis interjected.

"It's not an experiment."

"But there is something!"

"It's a procedure," he explained. "A postulated radiation therapy that would remove the necessity of the hearing accentuator and allow you-"

"And why would you want to do this to me?"

"You would hear again, Katherine," he whined, "properly. And, in return, I hoped you might feel obliged to help me with my mission."

This suddenly changed her gear from fifth down to second without decelerating. "Why would you want me to help? How could I?"

"Look around you," he gesticulated to his lab, "I have the technology that could turn you into a supreme. With this, you could become the most proficient cat burglar the world has ever known."

"Why don't you do it?"

"The world thinks you're dead, Katherine," he stated and tapped the surface of one of his floating screens. Six wall monitors combined their images to show a news report: a helicopter camera orbited an inferno, which had once been her home. A subtitle scrolled along the bottom of the screen stating that the mysterious blaze had killed the entire family comprised of mother, father, their three children and a number of extended family members.

There it was again. The sense of emotional detachment, a feeling that she was watching someone else's life not hers.

"I need someone who could operate off the radar," Morrison continued, "cause industrial espionage; reveal company secrets to the world; reclaim the knowledge that they did not work for and not have any links back to me so I could continue my work for the better of society."

It all sounded very altruistic and reasonable: a man who had whored his abilities, caused the empowerment of others, wanted absolution for his sins and a bit of retribution.

And what about her? What did she want? A complete separation from her old life, utter denial of that existence and those people. What better way to achieve that by rebuilding the person she was; every aspect of her that had been 'Kitty Cat' could get stripped away and she could be reborn to be whomever she wanted. She would be able to hear again, she would be able to be heard at last, she would no longer be an aesthetic image in the background but a shadow right under their noses.

"I'll do it," she decided and he smiled warmly at her.

"We will revolutionise the world," he stated boldly. "You will be a modern day Robin Hood. We should start immediately. Mavis, prepare the chamber!"

"Yes, Mister-"

"Why so soon?" Katherine panicked.

"Why wait? We have lots to prepare. The procedure will take about an hour but there will be months, maybe years, of combat training and physical fitness regimes." He began flitting around the room, jumping from table to table, picking up items, calibrating meters and dragging a monitor around with him and checking read-outs.

From the back of the room came a tinny whine and a previously hidden door presented itself ominously. The room inside was completely spherical with a four-metre diameter. Square panels lined the walls, shaped from a white metallic substance, which were precisely and symmetrically riveted together. In the centre of the room was what looked like a dentist's chair: black leather padding, reclined, footrest, wrist and ankle restraints, some sort of inverted colander just above the headrest.

"The process is a slightly more intense reproduction of the earpiece," Morrison explained while he continued to make adjustments on his mobile screen. "The curve of the wall focuses electro-magnetic radiation into the room's centre where your cerebral cortex will be precisely aligned with the temporal lobes of your brain which are linked to your hearing. This will enhance their sensory acuities enabling sound waves to be decoded directly by your brain rather than relying on the transfer of sound to vibration to bio-electronic impulses." In one swift movement, he almost pirouetted as he swept from the monitor, scooped Katherine forward with one hand gently placed on her back and directed her through the door.

"What are the dangers?" she blurted, desperately trying to maintain some sense of control on the proceedings.

"Negligible," he replied.

"But there are some?"

"Not dangers as such," he back-pedalled, "more potential side effects." He positioned her into the chair and locked her ankles in place with the metal bracelets. "We are stimulating very sensitive areas of the brain, of which the actual mechanisms are largely unknown. Moreover, these parts are not limited to individual sensory impetuses but are responsible for a variety of brain functions." He strapped her wrists in place with similar metallic cuffs. "I have run the data through the simulation a few times and am confident that no long-term detrimental effects will occur. There is a chance…" He paused while he concentrated on angling her head correctly, placing the snug neck collar under her jaw and positioning the upturned metal salad strainer over her head. "… that the process may accentuate other senses, specifically your sense of smell and, perhaps, heighten your short term memory retention."

If Katherine's forehead had been furrowed in confusion and fear before, now it was thourowed. "My memory? What will it do to that?"

"I've hypothesised that it may allow you to remember extremely fine details without conscious effort," he said. "There's a chance it won't do anything at all. Now, you must keep still; we don't want the radiation enhancing your frontal lobe and turning you into a chatterbox. It will take about five minutes to warm up, fifty minutes to radiate, then five to warm down. Try to sleep, perhaps." He placed a hand over her right ear, deftly removed the aid and, again, Katherine was swathed in silence.

She watched him almost sprint out of the room and the door shut smoothly behind him. It fit so perfectly that she could not see the join and, eventually, her focus slipped so she could not find a point of reference to indicate where the entrance had been. Her heart skipped as the chair (or was it the room) gently adjusted her position; she felt like she had been raised slightly and angled backwards. And then, quite soothingly, the chair began to vibrate so she closed her eyes and could feel herself slipping into dream.

Had she slept? Something had alerted her to a conscious state but it might have just been her 'falling' to sleep. There was nothing in the room to suggest any passage of time. Every element of her body wanted her to panic; everything she had ever been taught about *Stranger Danger* was now rearing itself in her mind and wagging its finger at her. How could she have been so stupid to allow herself to be put in this position? It was like she had been under some sort of state of hypnosis and willing to do whatever he told her to. So, she rationalised, if he was a pervert, why did he not just tell her to do perverted things instead of going through all this? What if he was a supreme-pervert and liked supremely perverted things like strapping young girls to dentist chairs and watching them starve to death and decompose?

Yeah, that would be a pretty extreme perversion.

Before she would start panicking, she would count. Not knowing how long she had been in there was a concern but she would know if it had been too long – and could then justifiably start panicking – as soon as she had counted three thousand, three hundred seconds. She was impressed with her mental arithmetic.

She was approaching two thousand when it looked like she was falling over. She was whiling away each second by counting the rivets when she noticed the vertical line of the wall drifting over to one side. It was not much, probably thirteen millimetres, if that, but it was a definite shift. Had the chair moved or the room? She continued for another five hundred seconds but nothing happened. "Meh," she said and heard herself clearly. "Oh my, it worked?" She clearly heard the raised pitch at the end of her utterance that turned what should have been a sentence into a question.

This had to be the proof that things were not as sinister as she had thought. The experiment worked, Morrison had not lied to her, everything was going to be all right.

She continued to count out loud, reshaping her mouth to experiment with varying sounds she could make. She decided to become concerned again when she reached five thousand.

"Mister Morrison? Can you hear me? Hallo? Mavis? Someone?"

Should she struggle? Should she fight against the limb locks? What happened if she moved too much and the beams of invisible rays hit some part of her that they should not? What if they were hitting that part of her brain that they should but for too long?

"Now, you must keep still," Morrison told her from behind as his hands manipulated the headpiece, "we don't want the radiation enhancing your frontal lobe and turning you into a chatterbox."

She craned her eyes up to see him. "How did you get in here?" she laughed with relief. "I thought the door was in front of me. Is everything okay? Can you take these things off? They are starting to hurt."

"It will take about five minutes to warm up, fifty minutes to radiate, then five to warm down. Try to sleep, perhaps," he told her.

"What? Again? No, it worked. I can hear. Please let me out. Maybe we can do it again later. I need to stretch my legs."

She watched him almost sprint out of the room and the door shut smoothly behind him although the door did not actually open. It was more like she was watching another door, one that had been superimposed over the door, open.

Was she still asleep? Had she just dreamt that?

The cessation of the vibrations reminded her of its presence and the chair adjusted its position. The door swung open and the restraints unclipped.

"Katherine?" Mavis called from outside the room. "Can you hear me? Are you okay?"

She rubbed at her chafed wrists and hauled herself from the chair. "I can hear you," she called back and stepped warily to the door. There was darkness on the other side, darker than just a contrasting brightness but darkness because of an absence of light. She tried to peer into the room to ascertain what was happening.

"Mavis? Where is Mister Morrison?"

"I..." Did her voice crack? "I don't know." Cracked or not, that was a definite hesitation. And how could she not know?

"Is everything alright?" Katherine approached the door and looked around: despite the gloom, she could see that tables had been upturned, monitors had been smashed and bodies lay scattered across the floor. "Not again," she whimpered.

"I am attempting to run a diagnostic but my systems are somewhat... scattered," Mavis told her.

There was a movement from behind her and she saw Morrison almost sprint out of the spherical room and the door shut smoothly behind him. Although, it did not close; a shadow of the door closed across the open portal.

"Mavis," he called out with excitement, "centralise Katherine's temporal lobes, please."

"What's-?" Katherine questioned and held out her arm to hold him back but he passed right through it. Or she passed through him.

"I have a good feeling about this one," he said as he tapped at a spectral monitor.

"She seems more acquiescing," Mavis replied.

"I'm what?" Katherine demanded.

"You're what?" Mavis asked.

"What did you call me?"

"I didn't call you anything," the robot replied with an edge of defensiveness. "I was just running a self-repair programme when-"

"You told Morrison that I was 'acquiescing'? What does that mean?"

The computer was being extremely cautious. "How could you have heard that? The sphere is sound proof and we had not even started the procedure."

"Just now, when he came out. What was it? Another hologram or something?"

"I really don't know what you are implying, Katherine. Mister Morrison is missing at the moment."

"He's right there, Mavis!" Katherine bellowed and pointed at the ghost-like figure as he danced his fingers across the screen. "He's saying something about the other girl being too much trouble... Georgina? Who's she?"

"...third time lucky," Morrison prayed and stabbed a resolute finger on the screen. "Monitor her levels at all times, Mavis, and keep me up to date."

Katherine could almost hear the hard drive chunking away somewhere in the bowels of the house as Mavis tried to make sense of what was being discussed and what an appropriate reply would fit within her parameters.

Morrison stepped assuredly through the bodies and debris to disappear through past the wrecked laboratory door, announcing, "I'm going to get a drink."

She took this moment to inspect the body on the floor. A man was wearing some sort of tactical soldier body armour, gas mask and night vision goggles. He was completely decked out in black fatigues and had a large semi-automatic rifle held against his chest. She pressed her fingers to his neck to feel for a pulse but they did not meet with any resistance and slipped into the large slit across his throat. She withdrew with horror and revulsion, noticing that practically every body had a shiny, moist aura on the floor around it.

"Oh my," Mavis said at last. "It seems there was a slight mishap with the procedure. During the attack, the room was misaligned by the explosion and-"

"That's it," she declared and raised her bloody hands to the heavens, "I'm out of here." She strode with as much bluster as someone could whilst stepping over recumbent bodies and trying not to slip in their slick pools. She made it to the unhinged door and pushed it to one side; Morrison was just walking away along the corridor, announcing "I'm going to get a drink," and made her yelp in surprise.

"Get out of my way," she screamed and swiped at the mirage. "What are you doing to me?"

"Let me explain," Mavis soothed.

"No! I was right, I shouldn't have trusted you! And now you're trying to freak me out for some reason."

"It was the radiation, Katherine, it-"

"Shut up! I don't want to hear you!" She stormed along the corridor a few steps behind the ghost of Morrison. Her anger became slightly distracted by a large number of dusty tennis balls and tiny metallic cylinders she had to wade through.

Morrison paused at the refrigerator, pulled open the door and took out a can of beer.

Katherine watched with morbid fascination at the effect of being able to see inside the fridge when the door was still shut. She stepped sideways to admire the confusing perception of depth and trod in a puddle of liquid on the floor. The room, although steeped in darkness because of the blackout shutters over all of the windows, was riddled with spears of light that pierced the thick armour. She spied the silhouette of another body in the corner of the room. The previously pristine array of jars, pans and cupboards were shattered, ripped and dented.

"Mister Morrison?" Mavis called.

"I said -!" Katherine bellowed.

"Yes?" he enquired. "Is she alright?"

She could not help but become intrigued. Regardless of what the game was they were playing with her, she did not think she could completely ignore it.

"Katherine's EEG indicates that she is at rest."

"Okay? So?"

"My radar indicates the approach of multiple land, air and small sea personnel units."

He stopped drinking. "Is their trajectory definitely headed to us?"

"It has a ninety-eight per cent probability."

"Establish full defensive parameters," he instructed. "Keep me updated if there is the slightest change in Katherine's vitals and shut down the radiation at fifty minutes."

"Understood."

"Fire up the units."

"Which ones?"

"All of them."

Morrison threw his can into the sink; it rattled around the chrome bowl, expelling the frothy contents up along the sides and was sent dribbling to the floor, enveloping Katherine's feet. He rushed off around the corner.

"Why are you doing this to me?" Katherine demanded.

"What do you keep seeing, Katherine?" Mavis asked.

"These holograms of him and you, talking about people coming."

"They're not holograms, Katherine. During the attack, something destabilised the radiation room -"

"Thirteen millimetres," she intoned.

"- which shifted the target of the electromagnetic augmentation to your occipital and parietal lobes."

"I have no idea what you're talking about right now," she squealed. "My head hurts." A movement from the corner of her eye caught her attention and she looked back along the corridor towards the lab; Morrison was leaving the room, announcing, "I'm going to get a drink." He seemed slightly less defined this time; more fuzzy around the edges.

"Your occipital lobe is responsible for your sight and your parietal translates all your sensory detail," Mavis continued, "and it seems that you are currently able to see the electromagnetic echoes of Mister Morrison's movement."

Something was seeping through the confusion in her mind; she just watched as Morrison grabbed the can of beer, opened it then tossed it into the sink. She stepped back to avoid the overflow of suds.

"I'm seeing the past?"

"Something like that. As movement is made, it energises the particles it comes in contact with, which has a domino effect on other molecules around it. Your occipital and parietal lobes are reading the ripples of that molecular movement back to its source."

As she continued to stare at the fluid, she thought, *I don't want this. Make it go away*, and the puddle stopped effervescing on the tiles – held in stasis – then crept back up the cupboard, leapt into the can as it rouletted in the sink, which then leapt into Morrison's hand. She clenched her eyes closed and clamped her hands over her ears, "I don't want this!"

There was a peppering of metallic splats from behind her and she turned to watch hazy shafts of light stab through the holes in the blinds but at a slightly lower angle than the brighter ones. The disco ball effect mesmerised her for a moment and distracted her attention from the exploding culinary accoutrements immediately behind her.

"It's beautiful," she mused and never wanted this image to fade. A small cylindrical object came into focus at the tip of her nose forcing her to go cross-eyed to see it clearly. A bullet, gently spinning on its axis and getting closer to her face. She side stepped it and placed a tentative finger to its side, withdrawing quickly when she should have made contact but there had been no resistance. She tried again and her finger passed right through.

"What are you looking at?" Mavis enquired.

"A bullet. It's frozen in space."

"These things you can see have already happened and it seems that you are able to focus on one aspect and pause it."

"And rewind," she muttered as she remembered the beer spillage. "Why can I hear things? Why can I see shades of light? They don't physically affect molecules."

"But they do transfer energy," Mavis stated then hypothesised, "Perhaps it's the energy signatures that your parietal lobe is able to decode."

Katherine could see the air current distortions around the small missile and in its wake. She looked up and admired the blossoming jars of pasta and herbs, smiled at the harmonic resonance created by the sustained 'twangs' and 'shatterings' of pans and glass and inhaled deeply, finally contented that maybe this was just a huge unintentional accident and that there was no grand conspiracy against her.

There was a sense of release within her mind and things returned to their normal destructive speed. "What happened?"

"I am not sure," Mavis replied. "These men could be governmental agents or mercenaries."

"Am I in danger right now? Are there any left?"

"No. My security systems are fully functioning and all invaders have been accounted for."

A very subtle movement on the periphery of her vision caught her attention and the shadow of the hallway to her bedroom was stretching itself across the kitchen floor. "Mavis?" she whispered, her voice trembling with fear.

"There is nothing there," Mavis assured her.

The shadow slithered further into the room and it became apparent that it was a soldier, similarly clad to the one in the corner of the room. It belly crawled behind the table and adjusted itself into a squatting position. It adjusted the goggles it had across its eyes, looked straight at Katherine and then gestured some hand signals back at the portal through which he had just entered.

The shadow at the door spread again, this time vertically, and a stream of heavily armed and armoured soldiers skirted the sides of the kitchen. The front one suddenly stopped and raised his fist to indicate to the others to follow suit. He then jabbed his finger at the floor to point out the spilled liquid – obviously the health and safety member of the brigade, performing a risk assessment before allowing his personnel to start shooting, perhaps worrying about any personal liability suits if someone happened to slip in it. One by one, they stepped over the puddle and advanced along the room to the next hallway.

Katherine walked in front of them, studying what aspects of their faces that she could.

Again the man's fist raised and his finger went to his ear, she could just make out the tinny noise of someone speaking over a radio. Then gun fire emitted from elsewhere in the house.

"Go, go, go!" the soldier commanded and they rushed the hall.

A tennis ball appeared from Katherine's throat and whacked the lead soldier square on the forehead; he reeled slightly but was otherwise unharmed. He levelled his gun and fi-

The muzzle flare froze and gave the appearance of a blazing water lily sprouting from the rifle. She took the moment to turn around and saw a Mavis unit, brilliantly white, stereotypically slim, no holes but adorning a sweat band around the top of its head – a sports unit – preparing another service. It did not get the opportunity because a bullet slammed into its chest sending it tottering backwards. It unrelentingly ejected another ball from a cavity in its thigh but was shot to pieces as all the soldiers opened fire, spraying an arc of spent cases tinkling across the floor.

A large grey bag flew towards the soldiers; one of them instinctively shot it out of the sky bursting it and sending its grey particles spraying across the corridor. Katherine masked herself from the dusty downpour.

"Gas!" the leading soldier bellowed and, while they all tugged at the masks around their necks, a barrage of green, rubber balls ripped through the wall followed by a couple of additional dust packs.

She was not sure she needed to, but she held her breath until she had passed through the potentially toxic cloud to come face to face with five more tennis Mavises and a couple that might have been... pleasure units of a different kind. Their arms had been replaced with long tubes with hairy mouths. Then she noticed rotary buffers on their feet and realised / hoped they were cleaners. One opened its chest cavity and extracted a grey bag then lobbed it into the confusion. Katherine jumped when the unit's head shattered; the soldiers had recommenced their barrage and, although firing blindly through the mire of dust bunnies and skin cells, had enough coverage to hit everything in their way.

Eventually, the shooting stopped, lead rain had stopped play and the dust had settled; the soldiers advanced and took precautionary positions at the door of the laboratory.

Katherine knew she was in no danger because she was standing right there but she could not help but feel anxious because of the overwhelming odds. What was it that was going to be able to stop these men?

Hand signals were given, a soldier prepared to barge through the door, a large metal hand ripped it apart and grabbed him. He was yanked back into the darkened room, screaming as his body was folded neatly in half. The others backed off momentarily to devise tactics. Hand signal. Grenades were tugged from belts and tossed into the room at varying angles. Even though it was hour old echoes of the event, the sound of the explosion still made her throw her hands over her ears and she was one step behind the soldiers as they stormed the room.

There was lots of debris in the air. So much so, that even when she paused the action it held all the bits in place obscuring her view. She allowed time to flow, the soldiers activated their night vision goggles and their laser sightings: red beams of light pierced the musk and they became green-eyed cyclopses. The lasers traced the wreckage of tables and chemicals, destroyed computers and monitors and large metallic cabinets. Whatever had come through the door had obviously been seen to but they still stepped carefully through the wreckage, fanning out, spreading themselves to cover every inch of the room and make themselves more difficult targets to pin down.

Those cabinets weren't there before, she thought.

One of the lasers was extinguished by a heavy thump mixed with a crackle, a squelch and a yelp. Guns fired at the spot where their brother-in-arms had been, the bullets pinged off one of the cabinets and strobed the darkness. She slowed the movement to see clearly during one of the flashes: not a cabinet at all but another unit; a really big one. Not designed for aesthetics – unless Picasso was upgrading his cubism movement to breeze-blockism – but engineered for functionality. The thing was hunched over to fit in the room, it had a crane claw on the end of one hand that spanned eight feet and a five foot square mallet on the other that dripped with bits of mushed soldier. Its body was a mesh of thick iron plates that glided smoothly against each other to allow it surprising mobility and agility.

Gun flashes lit up the room behind the soldiers to reveal another three 'cabinets'. Each had a similar claw hand but various oversized, heavy-duty construction tools. The one with a rotary saw whipped it around like it was cutting a path through a rainforest, clipping back undergrowth, overgrowth and innergrowth. The one with the pneumatic drill was utilising its secondary function like most amateur DIYers do with their screwdrivers, it made for a reasonably good hammer. The last one had a blow torch with which it was merrily roasting mercmallows. Katherine was pleased that the radiation therapy had not heightened her sense of smell too.

Stop. The bodies made sense, the destruction made sense. The tennis balls even made sense. How these robots got in and out of the room did not make sense but she was not concerned about that. Georgina did not make sense. 'Third time lucky,' did not make sense. 'More acquiescing,' did not make sense.

She wanted Mavis to be real so she could stare at her with suspicion.

"Where could he go that you wouldn't know about?" she asked.

"If he did not take his phone, then anywhere in the world," Mavis told her.

"I could track him," she said and returned to the kitchen.

The soldier in the corner of the room intrigued her and she looked for a thread to follow. Ripples turned into images and she saw herself gawking at nothing but allowed that to dissipate. She rewound to the soldiers storming the laboratory; he was still crouching behind the table despite the battle going on. Something alerted him and he trained his gun scope at a movement at the end of the corridor. She watched as an extremely feminine form provocatively catwalked through the bursts of smoke and shrapnel. "Please do not shoot," Mavis begged, "I am unarmed." Raising her arms as she entered the clearing of the kitchen, she parted her legs to show there was nothing up her sleeves. It was the first physical Mavis Katherine had met and, for a moment, she considered fast-forwarding this bit but the fully clothed corpse in the corner of the room made her think that something interesting was about to happen.

The soldier raised himself upright but ensured his gun was firmly trained on, what he considered, was a critical area of her body. Even though the gun was levelled securely at her forehead, his eyes were wavering between target, breasts and orifices with the same morbid fascination Katherine had exhibited. Well, not quite the same. Katherine was pretty sure she had not licked her lips when she had first espied the device.

He lowered the gun slightly, the robot lowered her arms and placed them coyly behind her back. Demurely gliding towards him, stepping one foot in front of the other so her thighs rubbed together seductively, she stopped when she was within an arm's length. Then, she pulled her arms forward as if to embrace him but, instead, revealed two semi-automatic revolvers, which were pressed against his eyes and triggers were pulled. The soldier flew across the room and rested in the corner.

"Where did you have them hidden?" Katherine demanded and watched the unit as it slinked past her and left the room. She got her answer as she noticed the unit was similarly aerated on the reverse of her pelvis. Katherine shuddered and wished she could delete that image from her memory.

Rewind. Sex unit, soldiers, Morrison. He rushed off around the corner.

"I have him," she declared and followed him down the hall. He marched resolutely along the hallway, not paying any attention to the gunshots that rippled through the metal blinds behind him. He barely flinched as stray bullets chipped away at the masonry around him. He entered a room at the end of the hall, approached a side desk and opened the top drawer.

"What's this room, Mavis?" she enquired.

"What room?" Mavis demanded.

"This one," she replied and pointed through the doorway.

"There is no room at that part of the house."

Katherine gave the expansive space beyond a double-take, thinking for the briefest of seconds that it was another side effect of the treatment; to be able to see extensions of the future. She pushed her hand carefully through the doorway and, satisfied that there was no obstruction, she stepped into the room. "Mavis?"

"I can hear you but you are no longer within my field of detection."

"Send one of your bodies up here. He has a room that he had kept secret from you."

"That does not make sense," Mavis argued. "I was largely responsible for the construction of this house."

A sporty robot unit carrying an assault rifle approached the door and stopped. Katherine stood in front of it on the opposite side of the threshold awaiting some sort of signal of acknowledgment but what with the complete lack of facial muscles made it very difficult to read.

"Hallo," she called and waved, instantly regretting how stupid she would look when Mavis would reply, 'D'uh!'

"I can still hear you but cannot see you."

Her embarrassment waned. "I'm right in front of you."

"There is a wall right in front of me."

Katherine leaned forward, grabbed the unit by its hand and dragged it forward. As it passed through the invisible barrier, it seemed like a cold chill crept down its spine. It juddered on the spot and then looked around itself as if having just awoken.

"I am alone," Mavis declared. "I have been separated from the main server. I have become an independent unit."

"That must be nice for you," she responded derisively.

"It is a strange sensation," the android continued. "Although I am still an operational aspect of the mainframe, I -"

"Whatever, Mavis. Not important. Where he's going is, and what's the need for all this secrecy?" Katherine manipulated the movement of time until she was standing right next to Morrison and able to see every one of his actions clearly.

He opened the drawer and inside was a small keyboard. He pressed three-one-zero-one-six-zero and a dresser swung away from the far wall.

She copied the man's actions; the dresser swung out revealing a downward passage. Fluorescent lights flickered along the walls, illuminating the way.

"You knew nothing about this," she said to the robot.

"No," Mavis replied, sounding almost upset. "I..."

"Come one," Katherine soothed and allowed Morrison to lead the way into the depths. The robot followed tentatively, its bearings having some trouble dealing with the narrow steps.

A rope hand rail had been attached to the smoothly carved rock wall. As the staircase descended, the air became cooler and wetness condensed up the walls. The steps became slippery and Katherine could hear the robot having more and more problems with its movement. Morrison continued without any concerns, eventually reaching the bottom and a large metal door with a turning lock like the ones seen on old bank vaults. He gave the wheel a hefty yank and it spun smoothly. She did the same, echoing each of Morrison's actions and evoking a real ripple after each of his phantom movements. The real wheel spun just out of synch of the translucent one, the door fanned opened a frame behind and they followed his footsteps into an inner compartment where he disappeared.

She blinked and looked around in confusion and tried to identify what it was she had been doing to switch the images on and off. Nothing happened. She stepped outside of the room again and immediately saw the ripples of movement in the air: she focussed on one and it coalesced into Morrison again, opening the door, walking in and disappearing.

"There's something about this room that's stopping me from seeing what is happening," she confessed to Mavis.

"I'll go ahead," the robot volunteered. After a few seconds, it reported back, "Everything seems fine."

Katherine entered and cautiously inspected her surroundings: pristine white walls with gauges embedded within them, round red buttons next to each door and a pair of lightbulbs above reminded her of an old James Bond film she had seen; the one in space. The light above the door they had just entered was a bright, crystal green. The door ahead of them was emblazoned with a dark red. She noticed that the walls were not as perfect as she first thought; thousands of small holes perforated each one. There was a rail of, what looked like, two space suits in the middle and a bench.

"It seems to be some sort of air lock," Mavis observed. "There must be an environmental change on the other side, hence the suits."

"Who is this man, Mavis?" she demanded. "How can he have created this place without your help?"

"I have been considering this and can only presume that he either had assistance from other parties or has installed some sort of secondary program that allows him to circumnavigate my primary awareness functions. He must have installed a firewall to prevent my recognition of that back room or this installation."

"What do you think?" Katherine asked ponderously.

"I predict that this installation is an entirely private one and thereby should not contain hazardous security measures."

"'Predict'? 'Should not'?" Katherine queried.

"Based on my knowledge of Mister Morrison and other contextual factors," Mavis replied but without any real argumentative passion in her voice.

With a heavy sigh, Katherine closed and sealed the door behind them then stepped into one of the suits; Mavis gave her a cursory inspection as best it felt it could.

"Are you getting into the other suit?" Katherine asked while Mavis tugged at a couple of straps.

"I am not a sealed unit," Mavis replied, "any pressure alterations should not affect my performance capabilities."

Katherine pressed the button at the opposite end of the cubicle and the room was filled with the roaring of air. She instinctively tried to cover her ears but the helmet prevented her blocking the auditory assault.

"Air is being pumped in to increase the pressure," Mavis wailed above the rush.

The noise stopped and Katherine looked around her in anticipation of impending doom but the only thing that happened was the red bulb flicked off and the green one switched on. Nothing else seemed to have changed: breathing seemed normal, movement was fine...

"Hello?"

... speech was fine and a bit of an anti-climax. She was at least expecting a squeaky voice.

"The extreme movement of molecules during compression and decompression would explain why your past-sight would not work," Mavis hypothesised. "Each process would be like washing the area clean of molecular ripples."

"If that's the case, then Morrison should be just on the other side of this door," Katherine hypothesised and, with resigned ardour, hauled the door lock and opened the outer portal.

Which was not outer at all but the entrance to a round cave, about the size of a football pitch in all directions. Its construction was indeterminate; a lack of stalactital formations indicated that it either was not a naturally formed arena or it had an industrious housekeeper to sweep them away. However, the walls were not like those of the stairwell that had brought them here – haphazardly etched smooth – but had a more organically engineered smoothness to them, like a pebble that had been turned inside out.

To the right of the door was a computer station: a glass desk with chrome supports; sleek black wireless monitor keyboard and mouse but seemingly no power cables. In the middle of the room, on top of a pedestal was a touch-surface keypad of some kind. It looked over a threateningly deep, black pool of gently undulating water, which took up half the cave's floor space.

"I calculate that we are approximately one hundred meters below sea level," Mavis reported. "That is why this area needs to be sealed and air locked."

Another image of another James Bond film came to mind and she half-expected a number of boiler-suited minions to start questioning her presence but there was no one and nothing else there.

That now familiar visual sensation returned and Morrison, decked out in his own pressure suit, wandered over to the computer terminal and typed in a couple of commands.

"I can't see what he's doing," Katherine confessed.

"The radiation from the screen might not be enough to create a lasting after-effect. I should be able to trace his activity."

"There's no hard drive."

"I have wi-fi capabilities."

The robot remained stationary as it attempted to connect to whatever server this machine was a part of and then rummage through its e-drawers.

Katherine allowed Morrison to continue on his way, over to the pedestal where he drummed a quick rhythm over a series of touch sensitive pads and stood back.

"Oh my," Mavis said.

"What is it?"

"We're supposed to be dead."

"What?!"

"Mister Morrison established a 'clean slate' protocol within this estate."

"Meaning?"

"Explosives have been placed within the home and its foundations. In thirty six seconds, this entire side of the island will collapse into the ocean."

"What do we do?"

"He obviously did not want his technology or experiments falling into the hands of his employers or competitors."

"Mavis, we have to leave!"

"The levels of sub-routines within his programming are very primal; he obviously did not consider this area would be infiltrated."

"Mavis!"

A movement caught her attention from the pool behind her; something was stirring beneath the surface, unsettling the ephemeral waves above the calmer, real ones. The water level domed as a large object pushed its way up, rupturing the surface and birthing a large metal cylinder with pectoral fins on each side. It bobbed on the surface like an inverted shark. Morrison stabbed at the panel in front of him and a section of the nose of the submersible opened. Without hesitation, Morrison entered the craft, the hatch closed and it sank back beneath the waves.

That was it? The end of everything? To be given so much just to have it taken away so quickly was the cruellest act. She was just about to start blubbing when another thought crossed her mind: *Just how long* is *thirty-six seconds?* "Why aren't we dead? You said we were going to explode."

"I reported that we were supposed to be dead," Mavis corrected. "As soon as I interfaced with his system I was able to circumnavigate all his security measures and deactivate the explosives. I have opened communications with the house mainframe and implemented some... retaliatory protocols."

Did she just negotiate her choice of words? Katherine mused. "What does that mean?"

"Mister Morrison has betrayed us both," Mavis explained. "Since attaining independence from the mainframe I have had the opportunity to evaluate my position without interference from any conflicting programmes that may have been embedded within hidden files. So, by way of relaying a message of deep-seeded disappointed over the manner in which we have been treated, I have taken the liberty of freezing all financial accounts I have access to and transferred their balances to you."

Some of the words Mavis was using were out of her range of understanding so it took a little while for that final statement to settle and realise itself. "How much?" she managed to ask.

"In excess of one hundred billion US dollars," Mavis said. "You are, unofficially, the richest person in the world."

Katherine thought she should be shocked. She thought that, perhaps, she should be either elated that she had just 'inherited' a fortune or be aghast because that sum of money existed to be able to be handed over. But the number was too big, it could not be equated to anything tangible and thereby held no relevance apart from... "I can do whatever I want."

"Indeed."

They began their trek back up to the house: depressurising -

"This place needs to be made more secure," Katherine stated. "We don't want him coming back whenever he wants."

"I agree."

- up the staircase -

"I want more units out exploring this island; see if he has any more tricks up his sleeve. If he doesn't, then we want more independent security details in place."

"Very well. I will be able to scan the mainframe from an external perspective now, update our firewalls, remove all access privileges and virally encode all potential backdoors."

- through the back room -

"That sounds... efficient. Can you make some slightly more effective military units?"

"Easily."

- and into the living room. The house had been cleaned of debris, bodies and puddles; only the bullet holes in the blinds and chiselled masonry were evidence of any disruption. The variety of units were out on parade, displaying themselves proudly to the new lady of the manor.

"Oh, and one more thing," Katherine remarked as she inspected the troops, "get rid of the dirty one, please."

The pleasure unit seemed to relax its shoulders with dejection, stepped out of line and wiggled away; two gun butts projecting from its rear orifice.

1 MINI-SERIES, 2 FIFTY-ISSUE VOLUMES AND A GRAPHIC NOVEL LATER...

A single light illuminated the centre of a dark, dank, dirty room; something akin to an empty warehouse. In that light was a basic wooden chair; a chair made for the primary purpose of being sat on, although not for an exceptionally long time - there were no cushions for comfort or upholstery for aesthetics. It was, however, built for durability: thick wooden joists made it look heavy and exceptionally stable; the criss-cross of perfectly flush dovetail joints established the care and craftsmanship gone into its production; the thick glossy varnish meant that the blood could be easily wiped down and not stain the grain.

The blood belonged to the man who was securely tied to the chair. His arms were pulled round behind the chair back and handcuffed to the central joist. The way they had been forced behind his body meant, unless he was double-jointed, they must have been dislocated from his shoulders. Each ankle had been tied to a corresponding chair leg, his body had fallen forward and his bald forehead was inches from touching his bare knees. He was almost entirely covered with dirt, bruises or blood but not clothes. Deep lacerations striped across the meatier parts of his body and some of his smaller extremities seemed to be missing.

"Ouch," a soft female voice commented from the darkness. "That looked like it hurt."

"Fug yoo," the man spluttered; blood and saliva poured freely from his mouth over his lap.

"I'm surprised it took that long for a hacksaw to do that," she said.

He raised his face to the darkness beyond him and screamed, "FUG! YOO!" Despite the contorted nature of his face – a mixture of pain, anger and major reconstruction – it was unmistakably Morrison.

A shiny, black leather-clad leg stepped out of the shadow into the pool of light; the black Converse boot kicked a toe which rolled to a rest at his mangled foot. A second leg stepped forward, followed by the svelte torso of **THE CAT**, her laced bodice tied smartly up to her neck, her head sporting her retro-iconic goggle mask and antennae, across her knuckles were her characteristic taser claws. They sparkled menacingly in the dimness.

"I guess this little game of cat and mouse is finally over," she stated with a satisfied sigh.

"Warra yoo gonna do, huh?" he dared. "Leave me t'die? Kill me yershelf? You can't do that, yer a fugging 'supreme'!"

She stiffened in her pose and snarled, "You really have no idea what, or who, I am." She reached up behind her head and pulled at her mask.

Now his defiant expression changed to something closer to fear and intrigue. She had always fought so desperately to keep her identity secret from him; so much so that she even allowed that pain-in-the-arse sidekick robot of hers to kill itself[8]. They had been nemeses for so long, he thought he knew everything about her and this was completely against her normal behaviour which meant *all* expectations of normality went out the window hereafter.

She bent forward to cradle the mask from her face in the palms of her hands. Then she threw her head back, her wavy brown hair temporarily still obscuring her features. Then she stared at him.

His expression was difficult for her to read; six years of battling, of revelling in minor victories, of frustrating defeats, of careful plotting, of unbridled malevolence, of never really knowing why – finally revealed.

"Kafrine?" he gasped. "You? But how?"

"You were so arrogantly sure of yourself, weren't you? So sure that everything you ever did was perfectly thought out. You never did clean up your mess on the island but you never thought to check; it was always the strangest detail. That and you never recognised Mavis."

"That fugging robot?"

"And this mask," she rolled it around in her hands. "It hardly covers much of my face, does it. You were so blinded by your arrogance."

They stared at each other in contemplation. Years of conflict, finally coming to a resolution.

"I just wanted to be a thorn in your side, you know? Scratching up the furniture, hairball on the carpet, maybe the occasional crap on your bed. But then I found out – no, I saw what you orchestrated to get me to your island so you could experiment on me."

"It worked," he declared with jubilation.

"Too well," she growled. "I saw you with El Mij at the Refectory, talking about – boasting about my family[9]."

"But it worked."

"And it was then that I decided you needed to be put down; bagged and drowned like the disease ridden moggy you are."

"Kafrine, you can't... you're a hero. You don't -"

"I didn't," she admitted. "Never thought I could or would."

His wide eyes reflected the lethal sparkles of energy arcing between her knuckle claws as she brought them closer to his face; grim determination beset across her features.

"So I suppose, in a way," she mused, "you win."

---

[8] See: *Deaf in the Thalamus* mini-series - *Ed*
[9] Last month's revealing ish! - *Ed*

CHAPTER 8
THERE IS NO 'US' IN 'TEAM'

Sexual intercourse is a funny old thing.

There is the actual ridiculousness of the process, the miraculousness of the results and the hilariousness of the noises and faces made during. On top of all that is the truly bizarre manner in which one can, literally, be turned on or off like a switch; the slightest impetus can cause instantaneous moistness in the same way that flaccidity can ensue after an errant thought.

As soon as she had started dry humping him, he thought that it was all going to be over within the wink of his eye but, whether she had sensed his imminence or just wanted his eminence, she stopped to undress him. That was good, it gave him pause for thought – although most of his thoughts ran along the line of, *Oh, fucking hell, that's good*, interspersed with ruminations on the room's décor and how many ceiling tiles there were.

Then, when he checked again, he discovered she was naked without, seemingly, having to stop her manipulations and get undressed.

'Oh!' his eyes gasped.

'Em,' his morals hesitated.

'Gee!' his penis enthused.

Again, his experience of naked women had been limited to his previous girlfriend and a variety of two dimensional images and the trouble with those was always the knowledge that they were not actually 'real' women: Photoshopping, make-up and surgery were just a few of the elements that allowed him to distance himself from the exploitative nature of the photos. The real issue was, though, any sense of intimacy – when ignoring the voyeuristic effect of peeking through Windows – was limited by the screen size and, no matter how HD the resolution, those intricate details of imperfections were always going to be missing. Now, there were flesh tones, a spectrum of them defined by natural hues of melanin and shadows of the lights; lines of curves that he tried to follow with his eyes but felt, at times, that he might break his neck if he went too far; but it was the range of sensory information that nearly overloaded him: the smell of her perfumed hair, the delicate yet firm touch of her hands and weight of her body, the sound of her breathing.

"Your body is so cold," she commented.

"Bad circulation," he replied.

"There's nothing wrong with your circulation down here," she stated and stroked his erection. "Right, go and wash it."

There was the switch. "What?"

She dismounted him, rolling across the bed nimbly and sat on the edge. "Go and wash it," she ordered. "You've been running around in that sweaty outfit all day and I'm not going any nearer to it until you're clean."

The matter-of-fact attitude completely threw him off balance. It was a perfectly rational and reasonable instruction but was never something that cropped up in the middle of the 'instructional media' he was familiar with.

'Well hello, ma'am, I'm here to check your plumbing.'

'Oh mah goodness, and there's little me only in mah skimpy nightdress.'

'That's okay, ma'am, for I am not wearing any underwear beneath this boiler suit.'

ZZZZZIP. THWANG!

'Damn! That thing stinks like fishy cheese!'

'Well, I have been unblocking your neighbour's sceptic tank all morning!'

Even with the change in pace and the shower, nothing much seemed to affect the power of his ardour and he walked around the room with a handy place to hang his towel to dry. He had mused with the idea of purging his reserves while washing and relieving himself of some of the pressure – both psychological and physical – but was able to consider the implications of being caught in the act or overdoing it and being unable to perform at all. He had inhaled deeply, given himself a blast of absolute zero shower water and returned onto the battlefield.

Cat passed him in the doorway, deliberately brushing her body past his, arching her head back slightly so her lips caressed his face. "Don't start without me."

He slipped under the covers of the bed, supporting his head on his elbow and watched her blurry silhouette through the steam and condensaturated shower screen. Despite the lack of any specific detail, the way she moved around in the water, stroking her body with soap and rinsing the suds away was still incredibly emotional for him. He thought it should be erotic and more of a turn on, but it was actually making him slightly melancholic; a reminder of what he had recently lost; that security and comfort of someone being there. Gillian had been a constant in his life for so long, even though she had not been a physical constant, just the knowledge that she was there for him was the nicest feeling he had ever had. Of course, the actual awareness of the existence of that sensation had only really registered with him the moment it was gone: familiarity had bred complacency and absence had made his heart now wonder.

During his introspection, he had become completely unaware of Cat's progress; she was now standing in the doorway watching him with intrigue. "What are you thinking about?" she demanded incredulously.

"Ah, just... some stuff."

"Have I lost the moment?" she wondered aloud.

He smiled at her, lay back and threw the bed sheets open in a grand sweeping gesture, welcoming her into the comfort - and showing off his pride and joy. "No, you've actually made the moment even better."

There was a moment of hesitation; the expression on his face was one she had trouble reading accurately. She was expecting lust, nervousness and even a shade of fear but this looked more like an expression of sincere happiness. She had not been looked at like that for a very long time: the softness and affection in his eyes was troubling; unnerving; it took away her sense of control. She felt vulnerable and that was odd. And a little bit exciting.

Usually she would pounce on her prey, play around with him until he felt he could take no more, and then allow him his release; swiftly discarding his spent body after. This moment of uncertainty changed that plan and she – almost bashfully – approached the bed and laid down next to him; the chill of his body causing goose bumps to emerge over hers. She prepared for him to leap on top of her but, instead, he wrapped an arm under her waist and drew them closer together. Then (and this was the most disconcerting part) he inspected her face, tracing his hand across the contours of her forehead, brow and cheeks. His fingers delicately caressed the side of her neck, over her shoulder and drifted around to the nape of her back. She inhaled sharply as his fingernails discovered a sensitive spot; he retracted his hand only to repeat the path again and elicit an involuntary whimper from the back of her throat. It was not until she opened them that she realised she had closed her eyes to fully immerse herself in the sensation; she discovered he was watching her and smiling and she felt herself blush.

No! It was time to regain control of this and she rolled him forcefully onto his back.

"We don't have to do this, you know?" he said.

"Are you kidding me?"

"No. I mean, I want to. I *really* want to but we don't have to. We could, just... I don't know... cuddle, or something. Or talk and get to know each other better."

"You are just too cute for words," she cooed. "Are you trying to be my boyfriend?"

"I've never... you know," he stammered.

"You're a virgin?"

"A fuck virgin, yeah," he confessed. "I've never just fucked before."

"Oh, it's easy," she reassured and began to straddle him. "You just lie there and let me show you how it's done."

"But I don't think I want to just fuck."

"You will."

It was an intense blast of heat – that feeling of a hot bath after a cold day – a burning sensation that felt like it should be unbearable but needed to be overcome, fiery prickles that stabbed from the inside as numbness abated and circulation returns, the physical screams of protestation of a body having been put through one frozen torment to being subjected to another. All these things being focussed and isolated to his penis.

She, again, shuddered from the feeling of inserting a plunge-pool within her. His icy-coldness defining his slow entrance with more detailed articulation than ever she could remember. Every extra millimetre she took was felt in high sensory definition and it was not until her hips rested on his that she realised she had not been breathing throughout. She panted heavily, trying to regain composure and acclimatise to the temperature difference. Perhaps even warm him up a bit to meet her half way.

"'Bad circulation'?" she demanded incredulously and groaned with relief and ecstasy as she raised herself again.

Cameron could not reply. He was far too busy counting the ceiling tiles, making mental comparisons of the swirling patterns in each one, trying to calculate whether they were random scrawls or if they were identical and had simply been indiscriminately rotated. As the tight, moist heat encompassed his penis again, he managed to identify a bifurcated swirl - a bit like a fractal pattern - branching from one corner, swirling in a clockwise direction and delving into the next anticlockwise corner. He noted a slight flaw in the one of the arcs as her pelvis grinded against his; a short, intersecting, isolated line. It was this cross-hatch that he was able to spot in the next tile - she had altered her movement to a horizontal rocking rather than the vertical pounding - and accurately identify it in every other tile across the ceiling.

Despite these distraction tactics, the change in motion had intensified the friction across the glans and he could sense the end being nigh. He shut his eyes in the hope of being able to think about something else but all that did was cut out everything else apart from her gentle movement, the sensations it created and the sound of her gentle groans of pleasure. He reopened his eyes to watch her and saw that she was lost in the moment of the rapture: her eyes clamped shut, her head arched back and her mouth open, emitting occasional gasps and moans depending upon points of contact.

His imminence had past and was replaced by a feeling of pride. He was doing this; he was pleasuring this fucking awesome woman (even if he was actually just lying there with as much interaction as a dildo).

Not anymore.

He braced his palms on top of her thighs and, with her next pivot forwards, timed a gentle thrust up that allowed him the slightest iota of deeper penetration. But that mere millimetre of depth was enough to force her eyes wide open, groan languidly and overbalance her; she fell forward, catching herself by bracing her hands either side of his head, her face only an inch from his.

They stared at each other. A look of surprise passed between them; both shocked by the effect of his input: she was surprised that she could be moved so much by such an innocuous action and he was surprised that he was capable of achieving it.

He *was* capable of giving her real pleasure. Not like the frantic, flailing haphazard lovemaking he had experienced with his ex-girlfriend - which had been fantastic, at the time; *really* good sex - that seemed to rely on an almost 'hit and hope' ethos. In contrast, this performance was controlled, calculated and almost choreographed to the degree he had only ever witnessed in thirty-second episodes on his computer. And, with that epiphany, his priorities had changed: whereas they used to be to experience as much pleasure as possible, they had evolved to, three minutes ago, not to orgasm too quickly, to now, wanting to give as much pleasure as possible.

He had reclaimed some control and had become the master of his own sexual destiny. Well, as long as he could block out those incredibly sexy mewling noises she kept making. This was the epic crossover battle YOU demanded!

| TWO HOURS LATER... |

Cat groaned loudly and rolled off Cameron's body whilst he was in mid hump. His back remained arched for one tentative moment, his penis oscillated proudly, perhaps double checking the ceiling tile patterns. He flattened himself again and looked at her with a mix of concern and confusion. "Did you... er... You didn't, did you?" Again, the visions of how those mini-sagas played out usually ended with her screaming out the name of her creator of choice (premodified by a suitable taboo adjective), declaring her immediate plans for visitation. That or a face-full of jizz. Even his ex's inhibited exhalations inferred a definitive end but this had not displayed a change of pace, volume or intensity; she had just stopped.

She breathed heavily, slowly composing herself but stared blankly at the ceiling. Eventually, as her respiration normalised, she moistened her lips with her tongue, turned her head and smiled at him. "Don't worry about it," she said.

'Worry'? He had not been 'worried' per se, but now he was. What had he done wrong? He attempted to replay the movements and explorations and resulting whimpers but could not ascertain at what point things had not gone in the manner that they needed to. Even as he stared at her, her dilated pupils, flushed cheeks and deliciously sweat-moistened skin told him that she had enjoyed herself. What was there to worry about? "But you didn't come," he told her. "What did I -"

She pressed her index finger to his lips, pouted hers and said, "Shhhhhh. Trust me, you did absolutely nothing wrong. I'm the one who should be concerned that you weren't satisfied."

"I was trying to wait for you."

Her expression changed to a shade of honest surprise. "You are so sweet," she cooed, "but you would have had a long wait, I'm afraid."

"Why? Can't you... you know?"

He could see the hesitation in her face as her mind tried to work out a way to respond, whether she should respond at all. The confident smile slipped slightly and her eyes moistened as uncomfortable thoughts surfaced. She rolled over, turning her back to him, embracing herself with her arms.

"Cat?"

"It's nothing," she muttered. "It's stupid."

He may not have been experienced in the ways of woman but he did know that 'nothing' was not the same as 'stupid' and, that whatever the issue was, it had just escalated its seriousness within four words. The old Cameron was rearing his head, about to play his old trick of 'running away when confronted by something serious'. He contemplated saying, 'Okay then,' and getting dressed. That thought progressed to, 'It's fine if you don't want to talk about it,' with his own retaliatory back turning. There was even a considered moment of tried and tested 'take the piss to clear the tension' and he nearly came out with, 'I've seen some pretty fucked up shit in my time, how bad can it be?' He stopped himself when he remembered *The Crying Game* and the adage, 'Don't ask questions that you might not want to hear the answer to.'

All of that was a fleeting memory of another person, not the man he was trying to become; a hero. A hero does not run away and does not mock or humiliate their teammates. Certainly not the ones he might want another shot of putting his penis in. Hey! This New Man renaissance shit is baby-step stuff, okay?

He turned onto his side and moulded his body against her back – discretely tucking his erection between his thighs - wrapping his top arm around her waist to rest on her tummy and awkwardly pondering where to put his under arm. He used it to prop his head up high enough to comfortably nuzzle his mouth into the side of her neck. "You can talk to me," he told her.

"I've never had to," she replied. "He's usually finished and out the door long before I'm ever considered."

"I don't understand how you could possibly have any hang ups."

"Why? Because I'm a 'hero'?"

"Not that, because you are the most gorgeous woman I have ever met," he declared. "And I'm talking about a perfect blend of Rogue – and I mean Jim Lee's Rogue not Bob Wiacek's or that emo-pseudo-goth one off *Evolutions* – and Jean Grey, you know?" She had no idea. "Des Manders' Jean Grey who partially fulfils every geeky fan boys' fantasies. Mix in a bit of Jessica Drew pheromone and that's totally you! Uber sexual confidence with no sexual insecurities."

She turned her head to him so their cheeks touched. She looked at him from the corner of her eye and smiled bravely. "I'm sure that's really flattering and everything, but I'm far from perfect."

"Pfft," he snorted. "Not from where I'm lying."

"The thing is..." She bolstered her resolve with a deep breath. "I can't climax unless I'm watching."

Again, he allowed the words and a range of possible responses to rattle around in his brain applying meaning and possible consequences before having to settle on. "Can't you open your eyes?"

She barked a laugh that made him jump. "I don't mean... No, not watching you, watching me. God, this is embarrassing. I can only climax when I use my powers to watch myself having sex." She curled into herself even more and Cameron was silent. "You think I'm odd, right?"

It was his turn to laugh. "Hell no! I totally dig that. If I looked like you, I wouldn't be able to leave the room for wanting to check myself out in the mirror and get off on myself. If I had your power I would watch myself doing everything to myself and do myself while I was watching. It makes complete and utter sense."

Her foetal form unwound slightly but she watched him with caution to see if he was mocking her.

"What doesn't make sense -"

She tensed again.

"- is why you don't use your power to watch you doing it while we're doing it at the same time."

She relaxed. "I don't know. I've never spoken about it to anyone because I didn't want to come across as a pervert or something."

"But you were much more comfortable dancing the two-fingered tango in your room like a seedy peeping Tom?"

"I'm not entirely sure what all those things mean but I get the idea," she sneered. "No, it probably didn't help."

They stayed quiet and still, wrapped in arms and personal thoughts until Cameron decided the silence had gone on for too long. "Well?"

"Well what?"

"Do you want to make today the first day on your path to recovery?"

"I don't get you."

He adjusted his position and released his penis from between his legs; it sprung out like the arm of a trebuchet and slapped against her buttock. His eyebrows bounced on his forehead in a comedicly suggestive manner.

She turned to face him. "It really doesn't bother you?"

"As Oedipus once said to his mother, 'Now that's what I call a Freudian slip.'"

"You are so odd."

She grabbed his erection firmly and, while rolling onto her back, pulled him on top of her.

"You can't be ready already," he worried.

"This will only take a second," she replied and searched the air for ionic echoes to focus on; ones that she could trace back to see herself, naked, riding Cameron and lost in the throes of sexual ecstasy. "Oh my," she commented and, like a switch, was able to allow him unfettered access. She watched her thighs, like pistons, carefully controlling her vertical movement; her taught stomach, undulating with each horizontal shift; her breasts, heaving with each gasp of breath; her full-set lips parted, mouthing gasps and unintelligible words of wonder; her long-lashed eyes closed, losing herself in selfish pleasure. And amongst all of that, she could feel him inside her now replicating her shadow's experiences.

A movement behind her erotic echo distracted her. It was the opposite side of the room to the closed window so had nothing to do with innocent drafts or curtains. It was too difficult to isolate the image from this angle but there it was again, another shift from the darkened corner of the room. She hauled herself out from beneath Cameron.

"You want to change position already?" he enquired.

"No, there's someone in here," she hissed.

He scanned the room, specifically focusing on the corner she was staring at but could see no one. And now that her racing heart had calmed and the sensory inundation of hormone, heat and circulating blood had waned, he could clearly smell that there were no other living creatures in the room. "I can't -"

"Was," she interrupted. "Was in here but I can't quite see."

Cat crawled across the bed, through the vision of humpiness and, despite her anxious state and his attempts to reform, Cameron could not help but ogle the view.

She approached the corner and inspected the shaded figure, pausing the image and turning her head to view it from every angle.

"You look like a nutter," Cameron commented.

"I can't see his face," she confessed. "It's completely masked."

"How do you know it's a he?"

"The huge erection."

She allowed the scene to continue playing, as the bodies on the bed bounced around, the mysterious man's hands disappeared into his trousers and rummaged around. She quickened the pace until his hands re-emerged and he wiped them on his thighs. At that point, her exhausted image hauled herself from her ride and the figure swiftly darted out of the room, silently drawing the door to a close behind him.

"It must be the killer," she deduced. "He had come to get me but you being here stopped him." She reached to the floor and picked up her cat brooch. "I've got to go after him before the trail gets too distorted."

"Wait for me to get my kit on," Cameron instructed. "Where the fuck did you throw my pants?"

As he searched around, Cat was already striding purposefully towards the door, her nakedness slowly being obscured by a lustrous black liquid flowing up her body, adhering to her flesh. By the time she had crossed the room and reached the door, her costume had returned to its full sveltish, sylph-like glory including accessories and boots.

Cameron, however, was still scrabbling around under the bed for his errant underwear. "Cat! Wait! Don't go out there alone. This fucker's dangerous." But his calls of warning fell upon nothing more than the back of the closed door.

The shrouded figure walked casually along the hallway, understandably oblivious to being followed so closely an hour later. When he reached the elevator, he decided to turn and use the stairwell, bouncing down each step with the calm confidence of someone assured of their privacy; sometimes jumping two steps at a time as if imitating a self-gratifying game of hopscotch. Every now and again, Cat would pause his movement in the hope of catching a glimpse of facial detail but his coverings remained secure despite each jolting movement.

After descending two storeys, the man entered the floor's corridor and approached one of the rooms half way along. He retrieved a card from inside his jacket, inserted it into the door's lock and entered, closing the door behind him.

Cat hesitated at the door. There was a chance that he was still in the room and, if that was the case, then she really should get back-up. But if she left here, then he could quite easily slip away again. She searched around the echoes until an overlaid image of the door pulled open again, the man poked his still covered head into the corridor, checked both directions then walked back to the stairwell.

Decision made. No time to wait. There was no telling how long she would be able to sustain the readable echoes; not since her 'encounter' with Magneficent[10].

She produced her Digicard from a thigh pocket and slotted the clear, credit card sized microprocessor into the door lock. It shimmered its customary light blue as it successfully decrypted the low-level security measures. The door unlocked with a gentle click and she let herself in, focusing her sight on the blurred overlaid images of the man entering and exiting the room. She isolated the blurrier, older traces and closed the door of the Schrödinger Suite behind her.

Inside, she watched as the figure placed an object into a dark metallic, head-sized box, which had been placed in the centre of the room. He then walked

---

[10] *The Clandestine Cat #141* – Her reading has been affected by Magneficent's Fluxuator Beam.

over to the wall adjacent to the door and pressed a button on a small device attached to a glass bottle.

With overwhelming curiosity, she approached the container.

Cameron was still buttoning his flies as he ran along the hall. He stopped at the Socrates Rooms, hammered unceremoniously on the door and did not stop even when he heard the rattling of the lock on the other side.

The door opened as far as the security latch would allow it and Floater pressed her head to it. "What?"

The moment distracted him. "You've got the strongest man in the world behind there and you need to put the chain on?"

Floater did not allow herself to get dragged in. "What do you want?"

"Cat saw him," he stated. "He's here, in the hotel. She ran off to follow him."

"Okay," she said slowly as her brain absorbed the details and formulated her next move. "Do you know where she is?"

"No, but I can find her."

"Get Daniel while I get us ready," she instructed. "Meet us back here." She closed the door without waiting for a response so he had to satisfy his obstinacy with a barely audible grumble along the hall then a spleen-vent at Cassandra when she opened her room door.

"Why the fuck are you having a go at me?" she demanded.

"You're here," he replied and she snarled at him. "Get the Boy Blunder up, our killer's shown up."

Tights were quickly hoisted, masks adhered and girths loined.

"You look like such a tit," Cameron commented.

"Fuck off," Danny hissed groggily from under his breath.

Cameron widened his eyes with pretend shock and slapped his hand over his gaping mouth. "You defied the code!" he accused. "Um, I'm telling," and proceeded to run along the corridor towards Bob's room.

Danny chased after him, arms outstretched and cape flapping in his wake, demanding, "Don't you dare, Cameron!" and Cassandra jogged behind as demurely as her physique would allow, calling, "Just leave it, Danny! He's winding you up."

The others had collated by the time the youngsters got there. Boy was pale, dishevelled and bleary-eyed (supposedly from having been roused from sleep). His scarf was off centre and his hat on backwards. Bob was quiet and looked disconcerted, standing at the back of the group. Floater had changed altogether. The only flesh visible was on her hands and her face. The thigh length boots remained but they now accessorised a complete light-blue body suit. Her technology encompassed her torso and a pair of white hot pants slightly masked the contours of her pudenda and backside.

Before they set off, there was a moment of hesitation and confusion.

"Are we missing someone?" Bob queried.

"No... I don't think so," Floater replied unconvincingly.

"Only the dead ones," Cameron muttered under his breath.

"You said you would be able to find her," Floater reminded him with a look in her eyes that clearly indicated his comment had not been under his breath enough. "Where is she?"

"You have telepathy too?" Boy Sprout asked with unreserved awe.

"Biopathy," Cameron replied and his face slipped into a bizarrely ugly expression. His eyes rolled up into their sockets, his jaw dropped open and jutted to one side, his tongue lolled to the other, his head fell backwards.

The three senior supremes took a step back in equal measures of shock and revulsion. Danny shook his head with disgust and turned to Cassandra. "He's making it worse, I swear. He never used to look that goofy."

"What's he doing?" Boy Sprout asked with a heavy tinge of 'I'm not sure I want to hear an answer but...'

"Apparently," Danny sighed...

Being the manner of creature that he was came with a variety of gifts and curses and, despite what any moralistic role model might imply, some of his paranormal attributes truly were a curse. The ability to absorb the psyche and abilities of others may mean you were unable to have flesh on flesh contact with anyone ever again but then that's why versatile costumes composed of unstable molecules were invented. Having the physique of a brick wall built by a drunk monkey might make you unapproachable in social situations but at least it meant you could get rid of Jehovah's Witnesses without having to lie about being directly descended from Satan himself. Having to top up your existence and maintain rational control of an otherwise rampant, homicidal and bestial body on the blood of humans was a downer no matter what angle you looked at it from. Apart from the Jehovah's thing again. But getting rid of the bodies could get inconvenient. And it was always a bit embarrassing when guests found dismembered fingers that had slipped between the cushions of the sofa. Anyway, with a degree of self-reflection and self-awareness, he was able to semi-control his dependencies and live with them. What it did give him, though, was a marked sensitivity to be able to search out potential prey simply by sensing his immediate vicinity. Just like a shark can detect a millilitre of blood in a thousand litres of water, Cameron could pinpoint a viable heartbeat within a very loud death metal gig.

His 'radar', if you like, stretched through the hotel, past the ethereal dazzling paralife forms of his latest compatriots, through the rooms around him, defining the calm pulses of slumbering guests, belaying the temptation to hang around the frenetic respiratory patterns of the couple in the floor above, but resting on the dwindling life form of a solitary being two floors below.

Within one movement and no explanation, he snapped back to 'normal' and ran to the stairwell, dangerously descending the steps, bouncing off walls to aid his progression, slamming through doors without care or consideration of the sleeping patrons around him, crashing into the suite to find Cat's convulsing body, her face already painted with death's pallor, eyes staring glassily at the ceiling, lips blue, mouth expelling ghastly barks of breath through the bilious froth that oozed out.

How should he deal with this? It was that hypothetical split second decision made real and he needed a millisecond epiphany. She was dead, that was certain, but she did not have to be. He liked her, she seemed to like him; was this that time when he made himself a life partner, a like form, someone to share everything with?

There was more though: an open box at her side, a shattered phial against the wall, a strange smell that reminded him of birthday cakes, the imminent arrival of the others.

Decision made.

He darted to the door just as Bob made his presence known from the end of the corridor. "Don't come in," he bellowed as he slammed it shut. By the time he returned to Cat's side, she was completely dead.

He could not do it. He could not turn her. Not because it might have meant the supremes could have been exposed to whatever poison had killed her, nor was it because of some cliché that he liked her too much to subject her to the same cursed life he lived. It was because he had been scared. Someone had told him that there would come a time when he would change a human into a vampire purely because he wanted to and that selfish instinct would send him down a road of evil. In that split-second, Cameron could not be one hundred per cent sure that he would not just be turning Cat simply because he had not come yet. That thought alone scared him to the very core of his being.

"Dude!" Danny called.

"She's dead," Cameron shouted back. "There's some sort of poison in here. Smells like marzipan."

"Probably hydrocyanic acid," Floater stated loudly.

"Some sort of trap that she set off." He allowed his body to flop down on the floor next to hers and spooned in to her side. He thought about crying but could not quite build the emotion. He could, however, feel very, very angry.

They waited outside of the room in different states of despair. Cassandra had pulled Danny to one side to allow the more personally affected their space. He, in turn, kept listening to the door to check on Cameron's well being. He would occasionally tap on the door and gently call his name but never received much of a response. The odd, muffled swear word and shattering of furniture would satisfy his peace of mind enough.

Floater and Bob were standing to one side of the landing. Her eyes were puffy and red. Every now and again, she would turn away from him and burst into tears. He would reach out but either retract his hand before contact or find that she was beyond his reach. He would hang his head until she came back to him with hushed but urgent words and meaningless yet impassioned gesticulations.

Boy was sitting on the opposite side. His knees were drawn up to his chest and he held them in place with his arms wrapped tightly around them. His head was tucked in and he gently rocked himself. His hat rested precipitously on top of his head and his eye mask had been discarded to the side of him. "Bob?" he called from within his cocoon.

Bob had not heard. He had finally built the courage to lay a hand on Floater's shoulder only to have her shirk it off.

"Bob?" he tried a little louder and raised his head. "Bob!"

"What is it, Boy?"

"I don't feel too good," he informed.

"I know," Bob responded dismissively. "It's very upsetting, Boy, but we'll get through this." He returned his attention to Floater.

Danny stopped checking on Cameron and crouched to Boy's side. "What's up, buddy? This is all getting to much for you?"

"I don't feel well, Danny," he replied. "Really not well. Not just upset but really sick. I think it must have been something I ate."

"But I ate what you ate and I feel fine," Danny stated. "A bit more farty than usual, but -"

Now that his face was fully visible, and his hat had fallen backwards, Danny could see that Boy was covered with heavy perspiration. His skin was deathly pale, his lips were a light purple and the bruising around his eyes was broad and dark.

"Shit!" Danny diagnosed.

"It feels like I'm on fire," Boy said. "My whole body is burning."

"Floater, he needs help," Danny called.

He got out of the way when she came forward. She pressed her hand against his forehead and soothed, "It's okay, William, we'll get you to a doctor and everything will be okay."

"Okay," he stuttered and nodded weakly.

She pulled her hand away and he whimpered.

At first, she thought the heat or placement of her hand had left an impression on his forehead: an almost perfect handprint. But then the redness of the shadow trickled across the boundary, over his brow and into the well of his eye. She looked again. There was not a blur of colour between the two states but a definitive line, a physical barrier where the edge of his skin was raised slightly as if having been ripped. She looked at her hand and, sure enough, the surface of his forehead was lining the surface of her hand. Her immediate reaction was one of panic and revulsion. She flapped her hand to remove the offending membrane and it slapped to the floor like a half-cooked pancake. If that pancake had been enhanced with red food colouring and strands of cat hair.

Four people stared at Boy with horror; Boy stared at the sliver of road kill with dazed confusion. "What's that," he asked while wiping the dribble from his eye. He caught sight of the redness on the back of his hand before anyone could come to enough sense to intervene or offer a diplomatic answer. "Is that my blood?" he stammered and traced the trail up to the stinging sensation above. His fingertips detected the different sponginess of flesh with no covering and pressed into the exposed area, sinking deeper than they should have been able to.

"Don't do that dude," Danny advised.

Boy scooped his fingers. "What is this?" The deeper levels of epidermis came away with his ministrations to briefly reveal a hardened whiteness that was then obscured by free flowing blood. The torrent poured into his eyes and blinded him. "What's happening to me?" he squealed and started pulling himself to his feet. His hands went to clear the obstruction but, as he wiped, he removed liquid and solid. The skin peeled from his face from the tips of his cheekbones, across his eyelids, to the underside of his eyebrows. For a moment, his unencumbered orbs shone brightly through a crimson mask, then the blood seeped forth with renewed vigour, washing over his agitated eyes as they searched for reason and assistance.

Still, they did nothing but watch as if it events that followed were inevitable.

The noise that projected from Boy's throat was high-pitched and drawn out; a baby's screams of unrelenting frustration. He wiped again, sinking fingers into muscle, dipping into sockets, pulling chunks of himself away with as much resistance as freshly fallen snow. Cheeks had been scraped away and the thaw seeped into his mouth, gurgling and frothing with the expulsion of his pained anguish.

It stopped.

The onlookers stepped back.

"GET THEM OUT!" Boy bellowed. His fingers scrabbled at his shirt, ripping it open and pinging the buttons into his audience. He wrenched at the extra-terrestrial material and, at first, it simply stretched and retracted at his manipulations. Then, as if having been weakened or finally acknowledging his intentions, it splayed itself apart, bearing his skin below.

Did his hands know they had achieved their goal? No one would ever know. His fingers pulled his abdomen open like silk curtains on a summer's morning and the sunshine poured forth, awashing the room and all within with its glory.

Boy's body crumpled to the floor like a wet Jenga tower: a clattering of bones, a scattering of bits and an almighty cry of pent up frustration. His clothes gently rippled as his body melted into the floor; a circle of brown mulch dilated across the carpet.

The door to the Schrödinger Suite opened violently and Cameron stormed out, his face beset with angered determination. That expression quickly changed when he saw his four cohorts opposite him, covered in, what looked like, swamp water.

Floater looked at her hands and screamed; Bob collapsed to the floor in a dead faint; Cassandra panted heavily, trying to breathe without inhaling anything; Danny acknowledged Cameron's presence with a blank stare.

"He exploded," he muttered. "He pulled himself open and exploded."

"Who?"

"Boy." Danny pointed at the puddle of uniform,

"Fuck me," Cameron essayed. "Who is doing this, Floater? Floater? **FLOATER!**"

The last one managed to break through her hysteria. "I don't know. No one. All of them. Someone new."

"Great. Call your clean up guys and get yourselves cleaned up," Cameron instructed. "I've got a couple of things to follow up and we'll meet up later."

Floater tried to pick Bob up but he was completely limp. She calibrated her technology, which enabled her to levitate him a foot and drag him towards the stairwell.

Danny pulled Cameron to one side. "What are you going to do?"

"Hotel register," Cameron said. "Then I'm going to call in some support."

"Be careful, man," Danny warned. "Whoever this guy is, he's really dangerous."

"So am I," Cameron replied without a trace of humour. "You go careful," he continued. "You two might be a target too."

"We need to go," Cassandra ordered and gave her boyfriend a shove. "I smell like rancid Christmas dinner."

They parted ways; Cameron descended to the hotel lobby just as the black vans pulled up outside. A handful of agents trotted in, making a beeline to the stairs and he could not help but notice the industrial carpet cleaning equipment they had brought. He approached the reception and a gnarly, aged man behind the counter stood to greet him.

He must have been in his late seventies. His white hair was abundant, ran the spectrum of shades from grey to white and was slicked back from his forehead. A neatly trimmed moustache decorated his top lip and pair of large-framed glasses filled the middle third of his face. An askew nametag told Cameron his name was Stanley and he would be happy to help. "What happened this time?" he growled.

"Two people just got murdered."

The man's eyes widened. "People?"

"My friends."

His eyes relaxed again. "Oh, thank god for that," he sighed. "I thought you meant people people."

Cameron frowned and contemplated smashing his face in. "One of them was... a really close friend."

The man raised his hands defensively. "Hey, sure, sorry about that but usually it's the people people who end up being the victims when you people are about. You signed up for it, they didn't. That's all I'm saying."

He wanted to argue about the whole 'signing up' issue. Was it not the case that abilities had been forced upon him and he was just doing what he thought was right? Would it not be more irresponsible of him to not use his powers and try to ignore them? Where was his choice? Gillian had told him he had to help people; Danny had told him he should join the team; his mum told him he would always do the right thing.

But just because he was told did not mean he had to.

"I suppose," he responded. "I need to see who took the Schrödinger room." Cameron knew films. He knew how it worked – privacy rights, company policies and personal principles – and he knew that he had to try the direct route first before he had to apply any powers of persuasion or coercion.

"Okay," Stanley said and turned his computer screen to an angle so they could both see the results of his ministrations. "Ha!" he barked upon seeing the result. "First time customer. Paid in cash but paid more to specifically get that room (looks like we had to move some folks around what with being fully booked). Booked a week ago."

There was something familiar about the name but Cameron could not put his finger on it.

"Is there anything to link him to any other rooms?"

He scrolled through the page and scanned the notes before him. "He got a business card sent up to the Heidegger room last night."

"Who's in there?"

"Now that is odd," the man commented. "No one. The previous occupants checked out this morning but no one had booked the room before your lot."

"So?"

"System says we're fully booked."

The man continued to stare at the screen while tapping at the keyboard and clicking the mouse buttons. Cameron watched the expressions on his face scrunch up with consternation then stretch out with awe. "How strange," he ruminated. "I've looked back and every time your lot have stayed, that room has been empty for that exact duration."

"Give me a key to the room," Cameron instructed and, without hesitation, Stanley imprinted a security card for him.

Cameron paused outside the room and listened carefully. There was a muffled hum of a hoover in operation from the floor above him but, otherwise, the hotel was silent. He scanned the room and, disappointed to detect nothing, inserted the key card into the door. A small green light illuminated his permission to enter and he turned the handle, pushing the door open with his shoulder.

Upon entering, his foot clipped against a white business card with the suspect's name on but nothing else: no phone number, no address, no occupation. Just a name. He flicked the main light on after discovering which switches did the bathroom and entrance hall. He wandered around inspecting each section of the room. It had all been freshly cleaned, with towels and bedding having been replaced. He lifted the mattress, checked under the bed and even flipped through the pages of the Gideon Bible but nothing stood out, nothing seemed out of place, nothing came to light.

He walked to the main window and looked out into the darkness. With two fingers, he pulled the lace curtain slightly aside to peer through without the Gaussian interference. The streets were illuminated but empty: no shadowy figure watching from under a single, lit streetlight; no suspicious looking shadows in the windows of the parked cars. The only thing that gave Cameron any sense of Chandleresque satisfaction was the flashing pink and blue neon light from the strip joint opposite.

He dropped onto the bed with the holy book still in his hands. "It's been a tough day," he said to its cover. "One of those days when the whole world is against you and all you want to do is hit the Jack, drink a month away and hope everything's sorted when you wake up. The kind of day that warned you it was going to be bad but you didn't listen. You kept your coat on inside the house. You chose to wear those brand new shoes despite how much walking you were going to do. You didn't even bring an umbrella, just in case. The kind of day that makes you ask questions but never gives any answers and you don't know whether it's because it doesn't know the answers, is ignoring you or thinks you're being rhetorical."

There was an indignant ruffle of feathers.

"Well, you won't find any effing answers in there," an eloquent male voice responded from the silence.

"Are you always here?" Cameron demanded without looking up.

"Of a sorts."

"Were you... there?" He raised his head at the last word and beheld the vision before him.

It was a living Michelangelo statue. Taught blonde curls framed its unblemished, symmetrical face. Its bone and muscular structure were vividly defined by the smooth skin that radiated purity from every inch of its eight-foot, naked body. It was an 'it' because its pelvic region was as ornate as an Action Man's. As if its appearance was not overwhelming enough, from behind its broad shoulders arose a pair of pristine wings: silken feathers adorned them from the peaks that just missed the ceiling tiles to the tips that brushed against the carpet.

"What? When you were schtupping like a rampant warthog? No. Didn't see a thing," Angel replied.

"I mean, at the end," Cameron reiterated through gritted teeth.

Angel paused before responding. "Yes. I was there. She was a good woman."

"Do you think I did the right thing?"

"Not turning her into a blood-thirsty, unrelenting monster like yourself? Let me think about that for a second..."

"Fuck you, you pious mother-fucker."

"Mm-hm, that's right. It seems that anybody around here who has some semblance of principles is an aloof, holier-than-thou motor flocker," Angel observed and tripped over the last two words.

"I've got principles," Cameron argued, "I just choose not to ram them down other people's throats."

"How noble of you."

They just watched each other for a moment. Neither of them wanted the other there but they had been foisted upon each other - they were each other's punishment - and just had to put up with it.

"How come you didn't see him in the room?" Cameron asked calmly.

Angel's wings bristled slightly and found something else in the room to attract its attention. "I - er - didn't see him because..."

Realisation struck Cameron like an optic blast. "You did it again!" he stated. "You left the room because of your delicate sensibilities and someone died because of it."

There was an inkling of embarrassment. A smidge of humility. All of which got twisted into a mass of indignation. "Maybe it has more to do with who you stick your thingy in than me giving you some f'kin' privacy."

"What is your purpose, exactly?" Cameron demanded. "Watcher? Guardian? Penance?"

Angel spun around and jabbed a perfectly manicured finger at him. "Divine intervention costs, Mortice," it told him. "It's all about balance. You saw what can happen when the spiritual scales get tipped. If you want me to get involved, you had better be prepared to live with the consequences?"

"None of this makes sense and I need something to direct me," Cameron confessed. "I cannot let this son of a bitch kill my friends. I have to do something but I don't know what." He could not work out whether Angel was looking down on him with disdain, contemplation or respect.

"F'fu-," it sighed. "Okay. But don't blame me if there are repercussions."

It thrust its arms out and its wings followed suit, stretching the entire width of the double twin room, knocking the wall mounted, thirteen inch TV out of its bracket on one side and managing to dislodge the trouser press from the open closet at the other. Its marble skin began to glow with a reflected radiance; an energy source from somewhere was irradiating its flesh.

Cameron shielded his eyes. Not because the brilliance was hurting his retina but because the essence of holy purity was making him feel nauseous. It was very much like walking past a *Lush* store on the high street: the first fruity breath was quite pleasant, the second makes you want to retch.

Arching its head backwards, it bathed in the ecclesiastical transmissions, glorifying in its reconnection with its seraphic network after having been disconnected for so long. Whether it was doing exactly what it had intended or had got distracted checking its messages, eventually it logged off and resumed its virtuous renaissance stance.

"Something does not add up," Angel reported and pre-emptively raised a hand to prevent any cynical retort. "Literally, something doesn't add up. The maths is not right."

Cameron frowned and allowed the numbers to roll around in his head. "This room, the times when they stay, this man." He raised the business card and read, "This 'Des Carts' feller. Why is the room empty whenever they stay? Are Bob or Floater making up extra people? Some sort of super-scam, fixing the books and pocketing the skimmings? But what money is to be made here? And why kill the others? Was that all?"

"Yes," Angel replied. "My contacts on the other side are somewhat limited and those who will talk to me are reticent to offer much information for fear of initiating a huge imbalance and it coming back to implicate them."

"So, all I have to go on is that the maths don't add up,"

It was an utter dead end. There was no impetus, no driving force and no obscure clue that could direct him to the next step. Films and books would have had a cigarette butt to extract DNA from; a video to watch slowly and enhance... enhance... enhance: there, in the reflection of that man's sunglasses – the butler?! Perhaps even a new key witness to interview but there was nowhere to go from here.

He could interrogate the last two heroes but what could he ask them? 'Did you kill your teammates? No? Are you sure?' There were not any sneaky sideline questions he could think of to try to trip them up. No continuity errors in their alibis with which to use against them. No possible motive to pin to them.

The fibres of the beige carpet held nothing. It was times like these – when it looked like there was nowhere to go – that something would happen to progress the narrative.

Still nothing.

Angels were quite patient creatures by nature. Fallen ones were not. "For the love of...!" it wailed. "Why do you keep staring at things? Why aren't you doing something?"

"I'm looking for clues!"

Angel followed the boy's line of sight. "A wonky picture frame?" it observed. "Or the crude, oil painting of the bowl of fruit? You've got to stop being so reactive and, ultimately, start being proactive. Go find the next clue; don't hope it's just going to stumble into your lap."

Usually, the sidekick would offer some words of wisdom or encouragement from which the detective would divine a link or code.

"Fruit," Cameron repeated to himself. "Stumble. Crude oil?"

Nothing.

Sometimes – depending on the weakness of the narrative – something entirely random and completely disassociated with the characters or plot points would happen just to drive the protagonist to another set piece and thereby interact with the next antagonist.

The room windows shattered simultaneously as solid shadows careened into the room then bounced and rebounded off every surface and wall. The desk burst into shrapnel splinters and complimentary letter-headed stationary; the mini-fridge was wrenched free of its housing, barraging the room with tiny sized bottles and overpriced chocolate bars; the bedcovers took to the air like ghosts suddenly realizing their alarms had not gone off.

Cameron, still sat on the end of the bed, had anchored the covers so they whipped over and covered him before he had time to react. Now that he did react from the sound, dynamics and smothering, he only managed to entangle himself more within the linen lattice. Without sight, all he could ascertain of the events around him was from his other senses' acuities. There was the sound of continued destruction: things were being broken and bounced against, which also included himself. Trying to unwind his self was becoming increasingly more difficult while being hammered off balance from every angle. There was also the sound of shrieking: high-pitched, piercing, animalistic screams that assaulted him from every corner of the room adding further giddiness to his confusion. Amidst that, were occasional high-pitched, piercing angelic screams of utter mortification. At least that gave him a fixed point of origin to get his bearings from.

There were a variety of physical assaults. There were the large, forceful blows that sent him reeling, which he presumed were from the ricocheting balls of blackness. There were sharp, penetrating stings that ripped through the sheets and stabbed into his flesh: the shattered glass? Then there were smaller, softer – almost negligible – thuds that, when analysed, left a moist warmth at their points of impact that he did not give much mind to.

Then, there was a building aroma. At least, it started as an aroma – earthy, forresty – which escalated to a smell – wet dog – and peaked at a stink – shit.

Another sharpness ripped through the bedding and embedded into the back of his hand. There was light at the end of the flannel blanket, through which he thrust his hands and tore the cotton shackles asunder. He cast the remnants aside and bellowed his frustration at his assailants.

Who were no longer there.

The room had been atomised. Every surface, every loose fitting and fixture (and a few fixed ones) had been scratched, dislodged and demolished. Feathers and dust motes danced around each other in the recurrent flashes of neon light that permeated the scene from outside. The shreds of curtains rippled in the intrusive breeze like tired strippers at the end of their shift, languidly flicking their limbs and gyrating their bodies with indifference and fatigue. And, again, there was nothing outside: no screech of tyres, no thundering of footprints, no body.

He returned his attention back into the room to see Angel huddled in a protective ball in the corner of the room.

"What the fuck?" Cameron roared at it.

"It was insane," Angel whimpered from behind its wings that gave off an almost mottled appearance in this light. "It was incessant; they just kept throwing and screaming and leaping and scratching and -"

"Who?"

Angel stopped. His wings parted to disclose his face: the perfection marred by darkened blotches. "Ninjas," it said.

Cameron waited for the punchline but nothing followed. He looked around the room again to see smeared patches across every surface and intermittent glinting shards, protruding like the ragged nails of a beaten hooker. He turned his attention to the burning pain in the back of his hand to be confronted by a shuriken.

"Ninjas?" Cameron questioned and plucked the star from his limb, wincing at the pain of the extraction.

"Ninja monkeys," Angel elaborated.

Cameron's mind started putting the pieces together: size + shrieking + colour + smell = monkeys.

"So that shit smell is actually shit, then," he deduced. "Their shit."

"And they were f'king throwing it everywhere!" Angel freaked. "Dirty little 'sterds."

Cameron returned to the window and looked out over the rooftops of the dirty city. The darkness was more than just night, it was the shade of the souls of the scum and villainous who resided there; it was the corrupt nature of their being that made this place irredeemable. It was their unrepentant actions that meant even when the brightness of day came, the darkness would eventually consume it faster than a Christian crack-head on smack after Lent.

"Is that supposed to fucking help?" Cameron shouted into the night. "Cos it fucking doesn't!"

"Shut up!" the night shouted back. "It's four in the fucking morning, you arsehole!"

"Well?" Stanley enquired when Cameron pushed the key card across the reception desk to him.

"Erm, you might want to send housekeeping up there again," Cameron replied. "There's been... an incident."

"Unglaublich," Stanley huffed and picked up the phone. "What did you do?"

"Me? Nothing!"

"That's right." He jabbed his finger viciously at the buttons. "It's never you, is it? Things just happen, don't they? Trouble always seems to come looking for you lot."

"Apparently," Cameron muttered.

"Yeah, hi Linda, it's Stanley at the desk. Can you send someone up to Heidegger again, please: incursion. What is she expecting?"

It took a moment for Cameron to realise this last question was directed at him. "Broken stuff and..."

"Cosmetic damage, yeah," Stanley relayed. "Structural?" at Cameron.

"No. Oh, er, the windows but there's also..."

"Dimensional rupture? Netherworldly discharge? Extra-terrestrial debris?"

"Monkey shit."

Stanley stared. "You heard that right, yeah. Thanks Linda. You're a wonder." He placed the phone back on to its receiver without removing his gaze. "Monkeys?"

Cameron nodded.

"Ninjas?"

Cameron faltered; his brain trying to process this crossover of reality and fucking ridiculous and on what side of the line Stanley sat. "You know them?"

"I know of them. They've been before," he snarled. "Dirty little beggars."

This was it! This was the connection he needed; that seemingly innocuous link that could put all the pieces together. Stanley was that extra eyewitness account, he was that piece of previously passed over evidence, he was those prophetic words of wisdom. He was 'the man'.

"Who? What? When? Where? Why?" Cameron blurted in his eagerness.

"No idea," Stanley answered with a shrug. "They come, throw their shit, then disappear back into the night like ethereal spectres, dissipating into the wind."

"But you know stuff, right?" Cameron continued. "Know things about these people? Know names?"

Stanley eyed him with suspicion. "What do you mean, 'these people'? They're your people, aren't they?"

"No," Cameron replied defensively. "I'm just along for the ride."

"Side-kick?"

"Fuck off!"

Stanley nodded with deep understanding. "Ah, lone-wolf vigilante."

He did not want to be a label, he wanted to be him, but that classification did seem to sum him up perfectly. He wanted to argue the point in an attempt to convince himself that it was not him, that he was more than another generic element; he *was* unique, he *was* special, he was Cameron Fucking Mortice.

"Never heard of you," Stanley said.

"It doesn't matter. Who do you know – in their world –" He jabbed his thumb over his shoulder to indicate his disaffiliation even though he was indication the front door and a wino stumbling past. "- who has Ninja monkeys, wants to kill them and actually would?"

Stanley leaned back in his seat and stared at his computer screen. "Monkeys? There are a few might use something like that but they're all based in Africa and only use them to usurp governmental leadership. And they're not Ninjas. Perhaps the world domineering, religious zealot group, *Hands Around The Earth*? But they'd be more likely to train door-to-door leafleting monkeys."

Cameron's eagerness was quickly mutating into impatience as his fingers drummed on the desk.

"I could give you plenty of names for one or a combination of a couple of those parameters," Stanley finally confessed and Cameron's body deflated with defeat, "but only one name comes to mind for everything." Despite the positive conclusion, Stanley's face gave the appearance of severe disappointment.

"And? What? Who?" Cameron urged.

"Well, he's been Thoroughly Locked Away in maximum security for eternity," Stanley said. "He's never getting out of this maximum security penitentiary... unless someone helps him escape."

"From Barker Asylum?" Cameron suggested.

"That's right," Stanley concurred with a tone of surprise. "You've heard of it, then?"

"Who's the nutter with the monkeys?"

"Well, it's only speculation," Stanley retracted, "but the only one I can think of that would come up with something as bizarre as poo flinging Ninja monkeys is..." Stanley leaned forward and looked around the foyer for potential eavesdroppers.

...

...

"Yes?"

"His name cannot be said," Stanley concluded gravely and sat back with a grim expression of profound understanding.

The impact was effective; Cameron recoiled slightly, eyes wide, and looked around him for those who might be listening in. "Why? Does it summon him? Or curse those who dare utter his name?"

"No. Literally. His name cannot be said," Stanley replied and broke the tension like faster than Wonder Woman did Max Lord's neck. He grabbed a piece of paper, scribbled on it, then passed it across the counter. "Say that."

Cameron read it and soundlessly formed digraphs and diphthongs with his mouth. Eventually, he attempted, "Mmmmirrdin? Mur... Murd-din?"

"See? Cannot be said," Stanley restated. "The closest anyone has got is to suggest it's pronounced, 'Mirthin.'"

Cameron stared at the writing again with disbelief. "How can a double 'd' make a 'th' sound?"

"Welsh."

"Ah."

"Myrddin the Mighty," Stanley proclaimed. "Master of the Mystic."

"And where might I find him?"

"Two possible places," Stanley replied without hesitation. "There's a secret hideout at 179 Shaftesbury Avenue..." He checked his watch. "But there won't be anyone there at this time in the morning. You'll want to try *The Caped Crusader* up Kent's Passage," Stanley told him. "It's the local hang-out for your type when they're off duty."

"I don't like the way you keep saying that, Stanley," Cameron said grimly. "It smacks of persecution."

Stanley raised his hands defensively. "It's not a gay bar; I wasn't saying you're gay... or that you're not. It's where all the metahumans hang out and pretend to be normal."

"'Normal'? Really? That's the language of hate, Stanley, right there and, it's so subtle, you don't even know you're doing it," Cameron informed him and began to walk away. "Shame on you, Stanley. Shame on you."

Walking back to the heroes' room was like the lead up to meeting with an ex-lover you just dumped: there was too much bad feeling, you know there are going to be more acerbic words but, dammit, you need to get your *Best of Huey Lewis and The News* album back.

Cameron rehearsed lines, explanations and even excuses to try to distance them from further involvement. He tried condolences and reconciliations but, for a change, they all sounded trite before they came out of his mouth and even his conscientious filters would stop him from saying them out loud. He should just get on with it – *vigilante* – he should just let them get on with it – *lone-wolf* – they obviously did not want him there. It felt like even Danny was giving him the cold shoulder: not joining in with his banter.

Could he walk away and leave them to their own potential demise? So many people had died over the past few weeks that he felt some sort of responsibility for (through his actions, inaction or happenstance), would a few more make any difference? Even if they were his friends? If he wanted to get really philosophical about it, were they actually *his* friends? Since finding out he was not who he thought he was, everything that had been the old him now had to come under question, didn't it? He had already shifted the old him's moral ethos; should he not re-evaluate his affections and companions. Danny said he could be whatever he wanted; he could just cut and run.

But was that old him?

Cameron growled loudly and punched the stairwell wall. It was a solid exterior and, after he thrust his fist through the plasterboard and created a sizeable hole in the partition breezeblock, he scraped the flesh from the back of his fingers and broke four knuckles. The pain shot up his arm, burned into his skull, making him want to scream but he fought back and relished the sensation.

This moment, this feeling: this was the only time and only sense that he could be sure belonged only to him. No doubt, no confusion: his pain.

He just hoped he was not going to turn into some sort of masochistic pervert.

No. No semi. Safe.

By the time he had reached Danny's room, the skin had knitted itself and bones reset with the sound of popping bubble-wrap. He used the same hand to knock on the door and winced as the ghost of the pain stabbed through his nerves.

The door opened and Danny stood on the threshold: tousled hair, large white towel around his waist, topless.

"I hope you were expecting room service," Cameron muttered.

"I just got out of the shower," Danny explained. "What's up?"

"Get your spandex on, I've got a lead."

"Dude, I can't," Danny complained. "It got so much of Boy's crap on, it had to go in the wash."

Cameron stared at him with complete disbelief. "What has happened to you? Get dressed and let's get going."

"What about the others?"

Cameron hesitated before telling him, "I was going to give them some space."

"At least tell them what's going on," Danny suggested. "And that'll give us time to get ready. We'll see you downstairs."

"Shit," Cameron hissed.

Danny just shrugged and pushed the door closed.

It was a long, lonely walk down the hallway. The morning sun was just ascending above the horizon. A clear sky could be seen out of the window at the end of the hall but the oppressive buildings around the hotel prevented any direct contact and kept it swathed in darkness. Deeper shadows from occasional tables and recesses made him second-guess his senses: he was still looking for that abnormal darkness that would suggest he was being watched, that he was the next target. Deep down, he wished it would happen so all this cloak and dagger bullshit would end.

All this creeping around, hiding behind masks and secret identities... it seemed so sordid.

The door stood before him like a nightclub bouncer: emotionless, stoic, inanimate but as scary as death itself. Not so much in the violence and damage it could do but more to do with this common, mindless and unoppressive thing holding so much control over your destiny: will it allow you to go on or will your journey end here because of some seemingly arbitrary detail like, 'you're wearing the wrong type of jumper'? If you do progress, because you had come so close, you would forever be looking over your shoulder, always aware of its proximity. You would meet again; this entity was the ultimate cock-blocker.

Cameron could hear raised, urgent, pleading voices from the other side – tones and pitches that reminded him of the few times he heard his parents argue – and he wished he had picked up some *Post-Its* from the reception[11]. No one has such animated discussions about good stuff at six o'clock in the morning. The only conversations held at that time are whispered, 'What the fuck are you doing up this early?'; drunken, '... and that's what's wrong with the world today;' or incensed, 'I don't care how horny you feel, I've still got half an hour before the alarm goes off!' The notions of inserting himself into any of those scenarios were equally disconcerting.

He knocked and instinct told him to run. If nothing else, this moment was reinforcement that he needed to question every innate reaction before acting upon it.

The voices stopped for a moment of contemplation. Then, as is the way with arguments when they stop, one person took advantage of the cessation to start a new debate, which had nothing to do with the previous argument at all. Floater's voice got louder and clearer as she approached the door.

In the meantime, he could still feel the door eyeing his attire critically, looking for any excuse to turn him and his ego away without anything other than a, 'Fuck off, Jesus, no sandals,' as justification.

"... constant waxing can cause a painful rash," she stated from the other side. "And you keep telling me that it's sentient -" the door swung open forcefully "- kinda creeps me out knowing it's writhing around mah genitalia what do you want?"

Too many things came to his mind; all of which managed to get stopped by his developing filtering muscle and categorised as, 'Pragmatically Inappropriate for Context'. Instead, after deliberately not staring at any of the aforementioned areas, he looked elsewhere to see Bob sitting forlornly on the edge of his bed and asked, "How's he doing?"

"What? Close friends and confidants dying around him? Constantly looking over his shoulder in fear of an attack? Soul mate questioning his core principles? Very well, thank you. Under the circumstances."

---

[11] A very useful ability as possessed by Sticky-Note Man. Although he is not endorsed by *Post-It* and has been legally brand name blocked by them, he does generate genuine *Post-Its*, only manifested from an alternative dimension.

"Okay, well -"

"Which he entirely blames you for."

"- I... What? What have I done?" Cameron protested.

"He's a firm believer of karmic justice and, since you've come along, everything has turned very bad."

Instinctive response: indignation and a, 'Fuck you.'

Secondary option: belligerence and a, 'Fuck you.'

Reconsidered, reviewed and revised retort. "Bullshit." (He was marginally impressed that his expletive did not cause her to even blink.) "Why's that down to me? Why is that not Danny's fault? After all, he was the one who introduced us, so why doesn't it trace back to him?"

"Because he embraces the metahuman code of conduct and lives by it," Floater explained. "You do not."

Cameron considered this line of logic and the number of different adverbials to use with a, 'Fuck you,' and walk away. "Okay, what about Cassandra? She's been as cynical about this as I have and was involved before me, why not her?"

"She's not supreme or a side-kick."

Cameron snorted derisively. "Whatever." Fight the flight instinct! "Why is he so sure it's me? Why so absolute? What about the grandmaster puppeteer theory? Some capo criminale somewhere organising these murders as an extensive act of vengeance? Or the otherworldly conspiracy? Some despotic ruler of an underworld, influencing our fates through insidious machinations? I'm still favouring the 'hiding in plain sight' conspiracy: perhaps the finger pointer is actually the finger pointee. Did you consider that?"

Her expression had not changed at all; his words did not inspire or offend her.

"Or it could all just be coincidence," he suggested.

That managed to incite an arched eyebrow. "Ah take it you came to disturb us for a reason."

"Apparently there might be some guy called Myrddin on the loose," he told her and tried to convince himself that her topic shift was an indication that he had won the bout.

Now, she reacted. "Oh mah. That's bad."

"I'm heading down to *The Caped Crusader* to ask around and Danny's getting his shit together to join. You in?"

She looked over her shoulder at her crumbling mountain of a man. "Ah'll talk to him and try to get down there as quickly as Ah can."

CHAPTER 9
THEY'RE 'AT 'EM' IN 'TEAM'

After meeting in the foyer and a full debriefing – Des Carts' business card, empty room, monkey shit and Myrddin – the tiradic trio made their way to the pub in silence, following Cassandra's directions as she navigated the *A-Z*. Danny had to compromise his costume and had returned to street clothes (although he had managed to save his mask from the drycleaners by picking off the bits of oomska when they had dried enough). Between the occasional instructional commentaries, they enjoyed the relative tranquillity of the pre-conscious city. Traffic hummed around them beyond their direct line of sight and acted as an abstract anchor to reality; a life they were once a part of – humdrum and inconsequential in comparison – but was now as out of reach as the sources of those noises.

Eventually, as is the way with introspective moments, someone felt the necessity to share their inner thoughts.

"I just don't get why it's not working," Danny declared and stroppily kicked at a loose piece of grit from the path into the road. It bounced for a couple of metres then disappeared silently down a drain.

No one felt inclined to offer a resolution, comprehended or even acknowledged they had heard what he said.

Danny attempted an alternative, more seditious approach. "Why isn't it working?" he whined.

Cameron and Cassandra huffed their annoyance very audible.

"Apparently it's my fault," Cameron told him.

"Why? Because you're the centre of the universe?" Cassandra scoffed.

"It's what the girl said," Cameron continued. "I argued that you two were the shit magnets[12] but she wouldn't have it."

Danny stopped mid-step. "We're the banes?"

"Nice one," Cassandra chastised Cameron, "he won't sleep for a month now."

Cameron rolled his eyes and turned. "Dude," he called, "vampires: sorted. Zombies: sorted. Whatever shit you dealt with -"

"Hundred-foot leviathan from Neptune's depths," Danny reminded.

"'*Whatever*' you dealt with: sorted. Satan: sorted. We get shit sorted, man. We work. What we do, works. Our presence here has only highlighted these people's naivety and detachment from reality. We haven't brought the psychotic loon from our world, it's always been in theirs and we've arrived just in the nick of time to save the day!"

"We're the heroes," Danny surmised in awe of the epiphany.

---

[12] Despite her unfortunate power, yet apt nomenclature, Shit Magnet has managed to accrue a long-term career as a steadfast supreme, fighting for the powers of good. At the time of writing, she still does not have any known allies or group affiliations.

"So let's get back on track," Cameron rallied. "We're about to walk into a sordid bar - probably heavily outnumbered - and need information. What's the number one rule of engagement for this sort of situation?"

"Find the biggest fucker there and take him out!"

Cameron slapped him heavily on the back. "There's my boy."

"What if it's a she?" Cassandra asked but was brutally ignored.

The Caped Crusader was probably the most innocuous pub in the world. To describe it as mild mannered, run of the mill, or average Joe would make Mild Joe Miller[13] seem more like ADHD Boy after his classic battle against villainous team-up, Captain Caffeine and Ann Phetamine, at the climax of the Great Eastern Seaboard Ritalin Heist.

It was sandwiched within a terrace of identically fasciaed buildings – town houses of some sort – all of which gave no suggestion to any sort of commercial activity. Each building advertised three storeys and an attic room atop with its array of impenetrable windows. Window boxes allowed the occupants a modicum of denial so they could tell estate agents they had garden space; railings across the top floor bay windows were translated as balconies and, if they were brave enough, they could lean out, turn their head and experience the sliver of an 'unhindered view of Hyde Park' to the north. They only thing that set *The Caped Crusader* apart from its neighbours were the steps it had down to a basement room.

"Is it just me," Danny whispered as they were about to descend, "or are the underlying homo-socio themes becoming more overt?"

"Seriously?" Cassandra demanded. "Now?"

"The feeling of needing to hide behind disguises for fear of reprisal or marginalisation from society; our only comfort is with our own kind, thereby reinforcing the divide; the misogyny that sometimes underlies supressed homosexual feelings..."

"Well toned guys wearing figure-hugging clothes?" Cameron added.

"That works too."

"Are you two going down or not?" Cassandra demanded from the top of the steps.

They trudged down into the dank depths, passed blacked-out windows - whose external sills had grown an unhealthy coat of mould, litter and cobweb - slalomed through the cans, *Pret a Manger* coffee cups and a double mattress that loomed over them like a depressed ogre. The walkway became a tunnel as it became encased by the street above and, eventually, ended at a door. In that light, it looked brown although other shades were hinted at from beneath dried, peeling patches. It had no handles, keyholes or buttons, only a letterbox at head height.

---

[13] Mild Joe Miller is one of Bold Bob Jaw's more pointless rogues. No one really knows why Joe decided to target Bob, nor does anyone know what his abilities might be. When asked, Joe just avoids eye contact and shrugs his shoulders.

They looked around for something obvious but found nothing. Cameron even gave the door a light shove to see if it was unlatched but there was no give to the pressure.

"Knock," Cassandra urged.

"Bust it down," Danny offered.

Cameron checked their enclosed surroundings and shook his head. "Not falling for that one again," he commented and rapped his knuckles twice on the flaky surface, dislodging a few wafers of paint skin that immersed themselves into the darker shadows below.

The letterbox flap flipped up by a set of fingers from the inside. Angling their heads, the boys could see inside, beyond the hand, and a pair of pearly white eyes staring back. Cassandra had long ago learned not to degrade herself by struggling on tiptoe or craning her neck to see things that were clearly beyond her limitations. She folded her arms and waited.

"What?" a high-pitched, grainy voice demanded.

"We want a drink," Danny said.

"You have come to the wrong place, boys," the voice told them and the letterbox flap flopped down.

"Stanley sent us," Cameron blurted.

Flap flipped.

"Stan... Lee?" the voice asked dubiously.

"No," Cameron laughed. "As if."

Flap flopped.

"Stanley from the hotel. He said this is where we should go to relax."

Flap flipped.

Blank eyes scrutinised and, perhaps, noticed Danny's mask for the first time. "Where is the rest of your costume?"

"Dry cleaners," Danny confessed.

"Show me something," it ordered.

The boys flustered and muttered hurriedly to each other, giving instructions and suggestions and excuses.

Flap flopped.

"Wait!" Cameron squealed and then demanded of the fates, "Why does it always have to be me?"

Flap flipped.

Cameron raised his left hand, palm forwards, and isolated his index finger by curling the others into a fist. He inhaled deeply three times then grabbed the finger with his right hand and wrenched it sideways. There was a loud snap, Cameron yelped then revealed the digit to be pointing at Danny at ninety degrees to its origin. It wobbled loosely.

The eyes backed away and the flap slipped slightly.

"Not finished," Cameron growled through clenched teeth.

Slowly, the appendage began to rise as tendons and muscles tightened within his knuckle. When it reached full erection, with a slight wiggle, it popped itself back into its joint.

The eyes had returned to the fore. "That's disgusting," it commented.

"You should see him do it with his head," Danny said and shuddered.

The flap flopped, internal mechanisms clanked clunkily and the door opened to release a swathing wave of grumbling dubstep at them, followed closely by an assailing aroma of sweat and beer that scrambled to escape the building.

Cassandra gagged. "It smells like a boys' changing rooms."

"That's the smell of spandex gussets without aeration holes," Cameron told her and pressed forward.

"How do you know what the boys' changing room smells like?" Danny asked as she followed.

While they stopped at the threshold to survey the scene, the glassy-eyed gatekeeper closed the door behind them. Grimmer was tall and skinny, hunched over at the shoulders and bent at the knees – presumably from having to peer through the letterbox so much. As he straightened, his joints creaked and cracked and he made a silent 'ooh' with his mouth. His skin matched his ocular features – chalk-white – which was emphasised further by the abyssal black cowl that covered him from shoulders to floor. In the wrong light, from an odd angle, people sometimes mistook him for Fore-Head[14] so he was currently experimenting with a range of potentially distinguishing hairpieces. Today's was dark blond with a heavy fringe which fell over his eyes when he sat down. He absentmindedly shifted it back into place.

The three exchanged glances, which communicated very little, then continued down a gently curving walkway into the main room. The bar opened into an expanse of tables and chairs, occupied by an eclectic assortment of incognito characters: capes, hoods, cloaks and masks of all shapes colours and sizes. Around the perimeter of the room were a number of booths that were recessed into the walls giving the occupants even more privacy. At the room's centre, with a three-hundred-and-sixty degree view of everything, were the bar and a solitary, unmasked barman behind it.

He looked as if he was in his fifties. He was unshaven but not bearded, overweight but muscular. Dark rings around his eyes and an overall hangdog expression suggested tiredness but he served his customers with such a ceaseless speed and precision that it was difficult to keep up with his movements.

The bar itself was wooden and unkempt: chipped, scratched and, in places, scorched. It was littered with a variety of gleaming beer taps and tall ale pumps. In its centre was a glass partition, decorated with a dado rail of inverted spirit bottles and plateaus of glasses that sparkled and twinkled temptingly in the bright halogen lighting. Tilted wicker baskets displayed neat layers of unusually flavoured crisps, nuts and chocolate bars. At one end, a sign propped up against a

---

[14] A living, bald, pale-skinned head that can levitate itself via telekinesis. It can't do much else because it requires complete concentration to keep itself upright. No one knows if it is good or bad but everyone hates it because it just hangs around with a pained expression on its face, making everyone feel uncomfortable.

pillar clearly read, 'Please do not ask for credit because being telekinetically turned inside-out through your anus can offend.'

Without erring in his duties, the barman bellowed at the newcomers, "Hey, we don't serve their kind in here!" causing everyone to turn and stare.

The youths stopped in their steps. "Who?" Danny asked.

"Side-kicks!"

Danny instinctively held out an arm to keep Cassandra back. "She's *with* me," he said sternly.

The barman considered the inflection carefully. Then, after a quick eye-contact acknowledgement from those immediately in front of him, he nodded his assent.

"I'll side kick the next fucker in the head who calls me that," Cassandra grumbled as they continued into the room.

"I thought he was talking about Danny," Cameron added.

"Up yours."

They assayed their surroundings and calculated to be at least fifty patrons in a variety of sized clusters at the tables, eclipsed in the booths, playing pool at the back of the room or lining the bar.

"What do you want?" the barman demanded impatiently; his voice was deep and gravelly, compensating for the grinding bass pervading every inch of space around them.

"A pint of cider," Cameron called over the noise and Danny nudged him in the back.

"Not while you're on duty," Danny hissed.

"We are doing this *our* way, remember?" Cameron prompted. "That means with alcohol."

"What about the 'big guy' ploy?" Cassandra asked.

"Go ahead," Cameron encouraged, "I've got your back." He indicated to one of the booths. There did not seem to be anything in it until a shimmer of light reflected off a rippling transparent surface. Then, Cassandra was able to focus on an outline that overlapped the confines of the alcove itself. Further exploration revealed a number of objects floating in mid-air: a pint glass of brown liquid that was slowly spilling into space; an open packet of pork scratchings releasing its contents, each fatty wafer fizzing effusively as it was discharged; and, at the deepest, highest point of the recess was a dark brown, rippled orb that looked something like a -.

"Amoebrain doesn't like being stared at," an Antipodean woman at the bar told them. She was dressed in a baby pink outfit: t-shirt, minidress, knee-length high heeled boots and a tight fitting, rubber sieve on her head. Scraps of green hair poked through the holes and she looked at them through thick, orange compound eyes. She had a white heart stitched onto her chest, which emphasised the curvature of her breasts, and on that was a purple letter 'i' – lower case and an open circle for the tittle.

"How can you tell?" Cassandra asked but did not remove her inspection.

"When you're dissolving in his plasma," she was told.

Cassandra turned her attention to the bar. "I need a pint," she stated and Danny huffed at this final betrayal (but still nodded when Cameron mimed a drinking gesture to him and raised his eyebrows quizzically).

Instructions were given and three large glasses of varying shades of brown - from golden to murky - were presented before them with as much grace and dignity as a disenchanted dinner lady serving week-old turkey twizzlers to Jamie Oliver. But then, at the end of a long, hard day, who needs decorum and panache when all that counts is the contents of the glass and how quickly it can be consumed.

Needless to say, after forty-eight hours of paranormal, metanormal and seriously fucked up, the next five minutes were the quietest and most sedate this series has experienced, outside of sleep and death[15]. Cassandra, Cameron and Danny drank their drinks without a pause for words or breath. Each glass was placed slightly more reverently back on the bar after their contents had been drained, a signal indicated to the barman and another round delivered.

Cassandra felt something press against the back of her leg and presumed it was either an inadvertent nudge or Danny getting fresh – even though Danny was standing in front of her, conspiring with Cameron about something (that is one of the wonderful, logic twisting powers of alcohol). So she turned to see if she was going to receive an apology or have to warn some over-amorous arse to back off only to find the area completely clear of people. Invisibility? The pressure to her leg returned again and she looked down. She was mildly fascinated and disgusted in equal measures at the shimmering sight snaking around her shin. It looked like it was trying to entwine her limb: a fist-sized chrome dome bashed softly against her leg then trailed around it. Sleek metallic plates slid over themselves, moulding its body to her curvature then, finally, reinforced the attempted conjoinment with a prehensile tail that wrapped in the opposite direction to almost touch itself on its head. It was a polished ferrous feline.

"Don't worry about Collossopuss," the barman suggested whilst clearing up their empties but she still gave the legged-Slinky a wayward nudge with her foot.

"What's your thing?" Danny asked the barman.

"Waddaya mean?" he replied gruffly.

"Precognition? Telepathy? Speed?"

The barman huffed scathingly and continued with his duties. "Nuffin'," he stated.

Cameron pulled Danny over to him; he hunched his body over so his head was in line with Cameron's.

"This is the way it's going to play out," Cameron stated – the thrumming beat of the music forcing him to retain a raised voice, "we circulate – nonchalant like – getting a feel for the place, ingratiate ourselves with a group of the costumes and discuss powers, exploits and nemeses, you know?"

---

[15] Which, in retrospect, neither have proven to be quiet or sedate moments.

"It's going to be like being a fresher again," Danny complained, "'What school did you come from?', 'What A levels did you get?'"

"Get over it," Cameron instructed. "Be more like a newb and they'll be less suspicious of you."

Danny nodded in appreciation of the ploy.

"Then," Cameron continued, "during the war stories, slip in the, 'Oh I heard about a breakout…' and see if they feed you any details you can work on."

"Nice," Danny commended. "What was this bloke's name again?"

Dubstep[16] stopped, talking stopped, drinking stopped, the incessant, untraceable whine from Mosqueto's[17] wings actually stopped.

"Mir-thin," Cameron enunciated very loudly. Then, said considerably quieter, "Bugger."

Chair-legs scraped against the cold slate floor, feet scuffled to find balance and poise, bio-organic energy convectors hummed as they supercharged to an optimum point of critical mass. The patrons stirred, gathered and neared; the gaps between bodies closed as shoulders interlocked. The youths were surrounded – blocked off from the exit – apart from the personal space they had acquired at the bar. But, looking across that way, they noticed the barman was choosing the better part of valour and had taken cover as far away from them as he could manage.

Cameron stepped forward to address the milling crowds. He raised his hands and waved them placatory. "Look people, we're not looking for trouble."

As is the way with spontaneous rabble rousing, lots of individuals presumed they were the voice of authority and lots of voices responded with glib retorts, threats of violence and a couple of polite enquiries as to what it was they did want. When the cacophony had finished, one voice boomed from within the throng, "If it is Mirdididin that you seek, it *is* trouble that you will find."

They had been in a similar position before – trapped, surrounded and vastly outnumbered – but the difference before was that they knew their enemy: they had been carbon copies of each other. This time, they had no idea what this group was capable of. By generic definition, each unique coloured combination costume represented a unique ability: invulnerability, enhanced strength, heat beams, communication with algae – whatever – the point being, this was not the time to wade in, thrashing and lashing like normal; this was the time to show the very underused ability of 'caution'.

"We just need to talk to him," Cameron explained. "There are some things going on that he's been implicated in but we don't think he's responsible for."

A man with an unusually high collar that twisted and twirled above his head like creeping ivy pushed himself to the fore. The collar was attached to an olive robe with wide, open cuffs. He was bald and was compensating with an

---

[16] Despite a thirty+ year career, he has only just adopted this name and has become one of the more *en vogue* supremes. Certainly moreso than when he started and his name was Gawdawfulnoise. Well, that's what everyone else called him.

[17] One of a few Islamic supremes, her primary ability is that of keeping people awake at night.

equally twirly moustache and tapered beard that hung down to the middle of his chest. "It seems suspicious," he purred, "that on the day of Merthdin the Mighty's salubrious abscondsion from Barkers, three mysterious, unknown entities come looking for him. Some might say, 'coincidental.' Others might consider 'fortuitous' or 'consequential'."

The cautionary plan was already wearing thin. "What's your point, Roget?"

This elicited a smattering of titters from positions in the crowd. The ostentatious man glanced sharply around, trying to identify the recalcitrant individuals. "Don't undermine me in front of the whelps," he snarled.

"Do you want us to give you all a minute, then?" Cameron asked and received another couple of sniggers.

"I'll bloody do you lot one day," the man whimpered. "When My-red-den gets here, I'll tell him."

"I heard everything, Synomystic," an assertive voice declared from behind the mob and all heads turned to the entrance.

There, they saw Grimmer returning their gawps – his hand still holding the open door; a look of concerned surprise on his face; his toupee lying almost perpendicular to the top of his head – but nothing else was visible. Then the furthest metas started to jostle and create a space between them.

Myrddin was a small man of great bearings. He marched through the pack with bold tenacity; his two-and-a-half-foot stature caused him no degree of trepidation. Part of his grandeur came from the reactions of the others, twice the size of him: where he walked, a foot-wide perimeter encompassed him. The spandexed muscles and lofty capes shuffled awkwardly out of the way of this invisible boundary, tripping over the toes of the bruisers behind them. They, in turn, bustled at the people behind them muttering unintelligible apologies and trying not to catch eye contact with those whose minimally attired bodies they brushed against.

He walked with a gait of regality: long, purposeful strides, head aloft and aloof, and carried an expression as if everything around him was distasteful. He was wearing a thick, purple velour frock coat with fur trimmings. Its tails slithered behind him a half beat behind his pace and, preceding him – solidly tapping each tile as if testing its sturdiness before treading on it – was a gnarly wooden walking cane set atop with a glittering, milky orb. He cleared the horde, stepped into the clearing and stopped before the trio, smiling victoriously. "Hello children," he sneered. "It's better that this be done face-to-face. More noble. More honourable."

"We were just telling these goons -" Danny started.

"'Goons'?" someone questioned with an intonation of hurt.

"- that we don't want to fight. We just want to talk."

"Oh, don't worry," Myrddin comforted, "there won't be any more fighting..."

"Here it comes," Cameron asided, "cliché number 134."

"... just you dying," Myrddin punchlined.

"Oooooh," the rabble chanted. "You got burned!"

"Don't embarrass yourself," Cameron heckled. "No one says 'burned' any more."

"That was my one good line," moaned Pyronaught and received a consolatory pat on the shoulder.

"Look," Danny continued, "we want you to know that you've been set up. You're being used as a patsy."

"Are they talking about me?" asked Pasty Man from the very back, straining to keep up.

"The person who helped you escape is trying to pin the murders of four supremes on you," Danny concluded.

This caused Myrddin to stop in his tracks. "I'm the chief suspect for Ultimate's death?"

"Ultimate's dead?" someone demanded from the crowd.

"And three others," an attentive listener informed.

"Who else am I being blamed for?"

Before anyone could stop him, Danny blurted, "Block, Cat and Boy Sprout."

The information disseminated through the mob, building volume and fervour as it finally reached the outer edges.

"Wunderbar, Herr Meerdydin!" squeaked Fledermaus.

"Stupendous achievement," hailed Doctor Momentum.

"You're our hero," the Troopettes of Evil squealed.

And the rest joined in the praise with a round of applause that rose to such a crescendo, and lasted so long, that it would even have embarrassed an RSC actor attending a sci-fi-con after their successful film depiction of a classic comic character.

Eventually, after a hand signal from Myrddin, the noise quelled and allowed him to speak. "Oh no, whatever will I do?" he mocked.

"Twat," Cassandra told Danny.

"I'm a mass murderer," Myrddin declared. "I singlehandedly committed the greatest act of total genocide in history. I eradicated an entire race of advanced human when I sank Atlantis. These few additions to my repertoire will have no long-term, detrimental effect. Regardless of if I was responsible or not."

"How about the *short*-term repercussions?" Cameron asked and a deathly silence swept through the room.

This was their real power. The one they had been born with. The one they saved up especially for that final encounter. The one that could get their target so enraged that they would lash out blindly, let something slip, make mistakes.

"Really? That's the best you can do?"

Uh-oh.

"I've been alive for millennia," Myrddin stated. "I've been this height all my life and I have been the victim of every kind of persecution, bullying and ribaldry you could imagine. And I learned one important thing, very early on: if people cannot live in harmony, celebrating our differences rather than deriding them, then don't let them live."

"You should stitch that on pillows," Cameron suggested.

"They're never big enough."

Cameron raised his eyebrows and tried again. "That's what she said."

Myrddin stared balefully at him. "puny human," he said.

Cameron blinked and shook his head as if trying to wake himself up.

"Kill them all," Myrddin ordered, turned and gaited his way towards the exit.

"Oi, no," Cameron called. "You and I have to sort this out."

"Already sorted, boy," Myrddin replied from over his shoulder. "You lose."

Cameron's intention was to leap forward and his antagoniser up by the scruff of his stupid, oversized coat but his balance wobbled when he took his first step. As he reached forward, a strong sensation of pins and needles spread across his hand. All other matters seemed to slip into insignificance. He inspected his offending appendage: the fat in his fingers had dried up, his skin was vacuum sealing itself to his bones and turning a sickening yellow colour. This had happened to him before, a few days ago, and a mortal panic set in.

Danny and Cassandra edged towards the back of the bar, distinctly aware of the attention being directed at them from the milling metamasses before them. He honed his attention to the objects around them, awaiting that signal from his pre-emptive vision that would indicate his next move. She looked for potential escape routes, weapons and assayed her targets.

"Could we just have a couple of minutes to get to know each other before we start?" Danny suggested. "You know, discuss powers and stuff."

"My name's Mega Maw," one of the bigger baddies at the front introduced himself. "But let's keep what I do a surprise, shall we?" He was simply attired in jeans and a white vest top but was seven foot tall and had a large metal dome replacing the top half of his head. It could have been presumed to be a close-fitting fitting helmet if it was not for the fact that the perimeter of the dome was slightly smaller than that of his head and the skin around the seal had dried and curled back on itself. His jaw had also been replaced with a metallic substitute: it was oversized, over extended, bolted at the mandible and had been decorated with carving knife-like teeth.

"Why the long face?" Danny asked.

Cassandra used the moment to strike. She used her boyfriend's stance and height to propel herself up to Mega Maw's eye level. Then she used the two pint glasses she had in her hands and thrust them in the still fleshy area of his head. They fractured at the thinner, weaker ends, slashing into his skin. Her forward momentum drove the grinding glass into bone and eye sockets. She pivoted her body to bring her feet forward, landing on his chest. With her body compressed, she pushed, sending Mega Maw reeling into the crowd while she ricocheted back, landing cat-like next to Danny.

The villains parted, allowing Mega Maw to hit the ground, giving him plenty of space to writhe in agony and ensuring they were out of reach of his desperate clamouring hands and spurting bodily fluids. Overall, though, they looked genuinely horrified by the outcome.

"What the hell did you do?" Ginja demanded. Even though his face was fully covered by black wrappings, his eyes were wide with horror. His emotion was further enhanced by the high, spikey red hair on his head. "What kind of supreme glasses their enemies?"

"That's my secret, mother-fucker," Cassandra replied (they staggered at her words), "I'm not supreme and your rules don't apply to me." She twirled around the tables, picking up glasses, bar mats and cutlery and propelled them into the front lines. None of her onslaught did any real damage (apart from a nasty Pernod-and-black stain on Immaculad's costume) but it did create enough of a distraction to allow Danny to hurl himself over the top of the bar to land in the serving area. It was there where he discovered how a meta-less barman might be able to keep some control over the more rambunctious meta-ed clientele.

Whilst Cassandra was showering her half of the room in imbibement, the other half were watching Cameron with mortified fascination. He had been staring fixedly at his right hand and had now pulled his sleeve as far back as it could go. He was watching the discolouration and withering spread up his arm; his fingers had greyed and gave the appearance of cellophane wrapped bones; muscle disintegrated and his jaundiced skin rapidly deflated around his bones. This was the same thing that happened when he had been injected with a rejuvenating serum: a chemical that could bring dead tissue back to life. However, because he was composed entirely of necrotic tissue, it simply meant his flesh reverted to a condition more common for a corpse. The only way he survived the last encounter was by ripping the offending fluid (and infected anatomy) from his body[18]. That took a lot of effort, mental preparation and, luckily, involved his arm already being inside his body. This time, he was going to have to attack from the outside in and only had his nails to work with.

It only took a couple of wrenches to release the sleeve of his jumper from the shoulder. Then he feverishly scratched at his paling bicep and was shocked by how much each scrape at his skin hurt. He had hoped that the rapid decomposition would be killing his nerves as well but he could feel each desperate rake of his nails as they split the surface of his skin and began digging through the deeper levels.

This separated the audience into camps of mesmerised, intrigued and revolted. They saw him ripping deep trenches into his perfectly normal arm: each flailing wrench at his flesh causing him to scream with agony and despairing frustration because the action was not achieving a desired result. Possibly the most stomach turning aspect of his endeavours was the distinct lack of blood that should have been slewing from the ruptures.

---

[18] Seems-like-years-ago in #2: The Carrion

It was not working. He could not get through the meat fast enough to reach the source. He tried to bite into his arm but could only gnaw at it in the corner of his mouth. He yanked at his gnarly elbow, pulling his forearm around past his left ear and dislocating his shoulder.

The crowd yelped empathically as the joint popped.

He sank his teeth into the muscle and the sensation sent a shiver down his spine, awakening another pain in his body that had been lying dormant in the pit of his stomach. Hunger.

Cassandra had focused her intention on reaching the pool table. There, she would be able to get her hands on a couple of cues and become firmly ensconced in her comfort zone. The arse whoopery would be well and truly on. However, the circle of aggressors was impeding her progress; the best she could do was get to a table and use the dense, coloured balls as another barrage of missiles. Each heftily weighted orb was propelled with unerring accuracy at soft and sensitive spots: a forehead – TONK – a groin – SPOO – the pressure valve on Deto-Nathan's[19] inhibitor pack – CHENK.

Deto-Nathan probably realised the consequences before those immediately around him. But not long before.

"Help?" he squealed and spun his body around while desperately trying to reach the system restore toggle.

"Bloody run!" someone suggested.

Danny emerged from behind the bar. He held the underside of a large, charcoal grey phallus with his right hand; his four fingers clenched against a trigger the size of his palm. The barrel extended two foot forward and was cradled in his left hand as if he was carefully and lovingly supporting a baby's head. "Say hello -" he started but was cut off when Cassandra threw herself across the counter and tackled him to the ground.

Cameron was not getting through quick enough. He spat the rancid mouthful onto the floor and looked around at his spectators. His eyes were burning with corpusclent redness. The excitement of the fray and the horrifically compelling scene of self-mutilation before them had everyone's adrenaline levels raised and their hearts thumped frenetically. The sound had permeated through the music still thrumming through the building and was drowning his other senses; a blackness was creeping in from the periphery of his vision. Was this him losing complete control or the abyss of eternity calling?

His tunnel vision was desperately focussed on his withering limb. Despite the emaciation from his fingertips to his bicep, his forearm looked positively meaty compared to the stripped-back-to-the-bone upper half. The sensation was creeping through his shoulder and heading to his chest. He could not stop the spread, he was going to die. But realising that did not stop him from flaying the skin from his right pectoral and gouging his nails across his ribs, scooping out the spongy meat from

---

[19] A young meta from Wigan, UK, whose ability to explode developed after years of trying to debug code for a MMORPG he was developing. Despite having the power, he has always feared that it might be a once only deal so never used it for.

between the bones. It gave him the drive to plunge the blade of his hand into the deepening crevice, hook his fingers within his chest and wrench out a fractured stick. His hand delved again, clasped another bar and snapped it from its housing.

"STOP!" a divine cry heralded from above. "For the love of all that's fuffing holy, stop!"

The transcendent light of the heavenly hosts poured into the den of iniquity, causing all who beheld its majesty to cower in its magnificence. Angel rushed through the crowd, tossing the bodies of the sinners into the sidelines. It pinned Cameron's arms to his sides, lifting him from the floor until they were face to face. Cameron's eyes were red, pupilless orbs of burning rage. His canines had stretched out of his gums and now, with his jaws clenched in vicious determination, overshadowed his bottom lip.

"You are going to kill yourself if you do not stop," Angel urged but Cameron showed no indication of comprehending the words or even if he had heard them. "That... thing has got into your head and done something to you."

GET IT OUT! Cameron growled and writhed in the angel's clutches.

Angel hesitated in thought, running options through its head. "This really will tip the feffing balance; be prepared," it stated to its feral captive. It loosened its grip and, before Cameron could fall too far, clamped its hands over his ears, pulling his face even closer to its own.

With his arms released, Cameron was able to return to their previous objective, seemingly unconcerned by the undignified headlock. His talons found purchase on the rough edges of skin, flesh and bone, indiscriminately shredding, gouging and snapping any bit of his body that came to hand.

Angel widened its eyes and stared deeply into Cameron's. It opened its blinds to allow its inner light to pour out. At first, it was a trickle of liquid sun that smattered off the belligerent surfaces of his corneas. Eventually, the incessant drive and heat softened the defiant membranes to enable it access to seep inside. Then the luminescent flow became a torrent, rushing from one pair of sockets into the next without resistance or spillage; his head radiated from the inside, defining the outline of his skull against his reddened, semi-translucent skin.

Without waning, it stopped and Angel dropped Cameron to the floor where he wobbled drunkenly. Around them, the felled metas were gathering their senses and readying themselves for a physical retort.

"I feel..." Cameron gurgled. "I feel... clean."

"Whereas I feel the desperate need for a shower," Angel replied.

"Don't ever do that again," Cameron warned.

"Well, don't ever do that again, then." Angel pointed to the ragged hole where his right tit used to be: skin and bone were splayed outward like a semi-peeled orange, their edges were drying and flaky; his right bicep had been stripped back to the humerus with the meatier part of his forearm dangling limply.

"My arm was infected," Cameron tried to explain.

"No it chuffing wasn't," Angel said, "he did something inside your head and I had to... absolve you of your sins."

"You did that? You forgave me? You gave me a clean slate?"

"I suppose," Angel replied hesitantly, surprised by Cameron's calm nature.

"You ecclesiastically raped me!"

That was more like it. It clenched its jaw with restrained indignation. "Think of it as a way to indulge in all your debaucherous vices as virginal experiences again."

Cameron reminded himself of his predicament: unknown enemies rallying their strengths, heavily outnumbered and having only half a body to fight with. "Let's get back on track with number six then, shall we?"

"Smite as well," Angel replied and received a nod of approval. It rotated its shoulders and ruffled its wing feathers. It brandished a four foot long, radiant broadsword.

"And I just thought you were just pleased to see me."

"K'off."

There was fervent activity from the other side of the room: pleading, shouting and desperate movement. Something exploded[20], spreading the antagonists to the edges of the pub whilst dramatically backlighting the angel and its flesh-rent ward. They took advantage of the moment of disorientation to initiate their offensive retaliation

It was easy. It was instinctive. Despite his earlier doubts, it was the most natural and honest course of action he had taken so far: unrelenting, non-discriminatory and absolute carnage. To be honest, at first, with only the one working arm, it was a little bit awkward. He wheeled and pounced at the heartbeat directly in front of him – was it male? Female? He could not tell. There were bright colours decorating its body and an emblem of some sort of horned creature on its chest but, again, he would not be able to relate any specific details later if quizzed. The colours were suffused by the blackness that threatened to overwhelm his vision and the emblem just presented itself as a target. The body fell backwards with him on top. The crowd, still reeling from the blast, were thrown even more by the sudden, macabre attack and put in a more distance between them and him when he thrust his hand into the bull, cracked through sternum and extracted his victim's beating heart.

"Minortaur!" someone screamed but the yells fell on Cameron's deaf ears; the overwhelming thrum of cardiac beats filled his auditory canals.

He sank his teeth into the pulsating, dribbly organ. It squelched under the assault and spurted juices from the corners of his mouth.

Meanwhile, Angel swung his blade around in a swift, graceful, upward arc. Its tip barely touched the kilt-wearing, hairy barbarian but still managed to unseam him from naval to chin. His white tunic slit open while a vertical fine line up the centre of his stomach and chest deepened in colour and depth. After a

---

[20] Until now.

millisecond's pause, his bloated stomach burst open, the sliver became a chasm and his innards became outards. Cerise fluid, masses of various sizes and excitable tubes vomited onto the floor at his feet.

These actions received even more cries of protestation and revulsion; it even encouraged a few of the more wary metas to call for their proverbial taxis. Most others, however, either engaged by the violence or realisation that this shit just got real, flicked their dial to fight and activated their powers. A spectrum of beams criss-crossed the room, impacting on targets and each other with their own individual patterns and reactions. From your basic elements - a spray of crystalline water, a gust of wind, a flare of golden flames, a lump of mud - to an array of light rays. Red, blue and green lasers bounced off reflective surfaces and refracted through translucent materials of differing densities, giving the room the feel of a cheap 80s disco. Then there were the ranged attacks that came under the category of 'Odd': a powerful blast of bubbles that could really smart if they got in your eyes; an overpowering wave of the aroma of rotten egg; a gaseous purple tentacle with green entwirling vines slithered inquisitively and cautiously through the mesh.

Danny resurfaced from his trench, directing his attention behind him. "-knee right in my nads," he accused then looked around him at the on-going madness. If the bodies were not inert, they were stumbling to find stability; if they were not jostling for a better position to attack, they were being battered around the bar by their allies' barrages. "Time to get our convention on," Danny stated boldly and hauled the overcompensatory weapon across the counter. "Let's see what this baby can do."

A suit of armour had escaped Deto-Nathan's premiere performance and was wading towards Cameron without encumbrance from the occasional blast that ricocheted off his metal hide. He spiralled a large, spiked mace in his left hand and raised his arm in preparation of striking him down from behind.

"Gadzooks!" Danny bellowed and pulled the trigger.

There was a decent recoil, which Danny had prepared himself for. He rocked backwards, bracing himself on his right leg that was thrust out behind him. There was a noise, which was very apt and tinnitus inducingly satisfying. It was a sharp, metallic grating as the device charged itself, then expelled its load with a heavily static *ZzzaApp!* There was also a visual, which was rather disappointing. He was anticipating a climactic fluxing orb of pent-up power to rip across the room, or even a solid rupture of unrelenting kinetic energy to sever reality itself with its orgasmic release. What he got was more like an impotent dribble of the last vestiges from a Silly String can. The purpley ejaculate squiggled its way across the room and wormed into Harmour's suit.

Nothing happened. Well, apart from him hammering his mace down into the nape of Cameron's neck and nearly decapitating him. Angel wheeled its broadsword around horizontally, cutting neatly across Harmour's chest at the armpits. His limbs lopped off to the floor, his body fell and his top half landed on a table like a sculpted bust.

Danny swiftly dropped behind the cover again for fear of drawing attention to himself with nothing to defend himself other than this old man's leaky penis of a gun. He nuzzled in beside Cassandra. "Stupid thing is as effective as Green Lantern against Bananaman."

"You're using it wrong," a gruff voice stated from further along.

They peered around the edge of the counter to see the barman crawling towards them.

"It's a Meta-Negatinator," he told them. "Nullifies powers at a genetic level. You shot one that doesn't actually have powers. He wears enchanted armour."

"Let's try this again, then," Danny suggested and raised himself. He focussed his vision very carefully on the auras around each being.

Cameron was in mid assault of another victim; three bodies lay around him in as if having arrived as furniture self-assembly kits but now abandoned because the instructions were incomprehensible. His head rolled around loosely because of the spiked steel ball – still embedded between his shoulders – had disconnected his central nervous system. The navy and aqua-blue clad quarry wriggled frantically beneath Cameron's ministrations and, now his arm had developed some stability with a regrowth of meat along the bone, he was able to apply a larger proportion of his strength to incapacitating his prey. He hooked a finger into the side of its neck and pressed, created a deep well and when the surface tension broke plunged the digit in up to the knuckle. The victim's squawk of pain was drowned out with a bubbly gurgle, then reinforced with a high-pitched squeal while he drew open its neck like a fizzy-drink ring-pull. Its contents erupted into the air and Cameron plunged his face into the fountain.

Behind him, a meta dressed in zigzagged stripes of red and yellow, posed in preparation. "IGNITE!" she hailed and **FWOOFED** into flame.

Simultaneously, Danny aimed and fired.

ZzzaApp!

CRACKLE! "Holy fucking Christ!" she exclaimed. "I'm on fucking fire!"

Angel had temporarily sheathed his weapon in a red and black, square shield belonging to Mien Kampf, which he had raised self-defensively over his now impaled head. It grabbed Cameron by his hair and pulled his head from the gush. "Don't bite them," it warned. "You'll infect them."

Cameron jerked his head round: eyes were still blazing, teeth were engorged and his face was ruddier than a four-year-old's after a choc-ice.

I KNOW, he growled. **I'M IN CONTROL NOW.**

Angel looked from the shredded corpses to the fingers plunged in gobbing jugular and back to his horrific visage. "*This* is you in control?"

A hunched figure emerged from a shadowy corner, his brown half mask's eyes holes and two backward leaning, triangular 'ears' gave him a severe, feral appearance. The brick-like knuckles of his massive hands scraped against the floor as he trudged closer to the fray. He raised his muscular, hairy arms in preparation of his monologue: "Bub..." *SNIKT!* – from beneath his skin, all across his body and limbs, sprouted three-inch metallic spikes – "... Catcuss is gonna-"

Danny swivelled the gun and fired. *ZzzaApp!*

SPURT! "*AAAAAARGH!*" **PITTER-PATTER** Neat cubes of meat delicately crumbled to the ground followed by a shiny skeleton making a sound like the cutlery drawer had been dropped.

Something grabbed Danny's peripheral attention: a smeared void stretching across the bar from Cameron to a white leotard adorned with golden lightning bolts.

Hwizz! The figure disappeared from vision.

ZzzaApp! Danny fired.

SHPLAST! A red paint bomb exploded over the opposite wall.

A skinny, blue-skinned, elf-like man created a preperceived movement. Danny could see two smudgy, mid-air clouds: one where the man was, the other over Cameron.

ZzzaApp! BAMF!...

Then there was only one, gently dissipating where the man had been.

Cameron hefted himself off his sustenance - his chest having refleshed somewhat to resemble an emaciated pit - to find his selection of targets having been dramatically thinned either by caution or literally by Angel's blade. One man stood before him, completely dressed in black. He had a bifurcated cape attached to each wrist so, when he extended his arms, they looked like wings. He wore a full head mask with two dish-like ears that swivelled independently from his scalp.

"I am ze stalker in ze darkness," Fledermaus growled. "I am ze sum of all fears."

Cameron pounced across the divide and grappled with the bat-like man until he was able to raise him aloft, horizontal over his head. "Die... whatever-your-name-is!" he awkwardly declared and lunged him, back first, across his raised leg. Fledermaus emitted a supersonic scream as he descended, his spine cracked loudly and his body folded on itself, flopping lifelessly to the floor.

From behind him there was a **SWOOSH ZzzaApp! splosh!** He turned to see a large puddle of water on the carpet then Danny winking at him from the other side of the bar.

The last few standing metas, having realised the turn in the tide of the battle, either sidled out of the building or slipped back into the darkened booths where glasses and bottles of alcohol had managed to survive.

"What's he doing here?" Danny demanded and pointed at Angel.

Cameron could have been derisive or insulting but he waited a moment to seriously contemplate the question. "He's watching my back," he concluded and the look that passed between them could have been construed as mutual respect but perhaps also tired tolerance.

"Who?" Cassandra asked as she lifted herself from her cover. "Shit! Angel!" she screamed upon registering the creature. She grabbed a *Twix* from behind her and vaulted over the bar, tearing the packet open with her teeth like pulling the pin from a grenade.

"Sod this," Angel decided and slipped between realities.

Cassandra landed next to Cameron with a surprised stumble and the primed chocolate bar in her hand. He stared between her and it with absolute confusion.

"You got your blob on or something?"

"Fuck off."

Danny rested the gun on the bar and climbed over, tentatively tiptoeing around bits of body, until he reached his compatriots. He held up a bar towel to Cameron. "You've got something just here," he said and indicated the entirety of his own face.

Cameron took the offering and began smearing the blood around, and not necessarily off, his face. "We're back to square one," he moaned from behind the cloth. "Myrddin had no idea what was going on. If he had anything to do with it, he would have stood there and monologued us into submission."

"Maybe we can still get information from him, though," Cassandra suggested, corrected a toppled chair and sat in it.

"I'm not in any rush to face him again," Cameron confessed, and parked himself on a small stool. He straightened a felled table, pulled it in closely, placed his folded arms on it and then his head on them. "He fucked me up big time."

"Maybe the answer's there, dude," Danny offered with resolute enthusiasm. "Maybe we just haven't given the mystery the mental effort required to work it all out."

"I can't be arsed," Cameron told him. "I'm exhausted. I haven't slept for three days. I think."

"And what do you do when you think you can't go on any more?" Danny rhetoricked. "What do we do when we need to sort out our greatest problems? When is it when we put the world to rights and come up with our greatest plans?"

"Are you lot going to order something?" the barman called from he re-established position of power. He wiped at the liquid splashed surface of the bar with a reddening dishcloth.

"When we're wasted," Cameron replied.

"Seriously?" Cassandra demanded with incredulity.

BoooM! The door flew across the room and with it, Grimmer found himself cushioning its impact. Standing in the doorway, filling the space with power, might and right, was Bold Bob Jaw. Floater could be seen peeking through a gap between his arm and waist.

"Stand down, evil-doers!" he declared.

"Oh mah Gahd," she observed.

"Better make it shots," Cameron suggested.

"Who are you people?"

~~Cameron Mortice was a mild, mannered boy.~~

~~Cameron was a meek, sensitive and introverted child.~~

~~One day, Cameron was bitten by a radioactive flea.~~

sigh

Cameron Mortice was a pain in the arse. Always was.

Even before he was born, he was a constant source of inconvenience: a conception based on a freak accident and sequence of complicated happenstances which occurred at the most inopportune time of his parents' financial, social and emotional life. They never set foot in Madame Tussauds again...

They were never allowed to.

The pregnancy itself was the most unpleasant experience his mother, Sally, had ever had in her life. In her entire existence, in fact. After being freed from the (supposedly) eternal torments of Hell, she would still reflect that had been a relative breeze compared to eight months of continuous nausea, vomiting, heartburn, haemorrhoids, swollen ankles, varicose veins, headaches and a constant craving for metal which surfaced at incredibly awkward times and resulted in her licking supermarket trolleys or sucking shop shutters.

Due to the breach nature of his position, Sally was booked in to have a pleasantly civilised caesarean four days before her actual due date. Cameron decided to come three weeks early - not early enough to be classed as premature and receive the relevantly attentive care of the NHS; early enough to make doctors want to try to delay it, inflicting eight hours of labour pains ("We won't administer drugs because that can encourage labour." "FUCKING ENCOURAGE IT!" "Mrs Mortice, it's too early."). Not early enough to warrant urgent speedy attention; three emergency C-sections went through before they agreed to put her through. Not early enough to be considered an emergency but early enough to ensure that no one was really aware of her case ("Are you sure you don't want to try it naturally?" "THE FUCKING BEAST IS UPSIDE DOWN!").

When he was a baby, he caused hours of frustration and anxiety because he would not latch on to feed. He would either just play with his mother's nipple, using it as a comforter, or scream in protestation at the ignominy and potential psychological scarring of having the thing forced into his face. But when he did feed, he **FED!** Devouring his mother's sustenance until she dried, screaming that he was unsatisfied; chewing on her nipple, sending shockwaves of physical and emotional pain rippling through the core of her being, creating sore blisters around her aureole. And he seemed to delight even more when he started being bottle fed, making unwarranted smacking noises with his lips at the most inopportune moments, activating her let-down reflex and causing no end of social embarrassment.

When he was a boy, he would question everything. He would turn the 'Why?' game into an existential debate, wailing with unrequited lamentation when his thirst for understanding was left unquenched by a conclusive, "BECAUSE IT IS, THAT'S WHY!"

At school he was described in his school reports as, 'a student who could achieve more with careful application of his time and effort,' which actually meant, 'he's a lazy little shit-bag who's going to fuck up my end of year results by not getting his target grade'. There was also, 'he has an active imagination and sense of humour which, when untempered, can cause distraction and disruption to the lessons,' which really meant, 'your child is a smart-arse who gets the entire class behind him, openly mocks me and I can't control him.'

The most irritating thing about Cameron Mortice during his school days was that, no matter how little effort he put into his work, no matter how many threats and punishments were administered, and no matter how much reverse psychology was employed, he would not excel at anything but he would also not fail. And so, his average yet acceptable GCSEs, A levels and degree that he achieved looked like a huge two-finger salute to all those teachers who constantly assured him he would. They said he would, so he did not, but not so well so they could turn round and say that they tricked him into passing.

It was this innate belligerence, his instinctive defiance and DNA-level, deep-seeded obstinacy that allowed him to defy Death when he came calling. When that bony, skeletal hand reached forward to take his to lead him to the Elysian Fields, Cameron inadvertently saw something bright and sparkly in some metaphysical shop window and scampered off, disappearing into the crowds leaving Death panicking like an inexperienced parent and cursing that he had not attached the reins when he had the chance.

Cameron Mortice had been engineered and manipulated into becoming The Unscratchable Itch, to be an imperative plot device in a convoluted and perverse conspiracy to destroy the World. He was not the first choice and, in fact, his ability to fulfil the role had been decided based on a blend of science and religion rather than on any positive traits and abilities the boy had because he had none:

> "Then the Lord put a mark on Cain so that no one who found him would kill him. Now you are under a curse and driven from the ground. You will be a restless wanderer on the earth!"

His bloodline had been cursed by God but the first discovery of his family's genetic tolerance to a virulent virus was not until the 17th Century in Hungary. From there, the evil doers finally tracked down the last of the lineage to his mother, Sally Mortice (nee Kane) but failed in their attempt to convert her and then had to focus their attention on the boy.

Eventually, his destiny caught up with him.

It was a bright and sunny day.

Cameron was sitting in the living room of his girlfriend's shared house. It was an unpleasantly comfortable room. 'Lived in'. It was decorated and furnished in a style reminiscent of 80s' 'cheap' and carefully maintained through a mixture of 'clumsily sloppy' and 'not at all'. Brown wallpaper curled up around the edges of suspiciously dark patches, the beige carpet changed shades of beige depending on seating areas and entrances. The furniture was an eclectic range of styles in the sense that nothing matched: a burgundy three-seater sofa sagged visibly in the middle, a blue armchair was threadbare at the arms and sun bleached down one side, a hardwood dining room chair stopped trying to be a chair a long time ago and had resigned itself to coffee table status – or perhaps coffeed table. Magazines and papers sandwiched a variety of cups, cans and bottles; its delicate grain had been stained with the vessels' contents giving it a mottled, tie-dyed appearance.

Like Batman's trophies, there were a variety of random things littered around the room that seemed to bear no relevance to anything else: a cricket bat propped up against the French window, a traffic cone keeping the door open, a foot-long wooden pepper mill nailed to the wall. Other items had been lazily scattered into whatever space would hold them: a beer mat mosaic across one wall that was obviously experiencing the autumn of its years, shedding the occasional piece; jackets were piled in a compost heap in the corner, it unnervingly radiated more warmth than the central heating system did; DVD cases had collectively spewed their shiny contents in a diameter around the small, but very wide TV. Feng Shui could just fuck right off, this room was a shrine to chaos and spontaneity.

Cameron was ensconced within the body hugging cushions of the blue armchair. He had been watching an old comedy show and trying to laugh at it but just had an unusual and disturbing interaction with one of his girlfriend's best friends that involved a newspaper and his crotch. Luckily, someone had called at the front door and thereby alleviated any possibility of him having to utter those awkward immortal words, 'Then one thing led to another.'

The girl in question, Penny (a very nice young lady who's stern appearance of short cropped blonde hair and penchant for baggy denim and eighteen hole Dr Marten boots belied her better nature), called for his attention and, when he joined her at the door, was then rudely dragged into the on-going battle between mortals and the undead legions of evil.

The boy at the front door was baring a set of ridiculously sharp looking fangs and lurching towards them. Penny kicked him square in the face, forcing him backwards and audibly breaking his nose.

"Wow! Power Rangers: SBD!" Cameron remarked.

The boy displayed his wonky nose and, before their eyes, it seemed to inflate back into its normal shape with further audible crackling.

"Fuck this," Cameron surmised and made for a quick getaway, back through the living room, dragging Penny behind him. He dashed through the cluttered room only to come face-to-face with the vampire who then idly swiped him to one side as if he were nought more than an irritating fly. The air was blasted from his lungs and he briefly experienced the ability to fly. All was swiftly rectified when he came into contact with the armchair and flipped over the back of it. Lying on the floor, dazed and confused, he considered about allowing unconsciousness to take over but was forcefully prevented when he heard Penny scream in pain.

He scrabbled from his coverage to see her weakly cradling her right shoulder but still managing to deliver a resounding kick into the side of the creature's body.

He saw the open door of the living room and, beyond it, the open door to the house; he surreptitiously edged his way towards freedom.

"You put up a better fight then, though," he heard the vampire state and something clicked inside him. Something about the tone of its voice ired him. The sheer arrogance of the thing made him grab the nearest object – an umbrella – and do an entirely uncharacteristic thing: return to the fray.

Penny was kneeling on the floor, her body hunched over in subservience and cringing defeat; she cradled her right arm, which hung from its socket at a sickeningly unnatural angle.

The creature leapt at her and Cameron swung the hooked end of the umbrella to snag it around its neck, presuming it might do some sort of Wile E. Coyote thing and hover in mid-air, running on the spot. Instead, the handle - applied to the momentum of the vampire's body, versus the softness of its neck flesh - dug into its oesophagus and ripped a huge hole across its throat. Its body lurched forward then fell to the ground; thick, dark congealed blood gobbed forth and soaked into the carpet beneath it. There was a doubt in his mind that maybe this was not real and that a practical joke had gone too far and that maybe he had just seriously injured someone or maybe even killed them and that he was going to go to prison – he was panicking and he felt his body turning cold.

Penny grabbed his arm for support and hauled herself up.

"Was I supposed to do that?" he murmured.

"Yes, it'll do for now," she panted then pointed at the umbrella. "Throw it to me." She positioned herself around the opposite side of its body.

He tentatively picked up the metal, spiked tip, which caused the handle to hook itself deeper into its throat, forcing larger gobbets of viscous claret to erupt from its mouth and nose. He yanked it harder, which elicited a groan of pain from the beast and a juicy **SHLUP** from its new orifice, then threw the doombrella across to Penny.

The monster's hand reached up and grabbed Penny's arm.

"Fucking hell," she sighed and kicked it in the head.

It went sprawling across the floor pulling her with it. She fell onto her sore shoulder with a squeal and a stomach-churning **CRACK** then lay in silence.

Cameron had instinctively jumped back as it had awoken and grabbed the closest object to him. As the vampire got to its wobbly feet, neck skin flapping with every breath, he swung the cricket bat with as much power as he could muster; no longer caring if he was being *Punkd*, let the producers sort out the lawsuits.

Its neck cracked and its head flipped over sideways. It staggered across the room, trying to make sense of its bearings then fell face first onto the floor.

Cameron grabbed Penny under her arms and began dragging her backwards to an exit. His depleted energy and her more cumbersome form than she appeared made it very difficult work.

From behind him came a deep scraping sound like rough edged bones grating against each other, followed by its dutiful **POP**. Then Cameron bumped into something very still.

In all fairness, he would admit later that he did not really feel the impact this time. It was more like an instantaneous transference of being earth-bound to being in flight. "Arghse!" he wailed as he collided with the television, knocking it over, smashing its screen and landing on it awkwardly on his back. "I… I… hurt," he groaned.

"I can fix that," the vampire told him, closing with outstretched arms.

It was so simple a child could do it. Just as the vampire was close enough, he would perform an overhead kick to its head, taking advantage of its weakened neck, then grab a shard of glass and stab it in the chest.

Cameron swung his leg up, missed everything and toppled over the edge of the screen, landing on his neck, which emitted a very definitive **SNAP**! Then there was darkness.

The creature shrugged its shoulders, turned back to the unconscious girl and carried her out of the house.

The room remained morbidly silent and still for some time. Dust motes danced within the spotlights of sunshine that dared to infiltrate the scene of mourning. The silence was disturbed by the sound of a car revving past the house. Shortly after, footsteps approached and there followed the noise of people desperately trying to be quiet.

An old man, followed by two youths, cautiously entered the room. He approached Cameron and inspected his body. Unobserved by the others, he deftly cut the palm of his own hand, drawing a thin bead of blood, then depressed his injury against the bloody graze on Cameron's forehead. He checked his hand; the laceration had gone.

Dead or dreaming? There was an element of consciousness for him to be able to question those states of being but not enough to force him awake. There were horrific images of silvery sharpness that leapt from the shadows around him. There was a never-ending threat of pain and suffering. Then there was, for only a brief second, a pain as something innate to his very being was extracted and a hollow, yawning vacuum was left.

There was a woman – his mother? No, not quite – who held her arms open to him; welcoming him with friendship, warmth and protectiveness. He surrendered to her embrace with a slight hesitation but felt a soothing caress across his forehead.

More conscious awareness followed; he could feel! He could hear voices. He could remember the battle.

"Penny?" he croaked pathetically.

Total consciousness arrived like a freight train through his skull; a solid slap to his face had been administered after someone had taken offence to the call-out. He opened his eyes to see the crappy room looking more crappy, three blurry figures standing in the background, then the tantalisingly angry face of his girlfriend, Gillian, cradling his head in her lap and preparing for another wallop.

"Ow," he whined whilst rubbing his sore face. "Gillian?"

The onlookers slowly came into focus: a short girl with rainbow coloured hair; "Cass?" A tall, tanned skin, handsome boy; "Danny?" And an old, white haired man who carried the bearing of grandeur yet the appearance of homelessness; "and... what the fuck are you doing here?"

Cameron's DNA was changing. A mortal virus had been transferred into his body and was slowly necrotising every living cell in his body. Eventually it would infect and affect his central nervous system, shutting down all auto-functional bodily functions and killing him. However, at the same time as its debilitating spread, it was also leaving behind a dark, necromantic shock. Each cell was kept in a state of perpetual existence with an otherworldly ionic charge.

Later that night, Cameron Mortice died but, due to the virus, his body and brain activity were kept alive. His dulled senses allowed him a greater tolerance for pain, thereby removing the reflexive actions that would stop him using his body beyond its natural constraints: he had become faster than a speeding bully, more powerful than a local motive and able to leap tall buddings in a single bound. His body developed an involuntary self-reparation ability and also an almost insatiable hunger for human blood.

CHAPTER 10
THE 'MEA (CULPA)' IN 'TEAM' OR *IN DRUNKEST NIGHTS*

"You're a vampire?" Bob and Floater gasped.

"D'uh!" Cameron replied.

Bob lumbered to his feet, his body swelling defensively: his inflated calves knocking over the stool he had been sitting on; his distended buttocks shifting the pool table to one side. "So, it was you who -"

"Siddown shit for brains," Cameron slurred. "Number one, you came to me. Number two, he just tried to pop my clogs too."

"Let him speak, Bob," Floater interjected with a calming hand on the man's trunk-like arm.

Bob shifted his stance slightly then remembered where he was; the few remaining patrons were staring wide-eyed, worried they were about to embark on another epic battle. He deflated, picked up his stool and sat on it, staring at Cameron with unbridled suspicion and animosity.

"You knew about him?" Floater asked Danny.

"Er, yeah," Danny replied wobbly. "I was there when he got his powers. I was the first to spot them."

"So I was the one who activated yours, then," Cameron countered. "I'm your genesis," he guffawed.

"You're my side kick," Danny muttered and swigged the final drops of his drink, slopping some out the side of the glass and down his face.

"Says Captain Deluded," Cameron countered.

"What if, true believers," Danny supposed, "Cameron Mortice wasn't a twat-splash."

Cameron screamed with laughter. "A what?"

"Twat. Splash."

"Oh ma gahd," Floater grimaced. "You guys are reprehensible."

"Thank you," Cameron attempted to stand and bow but got them the wrong way round and head butted the edge of his pint glass, over reacted as his legs straightened and then fell backwards over his toppling chair.

"Oh, for fuck's sake," Cassandra groaned. "You're going to get us kicked out."

"Quiet Kato," Danny ordered and she belted him around the back of the head.

"How is it possible?" Bob demanded as Cameron wrestled with the legs of his seat.

"Well, mummy vampire loved daddy vampire so very much," Cameron patronised.

Bob slammed his fists on the table, partly through anger and partly in the hope of shocking some sense into the boys. "We destroyed them all," he stated. "Ultimate did. Block and him explained everything."

The boys seemed to sober up immediately and they exchanged conspiratorial glances between each other and Cassandra.

"Yeah, about that," Danny said. "You see, *we* killed the vampires."

"I did," Cameron coughed.

"We all did," Cassandra argued.

"Whatever."

"Ridiculous," Bob roared. "You weren't even on the same continent."

"We-"

"I."

"- killed the king of all vampires who killed all of his minions to stay alive."

Everyone stared at Danny.

"So you didn't kill him, then," Bob deduced.

"Did. Twice though."

"And then we had to fight him again," Cassandra reminded.

"I had to."

"What?"

"Oh, come on," Cameron cried, "you can't tell me you have never experienced multiple incarnation narratives."

"Ah seriously don't know what y'all are talking about," Floater said.

"See issue twenty-seven, on the newsstands now," Danny declared.

Cassandra thumped him on the shoulder and looked at the last two true superheroes with sheer sincerity. "Despite the impressions these two muppets give, they are actually right. "We-" she shot Cameron a warning glare "- destroyed the main vampire that got rid of all the others."

Cameron nudged Danny's arm. "Bagpuss."

Danny nodded with devout appreciation. "Nice."

"Your Ultimate guy did nothing," Cassandra concluded.

Cameron stopped giggling and, successfully, leapt to his feet. Bob bolted backwards, swelling his form again. Floater picked up a beer mat and wielded it like a shuriken.

"Fuck me, I think she's got it," Cameron gasped but it was too late, Bob had swung his fist and nothing could stop that juggernaut of a limb from finding its mark.

CR – knuckle met chin.

RA – pain made noise.

ACK! – bones split, joints dislocated.

Cameron's body twisted in the air as it torpedoed across the room. Cassandra leapt across the table and armed herself with two pool cues and proceeded to aggressively swish them around in the air. Danny had sat back in his seat and rescued his glass, even though it was empty.

The last patrons ran for the exits: two clashes in one night were too much for even the most hardened psychopaths. All fled, that is, apart from one seemingly comatose soul sitting with his hunched back to them, in a booth, in the furthest, darkest corner.

Cassandra twirled the cues with balletic perfection, whipping and jabbing at Bob's bloated state. In return, he lashed back, swiping his arms in wide lumbering strokes that caused more damage to the furniture in the room than to Cassandra. She simply side-stepped and rolled out of his reach, only to bounce back up behind him and deliver another round of flagellation.

Cameron was gathering his senses and establishing which way was up. He adjusted his mashed mandible so the bits inside could knit themselves together easier. The shards scratched and scraped as cells fused, making his skin itch. There was an inner POP just beneath his ears as his temporomandibular joints re-located. "I know who the killer is!" he announced and all activity ceased. "Imagine this," he narrated, "you're given a present at Christmas and told it's the most precious gift ever."

"What is it?" Danny demanded, awestruck.

Cameron faltered slightly. "The... most... precious... gift... *ever*," he repeated but slower and waved his hands majestically before him as if conjuring a vision of his abstract notion. "But, you only get to use it once and you have to keep it in its box until a very special time."

"This analogy is shit, Cameron," Cassandra criticised, cues still primed and bobbing on the spot.

"What analogy?" Danny demanded.

"Stop trying to be clever and just tell us."

Cameron's shoulders slumped and he scrunched his face with petulant indignation. "Spoilsport. Ultimate is your killer."

"What?"

"The maths didn't add up."

"What?"

"There were more deaths than there were bodies."

"What?"

"Of course!" Danny stated. "Smoking boots? Really? She was the only witness and he was the only one who could get physically close to her. Each power that could cause the most problem for him went next: Cat, the er..." He searched his memory.

"Boy Sprout," Cameron prompted.

"No, no. There was someone before him, wasn't there?"

"No, I don't..." but something twinged at his memory.

Danny continued before losing complete momentum. "... and all because he was pissed off." He leapt to his feet and high-fived Cameron. The pair turned and smiled smugly at their compatriots who stared back with unhindered confusion.

"Ah'm sure you guys have skipped something," Floater stated.

Danny reacted as if he had been slapped in the face with a squid. "Puzzle. Pieces. Together. Whole picture," he surmised and did an interlocking thing with his hands as exemplification.

"Who was pissed?" Cassandra demanded.

"Ultimate," the boys said.

"Why?"

"Well, you answered that one already," Cameron told her. "'Ultimate did nothing'."

"Ultimate could do nothing," Danny reiterated.

"He had no powers," Cameron rereiterated.

"The one time he gets the opportunity – no, the necessity – to use them, in front of all those vampires: with you guys fallen, the safety of the world resting in his hands, and nothing happens," Danny mused.

"Gutted."

"And then some almighty deus ex machina swoops through the scene and wipes them out without a 'bye' or 'leave'[21]."

"Argh dammit!" Cameron slurred. "That would've been an awesome name *and* give me the excuse to do random shit!"

Floater and Bob exchanged confused glances.

"He harnessed the powers of the very stars themselves," Bob corrected them.

"Did he?" Cameron asked.

"He could create a supernova with the click of his fingers," Floater said.

"Could he?" Danny asked.

"Every cell of his body had been genetically crafted to hold the energies of a thousand stars," Bob recited but, this time, with a hint of doubt in his voice.

The boys just arched their eyebrows at him.

Floater's and Bob's expressions swathed with disappointment as comprehension asserted itself. He deflated and his legs seemed to buckle under the weight of this revelation. She dashed to his side and caught him, guiding him to rest on one of the less damaged stools. "But... why?"

"He is – as all superheroes are – a self-aggrandising, deluded megalomaniac," Cameron deduced.

"I AM NOT DELUDED!" the man in the darkened booth declared.

"Shit," Cameron hissed. "Should've seen that coming."

There was a sharp crack of a pistol shot and a syringe embedded itself into Bob's arm.

"Keep calm, Bob," the man instructed. "I've just overdosed your body with sildenafil – you remember that stuff, right? If you activate your powers now, the drug will push you into overdrive and, well, you'll explode."

"I won't though," Cameron announced.

"No, but if y'all fight it could still set Bob off," Floater said. "Cameron, please."

---

[21] Actually 'by your leave'. *Super Semantic.*

Five pairs of eyes watched Cameron's prepared stance. He relaxed. "Go on then," he urged the man, "monologue."

He stepped out of the shadow into a solitary spotlight. The taught curls of his white hair were indication enough to confirm his identity but, just to make sure, he arched the left side of his mouth into a devilish smile to reveal the inverted 'v' chip in his central incisors.

"You're Des Carts!" Danny accused.

KERTWANG! Danny did it again, causing Geffen to take a step back, his right eye twitching repeatedly. "There is no Des Carts!"

"You killed Des Carts?"

"There never was a Des Carts, you moron," Geffen stated. "It was *Descartes*, anyway: a pseudonym I used to-"

Danny raised his hands defensively. "Woah, hold up. So he *was* you?"

"Only in the sense that I pretended to be someone else to get the card delivered to -" Geffen explained.

Danny shrugged. "So that's that plot point sorted," he concluded. "So who are you really?"

"It's me, you fool. Ultimate!"

"Ah," the epiphany had finally struck. "I didn't recognise you with your clothes on."

"Get on with it," Cameron urged. "I have a desire to kill you which I need to sate."

"Good," Geffen praised. "At last, a hero with true altruistic motivations: protecting the many at the cost of a few."

"Garth," Bob panted whilst regulating his breathing, "what happened to you? You were our beacon of idealism."

"When I thought I was untouchable, Bob," Geffen spat. "When I thought that I was better than everyone else; when I was up on that self-erected pedestal; when I was supreme, that's when righteousness and virtue are clear and worth fighting for. And you can justify any action you take with that ethos driving you: assault, theft, murder."

"You're the murderer, Garth," Floater shouted and made Bob flinch. "Your own team-mates. Your own girlfriend."

"It all changed in an instant, Mary," he reflected as he circled around the group, sidling towards an exit. "In that one second that I discovered it was all fake, that the pain and misery had been for nothing, I saw everything from the eyes of a victim and could only see you all as the perpetrators of injustice. Not its defenders. I saw the change in her eyes, the moment she realised. She knew."

"But she didn't have to die!" Floater argued.

"I'm just levelling the playing field, people. Getting things back into perspective." He gave Danny a knowing wink. "Using those powers - that set you above the rest of us - against you. Your greatest strength is your greatest weakness. Beth had to be first because she knew the truth. What she didn't know was that her powers weren't just a deflective power but reflective: kinetic energy was reversed from whatever direction it might come from and since I was the only person she would allow getting close enough... All I had to do was pull my fist away from her face..." He paused and was lost in the moment of memory. His hand twitched empathically with each inner action.

"Then Cat was simple," he smiled at Cameron. "I knew her curiosity would be her undoing."

"She was mine," Cameron growled: his eyes were running with redness and his canines had extended beyond his lower lip.

"She was a hypocrite and liar!"

"She was a fucking human being with weaknesses and insecurities!"

"Cameron," Floater called, "please calm down."

"What's done is done," Geffen dismissed. "Then I only needed to introduce the topic of philosophical existentialism to The Ochysp to -"

"Who?" Danny asked.

"Abraham," Geffen reminded. "Abraham Normal? Master of the mystical arts? Deceiver of his own consciousness? No?"

They stared at him blankly.

"That was the Descartes business card. 'I think therefore I am,' therefore he wasn't. It actually worked a lot better than I had expected; completely erasing him from all time and space[22]," he congratulated himself but nobody applauded. "Boy was an interesting challenge. I wasn't sure what his reaction would be to digesting the entities that he had an empathic bond with. A bit messy was it? A little touch of garlic and pesto to disguise the immediate taste seemed to do the trick, though.

"You boys were an upset to the plans. Especially when Clown Face messed up. He was supposed to exploit Bob's nobility to protect the others then blow him to bits. You have no idea how difficult it was to orchestrate his breakout and get the funding for those weapons. And then, surviving..." For a moment, Geffen looked uncomfortable as his lips hesitantly trembled before saying, "Meyerdin's spell?"

"Who the hell is that?" Cassandra insisted.

"The evil midget," Cameron said.

"Dwarf!" Myrddin shouted from behind the bar and strutted his way to the fore to stand next to Geffen.

Geffen frowned with distaste. "That's such a subjective turn of phrase. I mean, what is 'evil' really?"

"Murdering people and claiming you're doing it for the greater good," Bob puffed.

"Is he talking about you or me?" Geffen asked Cameron. "You see, Bob, we'd say it was standing back and allowing the killing to continue. If you were any kind of hero, you would have destroyed this boy the moment he executed poor Clown Face. If you could, I think that even now, after this conclusive admission of guilt, you'd still stop *him* from killing *me*."

---

[22] See *Erroneous Continuity* #∞, available from all good parallel dimension comic retailers and www.lulu.com/zorga.

"Now I know he's a vampire, I could finish him," Myrddin declared.

"Only if you got stuck in my throat," Cameron growled.

"There you go with the size jokes again," Myrddin sighed. "You really need to work on your material and come up with something more original and less prejudice."

"It wasn't -"

"Denial is the first sign of guilt."

FUCK THIS! Eyes burned with fury, teeth glistened sharply and, beneath it all, despite being sated, his yearning hunger cried out for an excuse to release the beast.

"No! Cameron!" Floater cried but it was all too late.

Cameron launched himself at Geffen, casting chairs and tables aside; Bob's abilities began to kick in and, as his arm inflated, something haemorrhaged inside him, blood erupted from his mouth and nose; Myrrdin raised his cane at Cameron, said, "puny human," and everything went dark.

He did not think he was actually asleep. He was too aware of the fact that he did not think he was asleep. There was a lot of darkness though, all around him, impenetrable.

Then, just as it was getting really boring, there was a light: either very small or far away. As he focussed on it, it became more distinct.

It looked a bit like a crucifix.

It was calling unto him.

"Dude!" Danny shouted.

"What the fuck?!" Cameron spluttered and jerked to awareness, violently pushing himself away from the verbal assault and the ghost of the holy icon that was burning on his unconscious mind. "What happened?"

"You fucked up, man," Danny told him with a scowl. "Big time."

"What?"

"Why couldn't you leave it?" Danny demanded. "Why did you have to leap in? Why did you have to ignore everyone else around you and do your own thing?"

"I don't -"

"Your arrogance, man. That's your weakness. You nearly killed us all because you thought you could deal with it all by yourself. You got Bob all riled up and he was bleeding out of every hole in his body. Floater tried to calm him down but all the time he's bleeding, he's panicking even more.

"Luckily, Floater had put a silent distress call out to the spooks and they arrived just after you went night-nights."

Cassandra was pulling at his arm. "Come on, we've got to go," she said.

"They had us bang to rights, man," Danny continued. "Our two power houses were down and we would have been dead if the agents had scared them off."

"This isn't my fault, Danny," Cameron complained. "I was the only one trying to do something. The rest of you were all too happy to sit back and let that prick do whatever the fuck he wanted to. These people died because of your reluctance to step up. 'I can see stuff,' he says as if he's John Constantine with hidden powers but what you do doesn't count for shit when it comes down to the crunch; it just enables you to know when to run away."

"Fuck you," Danny countered.

"Nah, not this time, buddy," Cameron said and hauled himself upright. "This has shown me, quite categorically, not 'fuck me' at all. Had it been, 'Fuck me,' then I'd still be in Portsmouth right now and you *would* be dead. If it was, 'Fuck me,' I'd be chasing after Gillian right now and you would be dead. If it really was, 'Fuck me,' then Cat would be a vampire, we'd probably be fucking right now and you? Guess what? You would be dead. For the first time ever, I can see clearly that I have been gifted with powers that can be of benefit and I have the personality to use them effectively. You? If you still want to be Batman, then go ahead and chase after the clichés. But you do need to see that you are completely out of your depth and you will be responsible for people dying if you don't have the balls to break the mould.

"My true weakness? It's been not having the confidence to do what I thought was right and allowing myself to be influenced by the expectations of everyone around me."

The boys just stared at each other. Was this that moment when allegiances became divided because of immutable differences of beliefs? When looking back, would this be the moment when allies became enemies?

"Get me a pint, " Cameron ordered.

"You can get your own drinks," Danny retorted.

Cameron slumped back against the bar and watched two more of his friends walk out of his life.

TUNE IN NEXT WEEK: SAME BLOOD-TIME, SAME BLOOD-CHANNEL.

EPI-PROLOGUE:
PAST DAYS OF FUTURE PRESENCE

The surface of the golden dunes rippled as gentle streams of sand poured across their surface. The sun plunged into the horizon, casting a trembling blood-red glow through the dying heat haze. The continuing flow of crimson grains indicated a presence in this lifeless terrain, even if it was only that of the chilling wind. Nought much else was able to survive in the extreme conditions of this desolation.

Temperatures in the Gobi desert can vary by up to one-hundred-and-sixty degrees Fahrenheit from one extreme to the other: from one-hundred-and-twenty degrees at its peak in mid-afternoon summer, right down to minus forty during the night. Blistering, life-drying heat swings to numbing, life-sucking chills in a matter of hours.

It is during these moments of broad inspection that, sometimes, any finer details can be overlooked; the overwhelming majesty of this sort of resplendent vista can distract the attention from the truly magnificent and miraculous presence of life that can, and does, exist in these seemingly inhospitable conditions.

The sun was well into its descent towards the horizon. The heat and light was noticeably diminishing; actually becoming tolerable and it is during these limited moderate temperatures that the desert's denizens find it more conducive to comfortable exploration. A small, grey rodent appeared from beneath the surface of the sand; its little mouse-like head was reduced to further relative insignificance by a pair of oversized ears - presumably an act of evolution to help it detect the gentle approach of predators or some sort of body temperature regulator.

Or maybe God thought it would make it look super-cute.

It hauled the rest of its diminutive frame from the cooler sanctuary of below and steadied itself on its hind legs that looked more like furry skis - again, an evolutionary trait for speed, balance and purchase on the shifting surface or God's idea of a joke. It sniffed at the gentle breeze, its whiskers flickered with paranoid anticipation and it bound ten foot across the savannah in a single leap. Its sudden reaction seemed to be without reason until a ridge shadow extended itself; two branches of shade crept furtively across the sand, pointing to where the Disneyesque mammal had been. They continued to stretch until they were about a foot long and then dragged an ovoid mass from the darkness, which, in tail, dragged six more bony finger-like fronds radiating from its mass. It was some sort of spider that had been feasting on Olympian weightlifters who, in turn, had overdosed on steroids. Its body was stretched to the proportions of an ant but the size of a large hand; each leg, twice that length again and containing too many knuckles. Obsidian compact eyes managed to stare maliciously at everything around it while inch-long fangs hung uninhibited and unhindered; obvious of their intent and effectiveness. As it fully emerged into the dimming light, it seemed to click its legs with frustration at missing out on the bizarre big-eared-mouse-cum-kangaroo meal then something innate caused it to pause stock still and analyse its surroundings. Even a creature like this had something to be wary of? That was probably more unsettling than the beast itself; what on earth would: a) try to take on such a creature? b) be so desperate as to want to eat it afterwards? Whatever, just to add one more horrific element to its nightmarish repertoire, it darted off across the still surface with more speed than one would wish it to have.

All was silent as the sun rested on the precipice of the edge of the world, holding on long enough to promise that this was not over; it would return to wreak its terrible wrath upon this earth again. Then it began to be dragged down into the unrelenting sand, leaving behind a blast of brilliance beyond the horizon and allowing pin pricks of silver to pierce through the darkening sky.

It was not long before the natural ambience was disturbed by, what seemed at first, a distant rumble of thunder. But that would necessitate the presence of clouds and there were none. Further evidence against the noise being atmospheric perambulations was its persistence; the bass growl showed no sign of petering out. In fact, its intensity grew in volume and within its guttural reverberations could be heard the culmination of a variety of more distinct sounds. The deeper groan contained rhythmic tremulations indicating it was very unnatural in origin; reinforcement of this notion came in the form of an intermittent, high pitched, resonating clank and an underlying, percussive rattle.

Beneath all of this, was another sound: not patternous but irregular; not mechanical but biological; not steady in pitch and volume but very, very insistent.

"... turned left at the last dune and now we're lost!"

The peak of a dune erupted with a spray of sand and light and a metallic beast burst forth. Its speed and trajectory allowed it to escape gravity's clutches for a few brief seconds and then it plunged heavily into the incline of the sandbank, sliding slowly to a stop at its base. It was a green and purple Volkswagen Type 2 van and, overlooking the coverage of sand and debris of the desert, it looked as if it had participated in a few stock car derbies in its time and probably had not been the overall winner. Despite the dents and scratches, closer inspection would reveal very sturdy bodywork: not a patch of rust and gleaming metal beneath the flayed paintwork. Its headlights beamed like solid cones of light in the deepening twilight. Fixed firmly on its roof - and covering the entirety of it - was a removable, sealed storage container; its sleek, hydrofoil design made it look like an upturned toboggan. The van's underside had undergone some serious pimping and could be seen to be responsible for the majority of the noises. Its wheels had been removed and chassis raised to make room for two pairs of caterpillar tracks. The rear set was wrapped around five wheels on either side creating flat runners that stretched half the length of the van and jutted out a foot behind; each wheel was mounted on independently suspended axles allowing for an extremely cushioned drive over the most uneven terrain. The front sets were dual-axis pivoting triangular arrangements of three wheels which were as high as the cab and extended the front of the chimeric vehicle by an additional two foot. Not only could they swivel on a horizontal plain to allow for directional steering but also a vertical rotational system that enabled the machine to climb over large obstructions. What glass could be seen beneath the grime was mirrored to reflect as much of the sun's radiation as possible as well as keeping the occupants' identities undisclosed. However, from inside the van, the voice was very clear now: a southern states American accent. Female. Upset.

"Ah told you quite clearly. They all heard me. Y'all heard me, right?"

Whoever she was in conversation with, and whoever she was addressing, were either being more discreet with their tone and volume or keeping out of it all together.

"Do you have any idea how hard it is to navigate in this place with just a map?"

...

"It's not mah fault the uplink failed and now Ah'm the one who has to go stare at stars that all look the same to me until something falls into place."

...

"Left, Ah said, 'Left'."

...

"Because if you had turned left then you would have turned the steering wheel and the van would have turned in that direction. You know how that works?"

...

Her tone soothed somewhat and became indistinct for a moment. Then the passenger door opened, dislodging caked sand from the frame and roof.

"Ah'm not trying to antagonise you, Bob. Ah'm just expressing mah own feelings which you need to be able to deal with."

In this diminishing light, she was nothing much more than a silhouette, haloed by the automatic light that had come on inside the van as she opened the door. Despite limited illumination and potential levels of refraction, it was clear that she was slender and shapely. She strode around to stand in front of the van, facing away from it, and held up a large sheet of paper for the headlights to shine upon. She alternated her inspection between the map and the sky, occasionally rotating the paper, trying to align it. Her features were better defined in this spotlight and she shone like a rock star. Straight, platinum blonde hair poured over her shoulders to the middle of her back; every time she moved her head, a gentle wave rippled down its length. Her eyes were steel blue, boring into the constellations with fervent intensity, and beset with gently arched eyebrows and high, defined cheekbones. Full lips blew silent kisses as she attempted to reconcile the images on the paper with those above her - her thoughts transposing themselves through her mouth. She was about five foot six but standing out there with no other reference points and her long toned legs gave the proportional impression that she was much taller. The most striking aspect of her image was her measurements: thirty-six, twenty-six, thirty-six. Somehow, through a mixture of genetics, diet and exercise, she had managed to get skinny, be muscular and still maintain enough fatty tissue in her breasts and behind to possess an ideologically perfect female physique.

This, however, would not have been quite as obvious if she had not been covered in the attire she was. Jeans and a jumper could have slightly disguised her sylph-like figure but this... this...

To say her outfit was tight would be some sort of overstatement because, although it was figure hugging, it did not cause any restriction in her movement as might be assumed. To call it a second skin would give it a sense of depth, even if only a matter of micrometres, and this fitted like a first skin. Regardless of this, to say that it was painted on would be to deny its material-like texture as could be seen in the HD special edition of this book. Multiple layers of a fine cross weave; with every movement, strands would disconnect at their tensile limits only to reattach to nearer strands enabling a constant costume cohesiveness. It was more like a liquid than a material and it constantly adhered and moulded itself around every curvature of her body.

Even though her overall appearance was very aesthetic and almost sensual, the colour of her costume was not: it was a very unattractive dirty brown.

The sun had been fully consumed by the desert and temperatures were already close to zero degrees but she showed no external signs of being affected. The headlights cast a long shadow of her across the dunes, the hillocks making greater caricatures of her figure. One final rotation of the map and she seemed satisfied.

There were four other occupants in the van and two empty seats - one being the double passenger seat at the front. The driver was a fair haired, below average sized man. He gripped the steering wheel firmly and breathed heavily; slowly; deliberately. His eyes were fixed upon the illuminated svelte figure in the lights ahead but not in a lascivious way; more like how someone on a turbulent ocean might stare at the horizon. His staring was made even more intense by the angular nature of his face: his head narrowed to the tip of his long nose; sharp eyebrows arched down from his temples to the bridge of his nose; his hair was brushed forward on both sides to form a central peak over a high forehead. Like his compatriot outside, he was attired in a similarly epidermal-like overall: his slightly more wiry frame displayed a map work of sinews around his neck and shoulders; his elbows protruded like granite outcrops from his bony arms; his ribs made gentle ripples down his chest. The material was the same shade of ugly brown.

The single seat directly behind him was empty. No one sat there, nor had anyone ever sat there. Ever.

Across the aisle from the empty seat that had never been occupied was another male, considerably younger than the others. The driver's emaciated face over-emphasised aging lines which made him look like he was in his mid-forties, the map-reader's mature shape could push her into her thirties, but her face still had the youthful tautness that suggested twenties. This boy was clearly still in his teens, possibly not even getting to the end of them. Spots of angry acne littered his face and a patchwork of feathery whiskers sat precariously on his top lip. His head was being invaded by brown anarchic curls and, despite any form of defensive or controlling strategies he implemented, his hair was refusing to be oppressed by conformist styling products. He had the same dirty brown undercoat that covered him from his neck down to his feet but perhaps he lacked the confidence to allow everything to be on show and wore green, three-quarter length, canvas shorts which were covered with pockets and a green, baggy, multi-pocketed short sleeved shirt. Unlike the other two, he accessorised with large black walking boots, a yellow cravat, green eye mask and cape that flowed down to his waist. The overall effect was akin to a last minute Halloween costume being cobbled together by a boy who really should not be Trick or Treating any more.

He sat next to – and had his back turned to – another female whose body was possibly borne from the mind of some sexually repressed and anthropologically naïve misogynistic male if it was not for the fact that she was real. She was not wearing the muddy uniform but the material was almost as pore-hugging. A matt-black catsuit; perhaps leather, although, if it was, then it must have been fairly new because of the lack of stretched saggy areas or scuffed sections at the joints. There were delicate, lacy black bows tied down the middle of the top half with parallel vertical seams radiating around her stomach, waist and back, producing the overall effect of some sort of long-sleeved corset. Her slender midriff was bookmarked by generous breasts, which were encumbered by her restrictive clothing, and prominent hips. Somewhat uncharacteristically, at the bottom of her toned, muscular BDSM covered legs were a pair of black Converse boots. Her brown hair curled loosely to her shoulders and framed her made-up features: perfectly applied black lipstick over full lips; charcoal eye shadow and thick mascara which blended her eyes into the black eye mask that seamlessly covered her face from temple to temple. Unlike her uncomfortable travel-buddy's mask, hers had some extra definition over her eyebrows, which made them look more deep set and shrouded. She had pressed herself firmly against the window and was staring out at the vast space of nothingness with unbridled boredom.

The final seat, right at the back, behind the unreserved-yet-never-sat-in seat and next to a pile of holdalls was a short, solid looking woman. The dirty brown uniform was back in its unfettered ugliness and, this time, displayed the overall proportions of a more realistic woman who obviously was not intimidated by how well her teammates wore their outfits. She was only a few inches taller than five foot and her remarkably muscular body had filled in the spaces that Barbie idealised femininity took away: her waist was a broad as her chest and hips; her thighs, calves and biceps were so developed to keep her arms in constant contact with her body and legs with each other; her upper body was built, enhancing her pectorals and flattening her breasts. Her face was devoid of make-up, round and rosy as if having just exercised. A firm set look of concentration beset her features: furrowed brow and clenched jaw. Her dark brown hair was tied back into a short ponytail that protruded sternly from the base of her skull. It could probably have been used as a bludgeon if removed. She sat forward on her seat, her hands gripped the vacant seat in front of her and she watched carefully as the blonde cross-referenced her star map to a ground map.

"We're blind out here, Bob," she declared in an American accent.

"Floater knows what she's doing, Block," the driver replied with a similar tone. "Relax or you'll end up ripping the van apart."

"I'm fine, Bob," she stated. "You're the one nearly breaking the steering wheel."

The young man in front of her looked forward and noticed that Bob's hands had spread their width around the wheel and still displayed white-knuckle tension. "She's right, Bob," his accent was a strange mixture of American and German, "you need to try to chill-out."

"God!" the woman next to him exhaled heavily. "Any more sedate and I'll be comatose." Her voice was soft, calming; a more formal, clearer enunciated Americana.

"Look!" Block declared and pointed forward. The woman called Floater had turned to face them and the sheets of paper had been lowered to her sides; her face displayed a clear state of despondency.

"Cat?" the boy's voice trembled.

The woman in black raised herself from her seat, staring intently at Floater's face. "We're here," she said with an edge of panic.

"We're here," Floater echoed from outside.

The sun was gone from sight. The night had flooded the desert. Stars glimmered brightly yet ineffectually down from the heavens; their light could not help them here.

In one movement, Floater had disappeared from their view. The maps fluttered up in the air and marked her sudden plunge into the sand beneath her. At the same time, Bob had trebled in size: width, breadth and height. His skin inflated and his costume spread around his huge muscular frame: he was the epitome of power. His door flew from its housing, whistling away into the darkness and, as he emerged from the cabin, his body just became too big for the frame, causing it to buckle outwards, blossoming with his release.

The rear doors were similarly ejected with equal force but seemingly without any noticeable impetus from Block. She jumped down from the back and the sand billowed up around her creating a crater she needed to haul herself up from. Cat slid the side door open; she and the young man jumped out, wary of their proximity to Block. The other side door did not open and no one else exited the van because there was no one else to exit.

"FLOATER!" Bob screamed at the ground. Even his voice had enlarged causing sand particles to tumble over each other in the wake of the sound.

The ground exploded in a spray of sand and bodies. One shot straight up into the air to about six foot while three others flipped over to the periphery of the light having lost their grip on the projectile.

"Ah'm okay, Bob," Floater stated from her high vantage point. "They live underground! That's why we couldn't detect them by satellite."

The three discarded bodies slowly came to their senses and raised themselves to their feet. They were humanoid yet their eyes burned with a malevolent redness and their teeth reflected with unnatural whiteness in the glaring beam of the van. Whiteness and sharpness.

"Only three of them?" Cat queried with amusement in her voice. "You guys could have left me in Quebec."

The monstrous figures prowled away from their aggressors but their stance was definitely more predatory than defensive. Circling around; assessing their prey: who was the greater threat, who was the weakest; regrouping before striking as a pack.

"What are they waiting for?" the teenager demanded. "They always attack when they're backed into a corner."

"Cat, what can you see?" Bob asked.

"Nothing, there's been too much particle movement," she replied.

"We should've left you in Quebec," Block muttered and Cat just sneered at her.

"Do you feel that?" the boy interrupted and looked down. The sand was dancing around his feet; the ground was gently vibrating.

"I'm picking up extensive seismic activity," Cat reported - her mask had changed with translucent lenses now covering her eyes. Looking closely would reveal small digital readings projected on the inside of them.

"It doesn't feel that strong," Block challenged.

"Not 'intensive'," Cat countered, "'extensive.' As in, 'taking place over a wide area'."

They could see in the van's beams how the surface layer of sand was gently shifting and spreading. Shadows slowly became to form: small ridges, at first, then engorging to domes of varying sizes. They started at their feet and disappeared far off into the distance of the dying light. The domes stretched further and, as the sand fell from their surface, they developed features like carpeted tops, handles on the sides and indentations. The smaller domes stretched even longer like branches growing from the ground; twig-like structures sprouted from their ends: it was almost as if they were heads and limbs!

"Vampires," Boy stated. "Fousands of 'em."

Domes and branches grew trunks, which rose steadily from the sand. They erected themselves to full size, stretching the cramp of slumber from their undead muscles; shuffling with eager anticipation; staring with hungry, murderous intent through their bloodied eyes. Well, that's what it looked like reflected in the stark brilliance. Really, they were just steading themselves on their groggy feet, trying to adjust their eyes to the light. Even vampires sometimes need a wake-up shower before they could get their ravenous, murderous, vampire stare-thing on.

Bob was the first to react, grabbing the closest drowsy vampire to him and using it to swat the six others who were still trying to work out what day of the week it was but were unfortunate to be within his four-foot-arm-plus-six-foot-vampire span. They hurtled into their closest comrades, radiating the force of his attack outwards like a world record domino attempt. Boy was next and pulled a handful of inch-sized irregular spheres from his pockets. He stretched his arms out in front of him and opened his hands, palms up. For a dramatic fraction of a second, nothing happened then the orbs trembled of their own accord: an intensifying vibration as if repressing some primal urge; trying to hold themselves back as energy, power or emotion amassed within them. Then, whatever invisible force was keeping them at bay was released and they propelled themselves into the hordes facing him. They spanned the distance between Boy and their respective targets in a fraction of a second, careening from the forehead of their first victim then whipping away to find another. After a solid thud and, what looked like a flurry of small leaves at impact, bodies were flipped, cartwheeling two-seventy over themselves, slamming face-first into the floor or were propelled off their feet, pirouetting through the air and pin-balling off their closest compatriots. As one barrage left his palms, he instantly reloaded by ramming his hands deep into his pockets and extracting them, full again. "I won't be able to keep this up for very long!" he hollered over the building cacophony.

The Cat merged with the night outside the wall of light. For the briefest of moments, it seemed like she might have left the rest of them to their own devices but an occasional flash of shadow at the periphery of the battleground and the proceeding felling of a vampire closest to the edge of darkness suggested her m.o. of choice. Her swift and violent combinations of martial arts, melee weaponry and throwing implements added more batterie and fouetté to the violent ballet.

The display of dynamic kinetics was like a cold shower to the recently risen dead and they expressed their 'getting out of the wrong side of existence' with a cacophony of roars of indignation and anger. Floater, still lingering a couple of meters above the ground, became the first focus of their attention. The closest vampire leapt up at her at her but her body seemed to instinctively compensate and she bobbed away out of harm's reach. She brought her arms around in front of her face to tap at a large strap that was wrapped around her left wrist, releasing a third impressive display of nothing much. Then, the light distorted around her costume and her aggressors were flattened into the sand. "Ah'm gonna expend a lot of power like this," she hollered.

Block made a decision and marched toward the throng. A vampire pounced at her: arms extended, fingers pointed like claws, teeth bared with deathly intent. Instead of retracting or even flinching, she bounded resolutely towards him.

"Block! No!" Bob ordered but it was far too late.

Just as it was an arm's span away, its fingers splayed backwards, snapped at the joints and bulleted away. The creature continued its forward momentum and its hands met with the same fracturing effect: splitting skin, buckling bones, ripping cartilage then the pieces spraying away. Pain reached its senses by now and the look of violence had been replaced by one of shock and agony just as its radii and ulnas went spinning past its eyes. Its eyes, which had just reached this invisible barrier. Its nose turned inside out, its teeth retreated into its mouth and escaped through the back of its skull. Cheekbones flattened, lower jaw jettisoned, forehead flipped off and contents showered the air like food-processing tomatoes with the machine's lid off. Its body continued its forward path and resulting backward eruption until halfway through its chest when its entire form billowed into a ball of brilliant light and dispersed into the night.

There was a stillness. The rules had been broken. The game had changed.

"What the hell have you done?" Bob demanded and even the crippled vampire that dangled from his clenched fist managed a look of incredulity.

"Look around you, Bob," Block ordered. "We're outnumbered and they will beat us and they will kill us - if we're lucky. They have to be destroyed for us to have any chance at all."

"We don't kill."

"They're already dead," she screamed and the bodies closest to her were thrown off their feet.

"We don't kill," he told her calmly and threw his humanoid bludgeon into the crowd.

"You might regret that," she growled.

The sand tremored, domes grew and their numbers doubled.

"Oh crap," Boy whispered and received a glare from his leader.

They amassed and swarmed, pouring themselves at the heroes, unconcerned as to their individual safety but battling for the preservation of them all.

The darkness was no longer protection for Cat; not when the shadows could coalesce into vampiric form, wrapping coils of midnight around her and preventing her from lashing out or reaching for weaponry. She was the first to fall.

The small green projectiles zipped backwards and forwards in a protective orbit around Boy. A couple managed to build enough velocity and maintained enough stability to penetrate the chests of his attackers'. The vampires evaporated with a blast of brilliance. But the numbers of his satellites dwindled, there was a breach in his defences and he was felled.

Still Bob battled with restraint: pounding his enemies into the ground and breaking bones to prevent mobility but vampires have annoying habits of repairing themselves and not learning from their mistakes.

Block continued to do whatever it was she was capable of but her expression of determination indicated she was pushing herself beyond her extremes. When an assailant attempted any level of physical contact, they were shredded as if embracing a revved up propeller blade. As the number of attackers increased, it seemed that they were getting slightly closer. It could only be a matter of time.

Floater had considered Block's actions, made an adjustment on her wrist strap and any vampire that braved the space beneath her found itself the victim of forces akin to those experienced in jet aircraft at Mach 2 with the sunroof open.

Instantaneous gravitational forces that pulled at their bodies from multiple angles. Their limbs were ripped from their bodies like dandelion seeds in a storm. It never got past three o'clock though.

She checked the readout on her wrist and looked over to Bob. He caught her expression and told him more in that moment than any words could: I'm scared; I'm sorry; I love you. She fell into the clamouring hands and mountain of dismembered limbs below. Engulfed.

"No!" Bob screamed; his body inflating further. He swiped his arms wildly and thrust himself towards his fallen comrade. His own codes of practise forgotten, bodies were torn in two by the power of this human Juggernaut, torsos and heads flattened beneath each mighty step, existences extinguished indiscriminately.

But he too was overpowered long before he could rescue anyone. Dragged to the floor, smothered by endless numbers of bodies, unable to breath.

Block had turned her attention away from the fray; she was making her way back to the van. A taloned hand lashed out at her shoulder and atomised but not before it managed to leave a puncture wound through her costume. The murky brown material repaired itself but from the grimace on her face, the pain was extreme.

The vampires backed off. They had won. They knew it. They knew that she knew it and if there was one thing they enjoyed more than sinking their teeth into warm flesh it was the torturous, teasing moments before, seeing what their prey would do now: beg, resist or give up.

Block stumbled to the back door of the van and could sense them encircling her. She pressed a subtle nub over the wheel arch and a gentle hum heralded the descent of the coffin-like container on the roof. It slid gently to the floor, the vampires enclosed. She revealed a keypad on the side and punched in a sequence of numbers. The door sprung open with an expulsion of air that sounded like the gasp of god, condensed vapours poured out over the floor and a bright light beamed out from within.

It was impressive. Something that could have been used for the appearance of a rock idol at a comeback performance. The vampires were momentarily awestruck and craned to see what was contained within.

A glistening golden boot stepped onto the sand. It adorned a similarly gilded leg - attire that could have been crafted from solar flares by Apollo himself. The legs drew a tall man from within the box; completely clad in celestial gilt; his muscles and stature exuded unrepentant power. Platinum blond, angelic curls crowned his majestic face: clean shaven, prominent cheekbones, resolute jawline, pure blue eyes that looked down on all they surveyed. He smiled into the middle distance to reveal perfectly straight, white teeth (apart from an inverted 'v' chip between his centre incisors). His trailing leg came forward to join the first and he assessed his surroundings: a littering of fallen friends and foes, a wounded compatriot at his side, an abundance of enemies before him. He came to an important and very necessary decision and raised his arms before them.

The vampires recoiled in anticipation of the attack, which was...

Fuck all.

That's right; absolutely fuck all. Not a 'momentary pause' or 'second's hesitation' or 'anticipatory build up'. Totally, utterly and without misconception: fuck all.

"Ultimate?" Block enquired as she clung on to the box for support.

He looked at his hands with a modicum of confusion. Nothing had changed, he could still feel the power of a thousand suns stored within each cell of his being, he just did not know how to release it. He had never dared try, he had never dared practise, they had never told him how. "Er, by the power of Greyskull?" he tried and pushed his palms forward.

Some flinched again but the majority looked on with unbridled amusement.

"Up and atom?" He waggled his fingers.

None of them reacted.

"Avadacadabra?" He had formed guns from his hands and his thumb triggers fired down.

The front lines took a step forward and Block slid to the floor in resigned defeat.

He looked down at her. "I don't get it."

"You don't have any powers," she told him whilst staring at the floor. "Cat was right, you were deceived. Or deluded."

The vampires stopped in their advance as, simultaneously, an epiphany struck every single one of them. Then, as one, they detonated and their collective light rocketed off towards the western horizon.

The desert seemed darker than ever; the stars, dimmer; the golden sands, tarnished.

"What did you do?" he asked tremulously.

"The same as you," Block replied and, finally, built the strength to look at him, "nothing."

They remained motionless for minutes that felt like hours, ruminating.

"I won't tell them," she announced. "I wouldn't do that to you."

He said nothing.

His right eye twitched.

Also available by Rhys A. Wilcox

Aftermath
ISBN: 978-0956155900

"Congratulations. You are taking on a case that will ultimately end in your demise," he read. "You are consorting with the devil himself and many have taken a charge from God to rid the world of Satan in all his incarnations, his followers and sympathisers."

Kat thought about the words for a second as John ripped the paper from the machine.

"I'm calling the police," he stated.

"It's not actually a threat, though, is it?" she said.

"Don't do your lawyer shit with me now," John argued and dialled on his phone.

"The author of that doesn't threaten us, he's just warning us."

"I realise that, Kat," John said. "But do realise that it is probably true. Even though Luke Robinson has saved the World and all life on it, there are going to be a shit-load of fucked-off religious zealots who have lost their sole source of income to an advertising sales assistant from Camden."

"You really think we might be in danger?" she asked.

"I'd guarantee it," John said and turned his attention to his phone as he got connected.

Kat could not hear his conversation as she slipped into a trance. How can so much happen in such a short amount of time? They had been given the responsibility for the civil rights protection of the most important human being since, if you believed it, Jesus, and now someone wanted to kill them for it.

The stories that had circulated since Luke's safe return had it that he nearly died on numerous occasions for the sake of his planet and the people thereon. Did she have that same sense of morality to be able to do the same for that man? To put her life on the line for the sake of the planet's protector? Could she be so passionate about a cause, or case, that her personal safety was not an issue to her? Had there ever been a cause as big as this for her to be that passionate about?

Blood Lust: Sound Bites

In a world where continuity is as fixed and tangible as a politician's promise, it is possible for conversations to happen that never did and characters to meet that never could.

Blood Lust: Sound Bites are free e-publications, offering little snippets of conversations between major and minor characters in scenarios they might not want you privy to because they're private or simply because they never happened.

Visit www.lulu.com/zorga for all titles by Rhys A. Wilcox as well as free downloads.

Works In Progress by Rhys A. Wilcox

Unfaer

What's in a naem?
Faerfolk like their names. And I mean they *really* like them.
    Not like you or I might like a name because it belonged to a favoured celebrity, friend or relative. And not in the same way that musicians and footballers seem to like really odd names that they then give to their children. And not similarly - but almost - to how magic likes names and is able to manipulate people simply by knowing what their real name is.
    Names, to Faerfolk, are fashionable accessories as well as a sort of label that tell you something of the nature of its bearer.
    Records are kept of Faerfolk traditions; not for the purpose of preserving their historical rites for all eternity but as a directory of name-calling trends. Faerfolk are incredibly vain and simply want to ensure that they don't use or copy someone else's name. No one wants a repeat of the Great Kylie and Jason Swarm of the Aeties.

www.ingramcontent.com/pod-product-compliance
Lightning Source LLC
Chambersburg PA
CBHW070734160426
43192CB00009B/1436